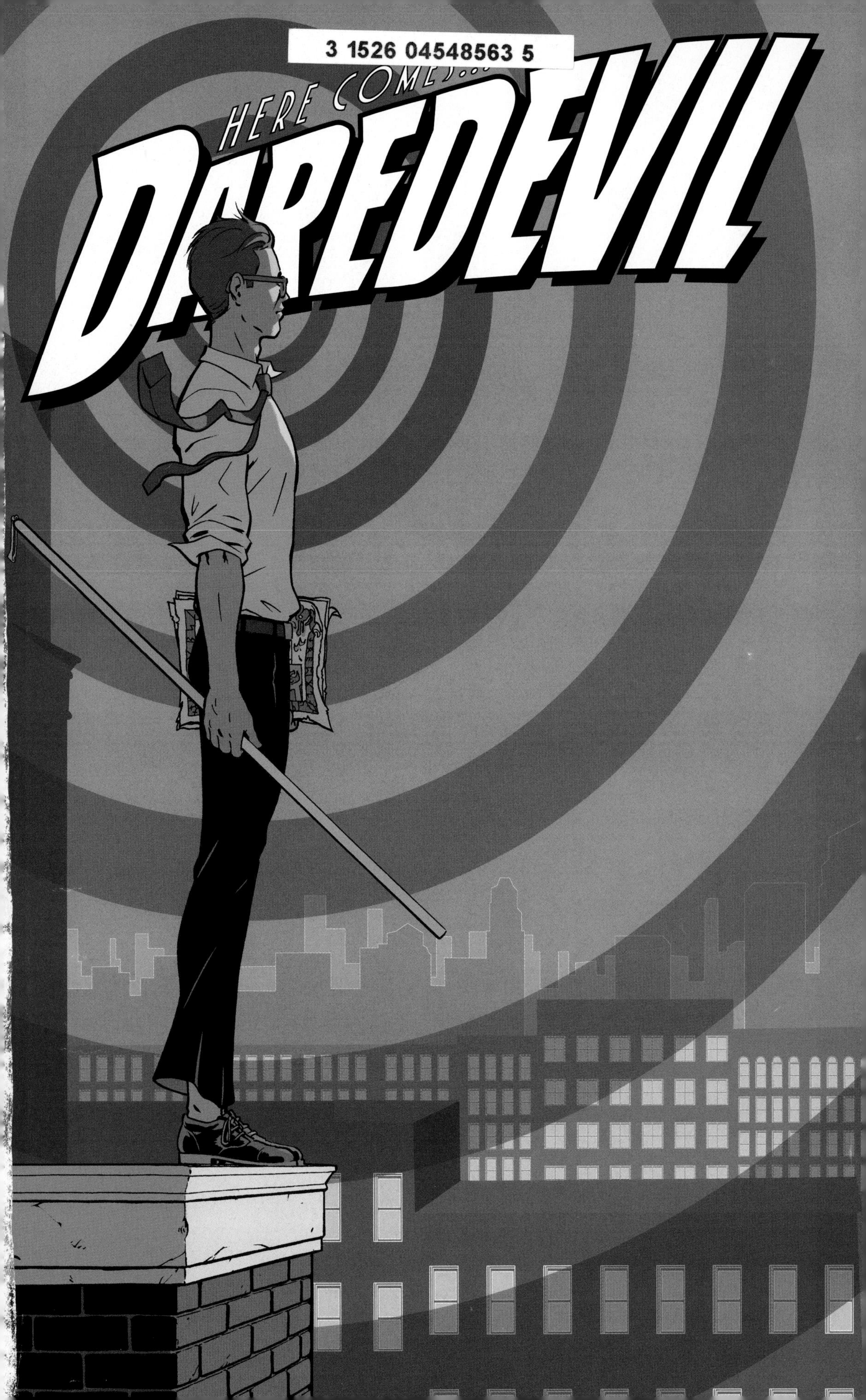
HERE COMES...
DAREDEVIL

WRITER
MARK WAID

DAREDEVIL #31-32 & #35-36

ARTIST
CHRIS SAMNEE

DAREDEVIL #33

LAYOUTS
CHRIS SAMNEE
ARTIST
JASON COPLAND

DAREDEVIL #34

PENCILER
JAVIER RODRIGUEZ
INKER
ALVARO LOPEZ

COLOR ARTIST
JAVIER RODRIGUEZ
LETTERER
VC'S JOE CARAMAGNA
COVER ARTISTS
CHRIS SAMNEE
& JAVIER RODRIGUEZ
ASSISTANT EDITOR
ELLIE PYLE
EDITOR
STEPHEN WACKER

COLLECTION EDITOR **SARAH BRUNSTAD**
ASSOCIATE MANAGING EDITOR **ALEX STARBUCK**
EDITORS, SPECIAL PROJECTS **JENNIFER GRÜNWALD & MARK D. BEAZLEY**
SENIOR EDITOR, SPECIAL PROJECTS **JEFF YOUNGQUIST**
SVP PRINT, SALES & MARKETING **DAVID GABRIEL**
BOOK DESIGNER **NELSON RIBEIRO**

EDITOR IN CHIEF **AXEL ALONSO**
CHIEF CREATIVE OFFICER **JOE QUESADA**
PUBLISHER **DAN BUCKLEY**
EXECUTIVE PRODUCER **ALAN FINE**

DAREDEVIL BY MARK WAID VOL. 7. Contains material originally published in magazine form as DAREDEVIL #31-36. First printing 2014. ISBN# 978-0-7851-5442-6. Published by MARVEL WORLDWIDE, INC., a subsidiary of MARVEL ENTERTAINMENT, LLC. OFFICE OF PUBLICATION: 135 West 50th Street, New York, NY 10020. **Printed in the U.S.A.** ALAN FINE, EVP - Office of the President, Marvel Worldwide, Inc. and EVP & CMO Marvel Characters B.V.; DAN BUCKLEY, Publisher & President - Print, Animation & Digital Divisions; JOE QUESADA, Chief Creative Officer; TOM BREVOORT, SVP of Publishing; DAVID BOGART, SVP of Operations & Procurement, Publishing; C.B. CEBULSKI, SVP of Creator & Content Development; DAVID GABRIEL, SVP Print, Sales & Marketing; JIM O'KEEFE, VP of Operations & Logistics; DAN CARR, Executive Director of Publishing Technology; SUSAN CRESPI, Editorial Operations Manager; ALEX MORALES, Publishing Operations Manager; STAN LEE, Chairman Emeritus. For information regarding advertising in Marvel Comics or on Marvel.com, please contact Niza Disla, Director of Marvel Partnerships, at ndisla@marvel.com. For Marvel subscription inquiries, please call 800-217-9158. **Manufactured between 2/21/2014 and 3/31/2014 by R.R. DONNELLEY, INC., SALEM, VA, USA.**

10 9 8 7 6 5 4 3 2 1

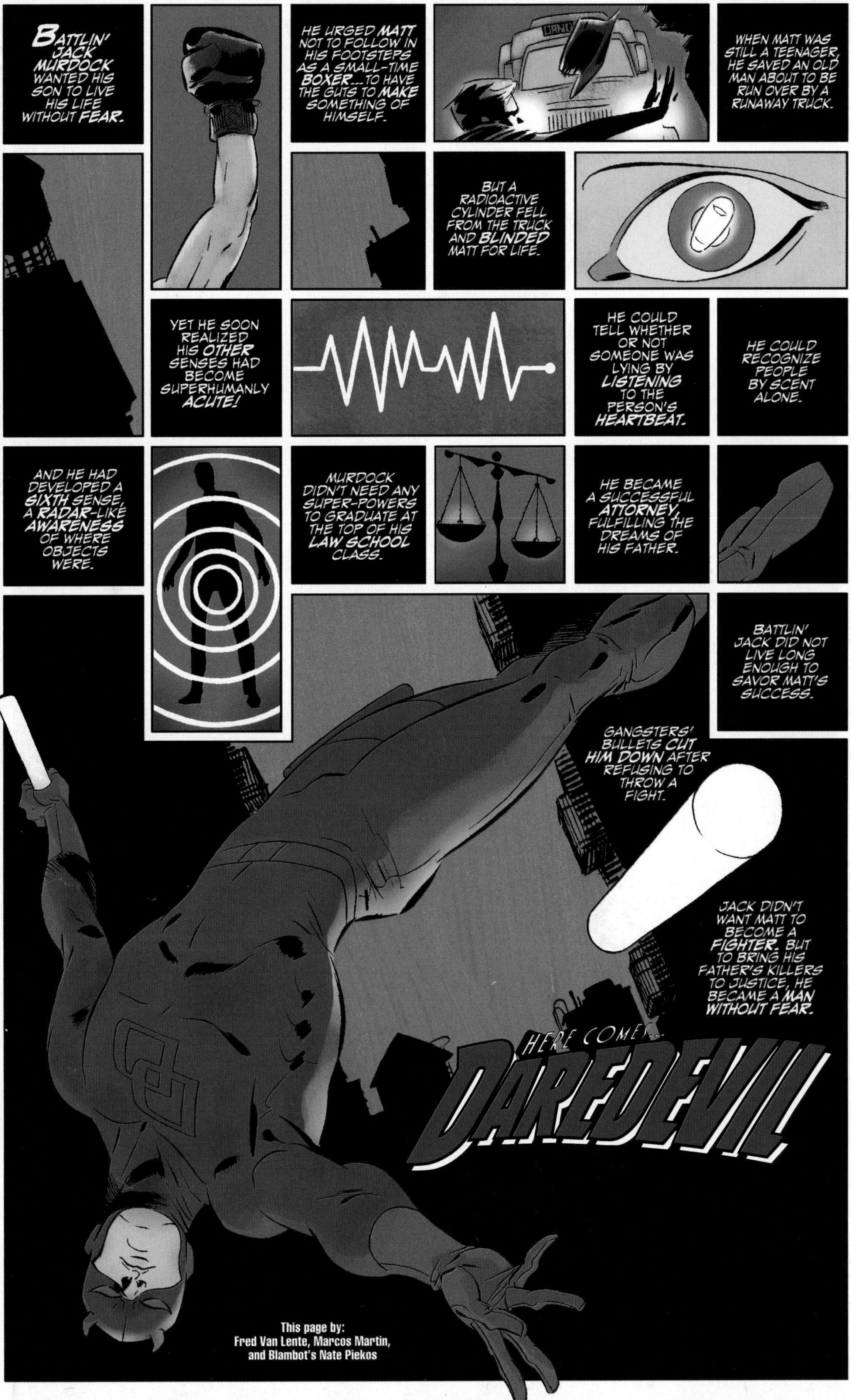
BATTLIN' JACK MURDOCK WANTED HIS SON TO LIVE HIS LIFE WITHOUT FEAR.
HE URGED MATT NOT TO FOLLOW IN HIS FOOTSTEPS AS A SMALL-TIME BOXER...TO HAVE THE GUTS TO MAKE SOMETHING OF HIMSELF.
WHEN MATT WAS STILL A TEENAGER, HE SAVED AN OLD MAN ABOUT TO BE RUN OVER BY A RUNAWAY TRUCK.
BUT A RADIOACTIVE CYLINDER FELL FROM THE TRUCK AND BLINDED MATT FOR LIFE.
YET HE SOON REALIZED HIS OTHER SENSES HAD BECOME SUPERHUMANLY ACUTE!
HE COULD TELL WHETHER OR NOT SOMEONE WAS LYING BY LISTENING TO THE PERSON'S HEARTBEAT.
HE COULD RECOGNIZE PEOPLE BY SCENT ALONE.
AND HE HAD DEVELOPED A SIXTH SENSE, A RADAR-LIKE AWARENESS OF WHERE OBJECTS WERE.
MURDOCK DIDN'T NEED ANY SUPER-POWERS TO GRADUATE AT THE TOP OF HIS LAW SCHOOL CLASS.
HE BECAME A SUCCESSFUL ATTORNEY, FULFILLING THE DREAMS OF HIS FATHER.
BATTLIN' JACK DID NOT LIVE LONG ENOUGH TO SAVOR MATT'S SUCCESS.
GANGSTERS' BULLETS CUT HIM DOWN AFTER REFUSING TO THROW A FIGHT.
JACK DIDN'T WANT MATT TO BECOME A FIGHTER. BUT TO BRING HIS FATHER'S KILLERS TO JUSTICE, HE BECAME A MAN WITHOUT FEAR.
HERE COMES...
DAREDEVIL

This page by:
Fred Van Lente, Marcos Martin,
and Blambot's Nate Piekos

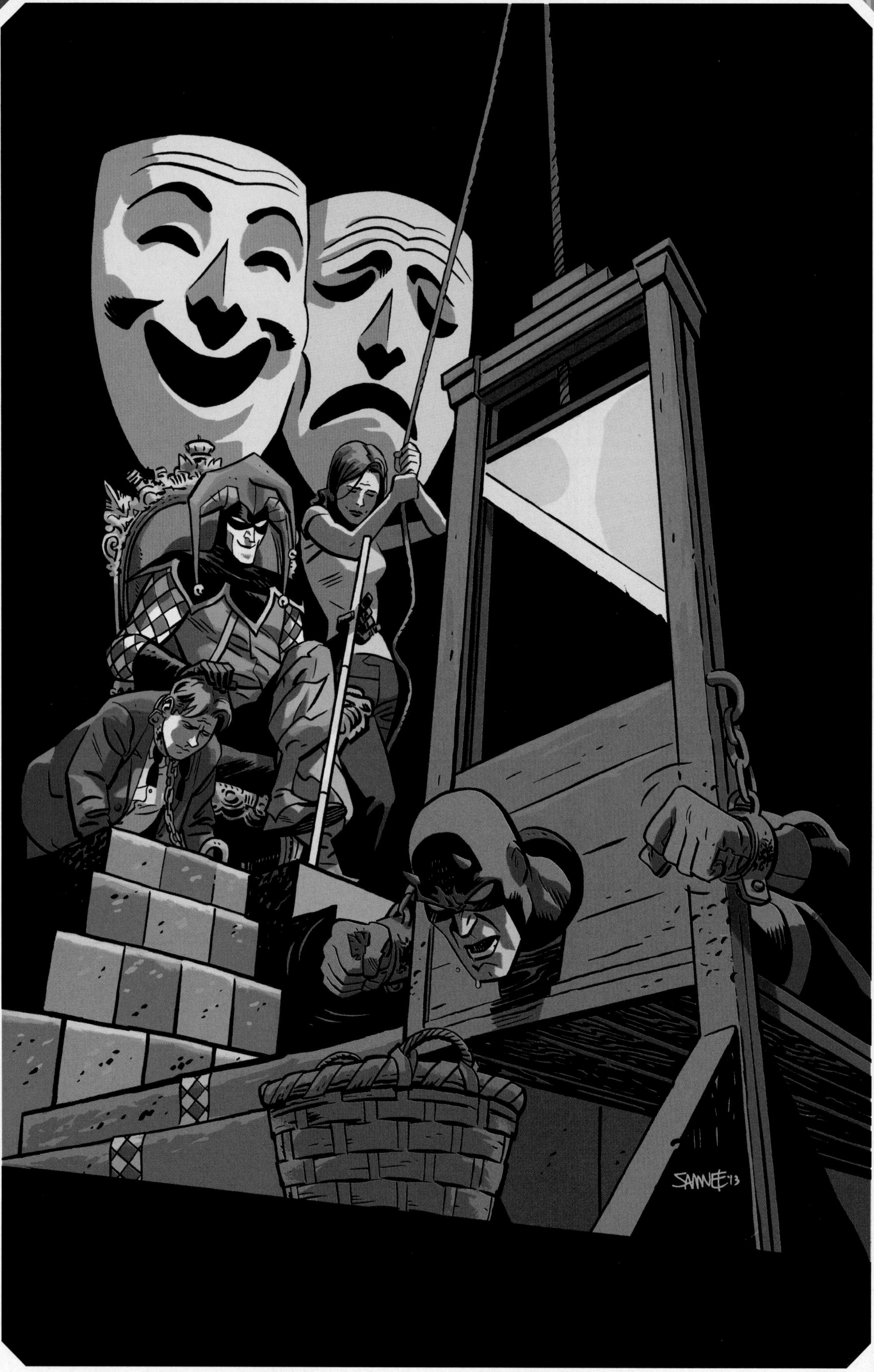
SAMNEE '13

DAREDEVIL #31

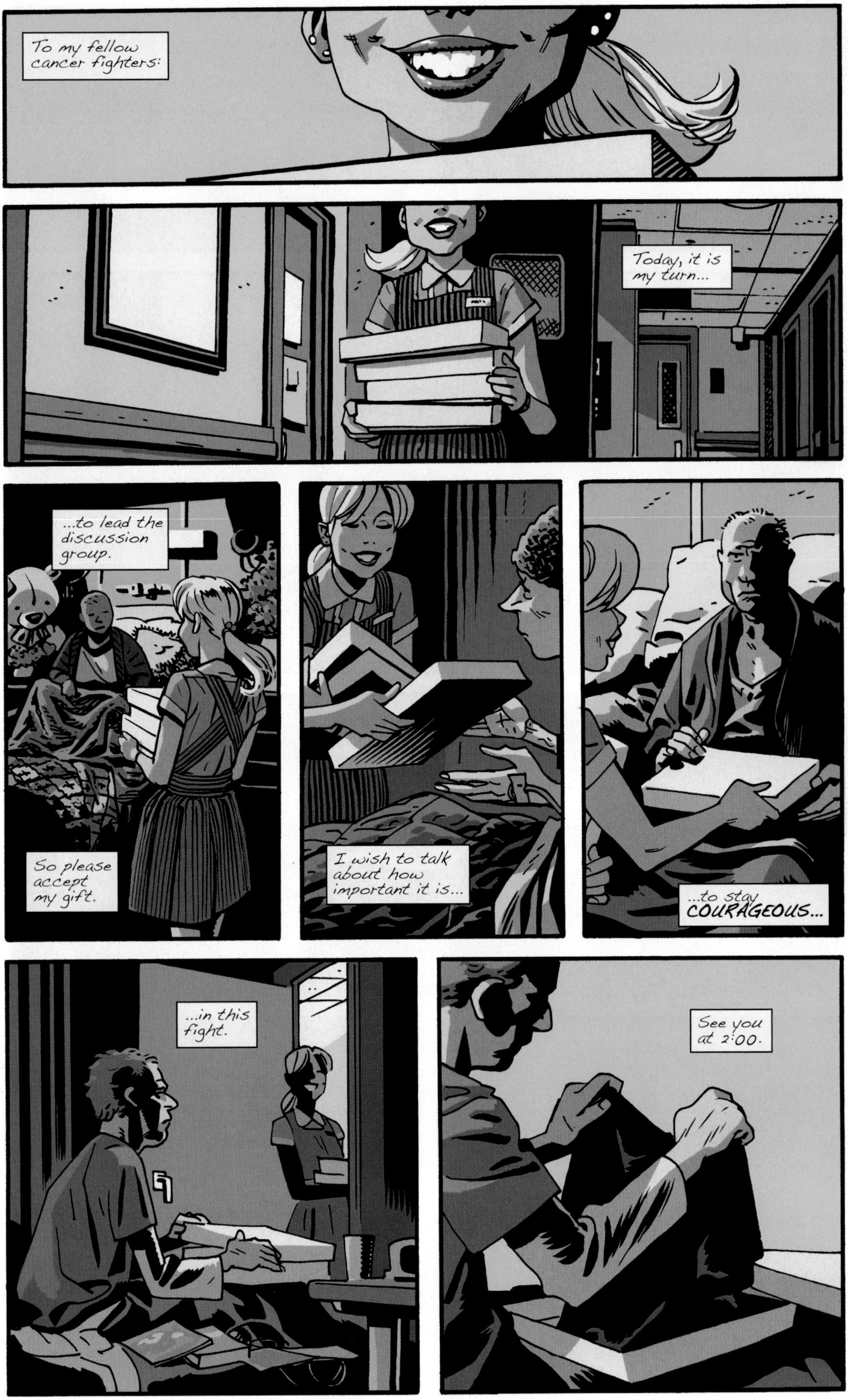
To my fellow cancer fighters:
Today, it is my turn...
...to lead the discussion group.
So please accept my gift.
I wish to talk about how important it is...
...to stay COURAGEOUS...
...in this fight.
See you at 2:00.

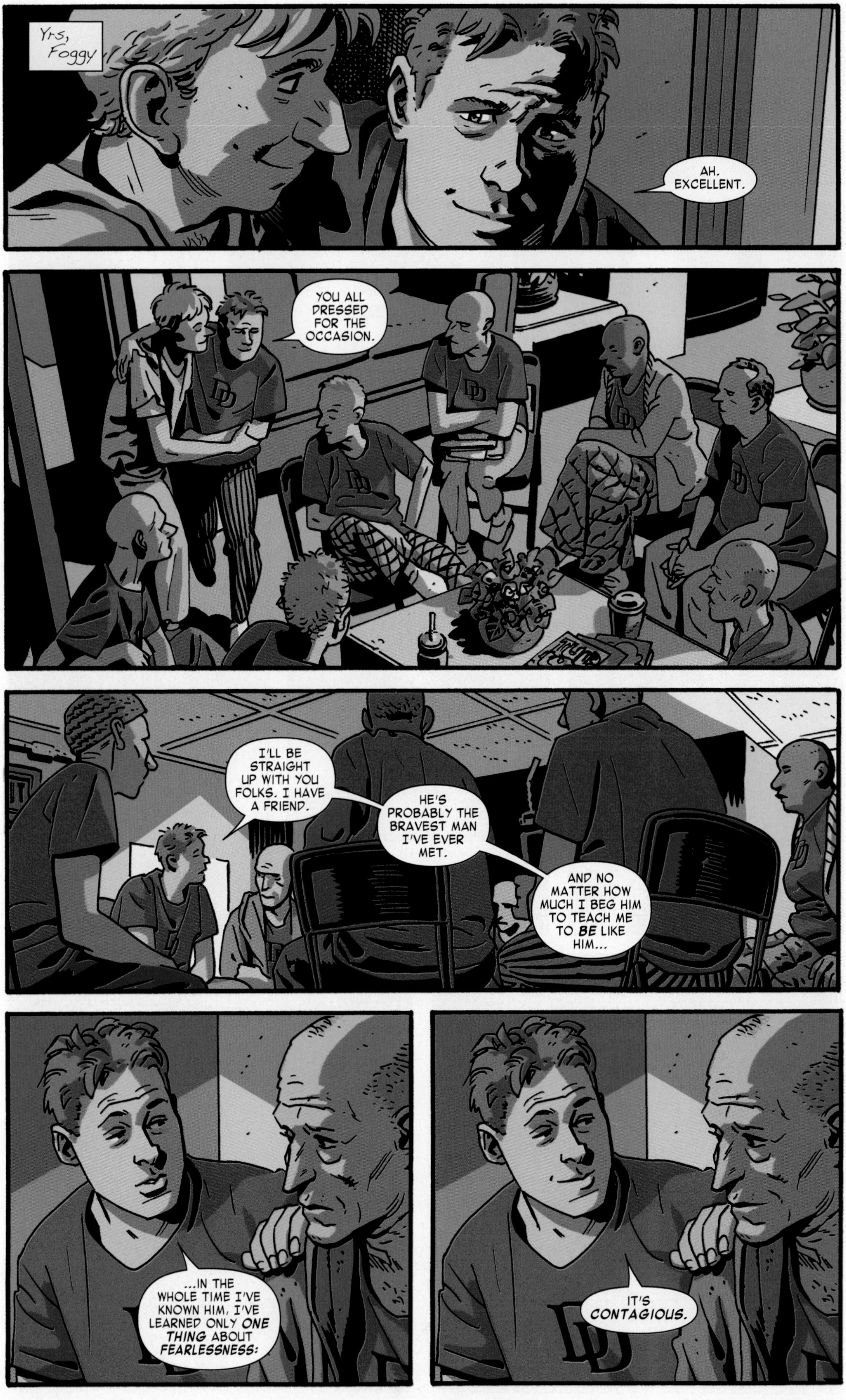
Yrs, Foggy
AH. EXCELLENT.
YOU ALL DRESSED FOR THE OCCASION.
I'LL BE STRAIGHT UP WITH YOU FOLKS. I HAVE A FRIEND.
HE'S PROBABLY THE BRAVEST MAN I'VE EVER MET.
AND NO MATTER HOW MUCH I BEG HIM TO TEACH ME TO BE LIKE HIM...
...IN THE WHOLE TIME I'VE KNOWN HIM, I'VE LEARNED ONLY ONE THING ABOUT FEARLESSNESS:
IT'S CONTAGIOUS.

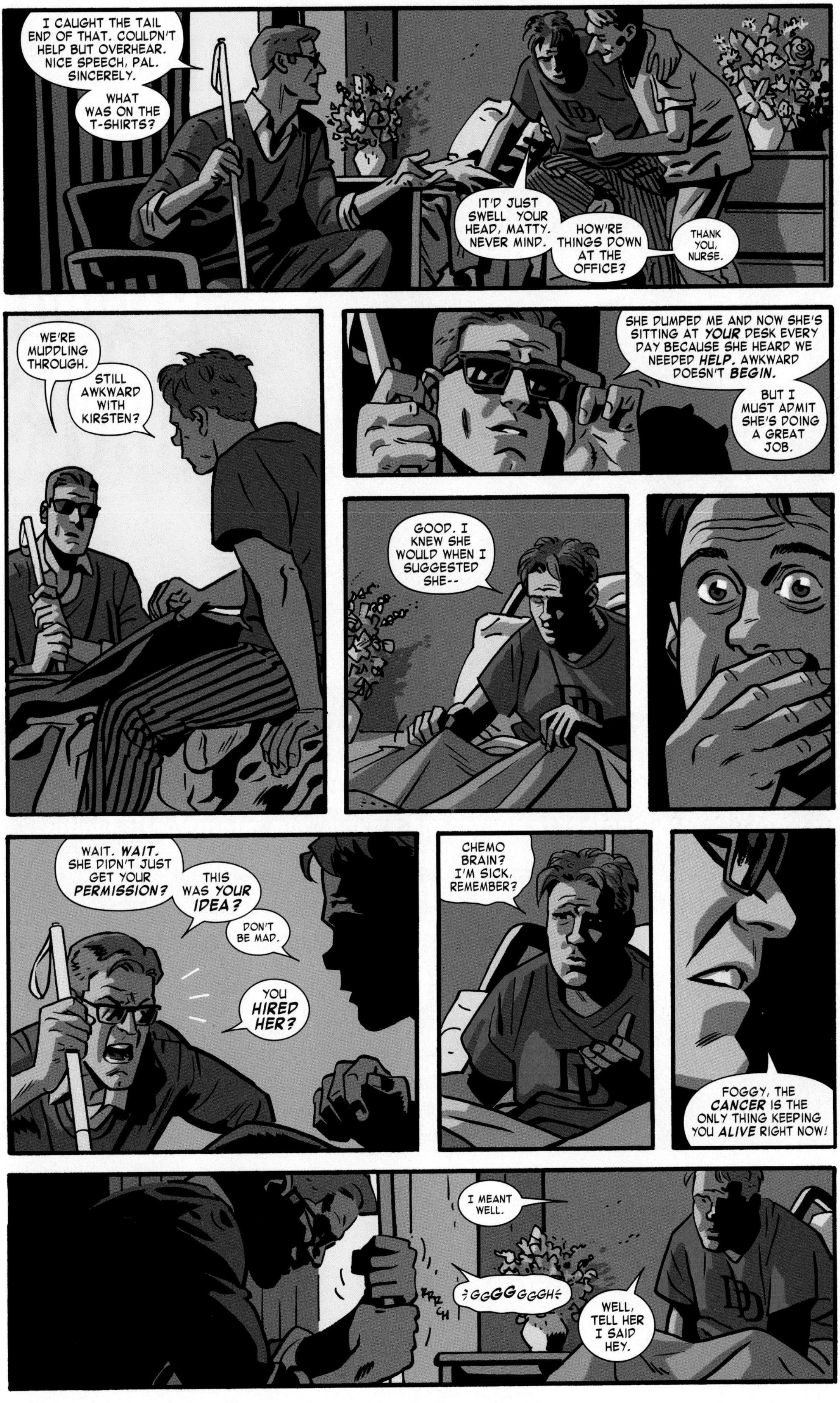
I CAUGHT THE TAIL END OF THAT. COULDN'T HELP BUT OVERHEAR. NICE SPEECH, PAL. SINCERELY.
WHAT WAS ON THE T-SHIRTS?
IT'D JUST SWELL YOUR HEAD, MATTY. NEVER MIND.
HOW'RE THINGS DOWN AT THE OFFICE?
THANK YOU, NURSE.
WE'RE MUDDLING THROUGH.
STILL AWKWARD WITH KIRSTEN?
SHE DUMPED ME AND NOW SHE'S SITTING AT YOUR DESK EVERY DAY BECAUSE SHE HEARD WE NEEDED HELP. AWKWARD DOESN'T BEGIN.
BUT I MUST ADMIT SHE'S DOING A GREAT JOB.
GOOD. I KNEW SHE WOULD WHEN I SUGGESTED SHE--
WAIT. WAIT. SHE DIDN'T JUST GET YOUR PERMISSION?
THIS WAS YOUR IDEA?
DON'T BE MAD.
YOU HIRED HER?
CHEMO BRAIN? I'M SICK, REMEMBER?
FOGGY, THE CANCER IS THE ONLY THING KEEPING YOU ALIVE RIGHT NOW!
I MEANT WELL.
KRRRCH
GGGGGGGH
WELL, TELL HER I SAID HEY.

FINAL ★★★★

DAILY 🎺 BUGLE®

NEW YORK'S FINEST DAILY NEWSPAPER

SINCE 1897
★★★★
$1.00 (in NYC)
$1.50 (outside city)

INSIDE: NOVA CHECKS OUT MANHATTAN; PHIL URICH ESCAPES CUSTODY; SPIDER-MAN OUT OF TIME

COSMIC WAVES

Daredevil and the Silver Surfer were spotted hanging ten throughout the New York skyline earlier this week. An unnamed source close to the Man Without Fear said that the Silver Surfer and downtown's Crimson Crusader were working together to apprehend a dangerous intergalactic fugitive named Ru'Ach. After successfully tracking down and capturing the cosmic criminal, the two parted ways and... (continued on page 2)

LEGAL AID

Esteemed litigator Kirsten McDuffie has recently joined the law firm of Nelson and Murdock to take Mr. Nelson's caseload while he undergoes cancer treatment. Whether or not Murdock and McDuffie are once again forging a personal partnership as well as a professional one remains unknown. At press time, Mr. Nelson could not be reached for comment. MORE...

HOW'S FOGGY?

HE SAYS HELLO.

HE SAYS A *LOT* OF THINGS.

WELL, I'M GLAD YOU'RE BACK.

YEAH?

WORD IS, THE *BAINWOOD* VERDICT IS IN.

OH.

I am very protective of the jury system in this country.

It's far from perfect, but it gives citizens a *voice* in how justice is achieved, and that voice is generally reasonable and trustworthy.

And then there are days like these.

MR. FOREMAN, HAS THE JURY REACHED A VERDICT?

The *Bainwood* case has had the whole nation riveted--and sharply divided--for months.

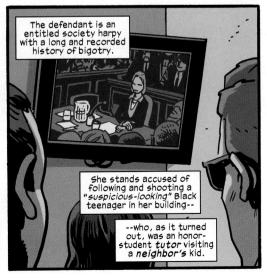

The defendant is an entitled society harpy with a long and recorded history of bigotry.

She stands accused of following and shooting a "*suspicious-looking*" Black teenager in her building--

--who, as it turned out, was an honor-student *tutor* visiting a *neighbor's* kid.

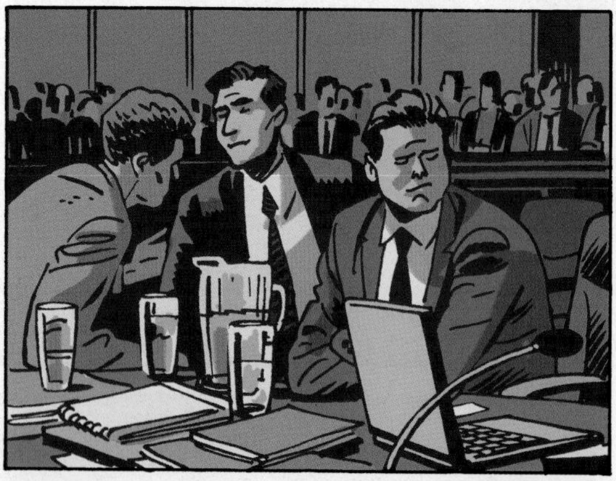

Her team has been exemplary. They've built their strategy around self-defense, exploiting the fact that there were no witnesses but there were clear signs of a struggle.

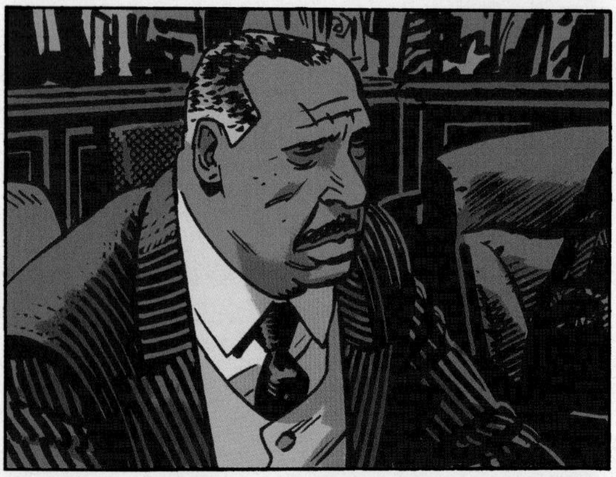

The ***prosecution,*** by contrast, paints her as a racist, armed vigilante who provoked a confrontation with an unarmed boy.

And the ***media*** has turned the ***prosecutor--D.A. James Priest***--into a ***folk hero*** to the African-American community for his ***diligence*** in this case...

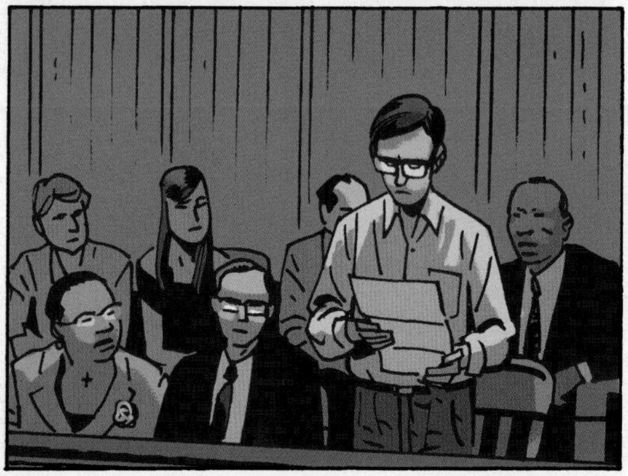

...despite my growing doubt that he'll win...

"WE FIND THE DEFENDANT ***NOT GUILTY,*** *YOUR HONOR."*

...because the evidence can't overcome reasonable doubt.

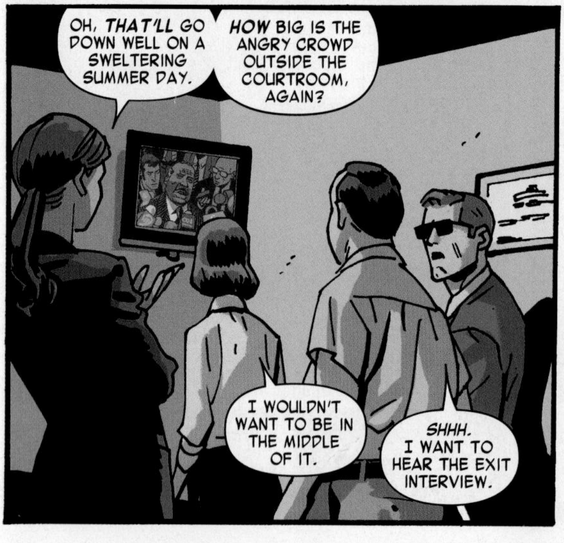
OH, THAT'LL GO DOWN WELL ON A SWELTERING SUMMER DAY.
HOW BIG IS THE ANGRY CROWD OUTSIDE THE COURTROOM, AGAIN?
I WOULDN'T WANT TO BE IN THE MIDDLE OF IT.
SHHH. I WANT TO HEAR THE EXIT INTERVIEW.

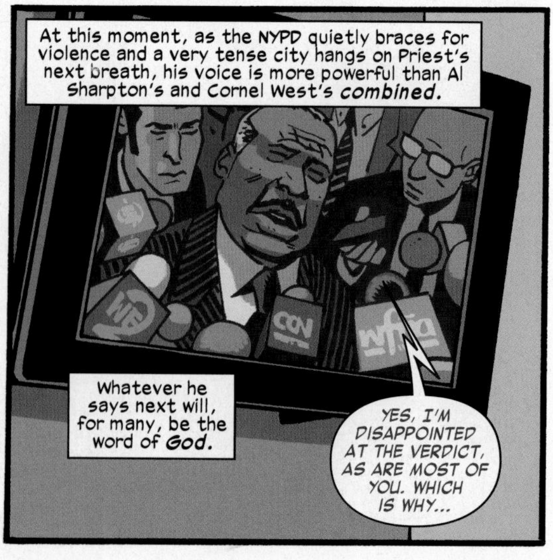
At this moment, as the NYPD quietly braces for violence and a very tense city hangs on Priest's next breath, his voice is more powerful than Al Sharpton's and Cornel West's combined.
Whatever he says next will, for many, be the word of God.
YES, I'M DISAPPOINTED AT THE VERDICT, AS ARE MOST OF YOU. WHICH IS WHY...

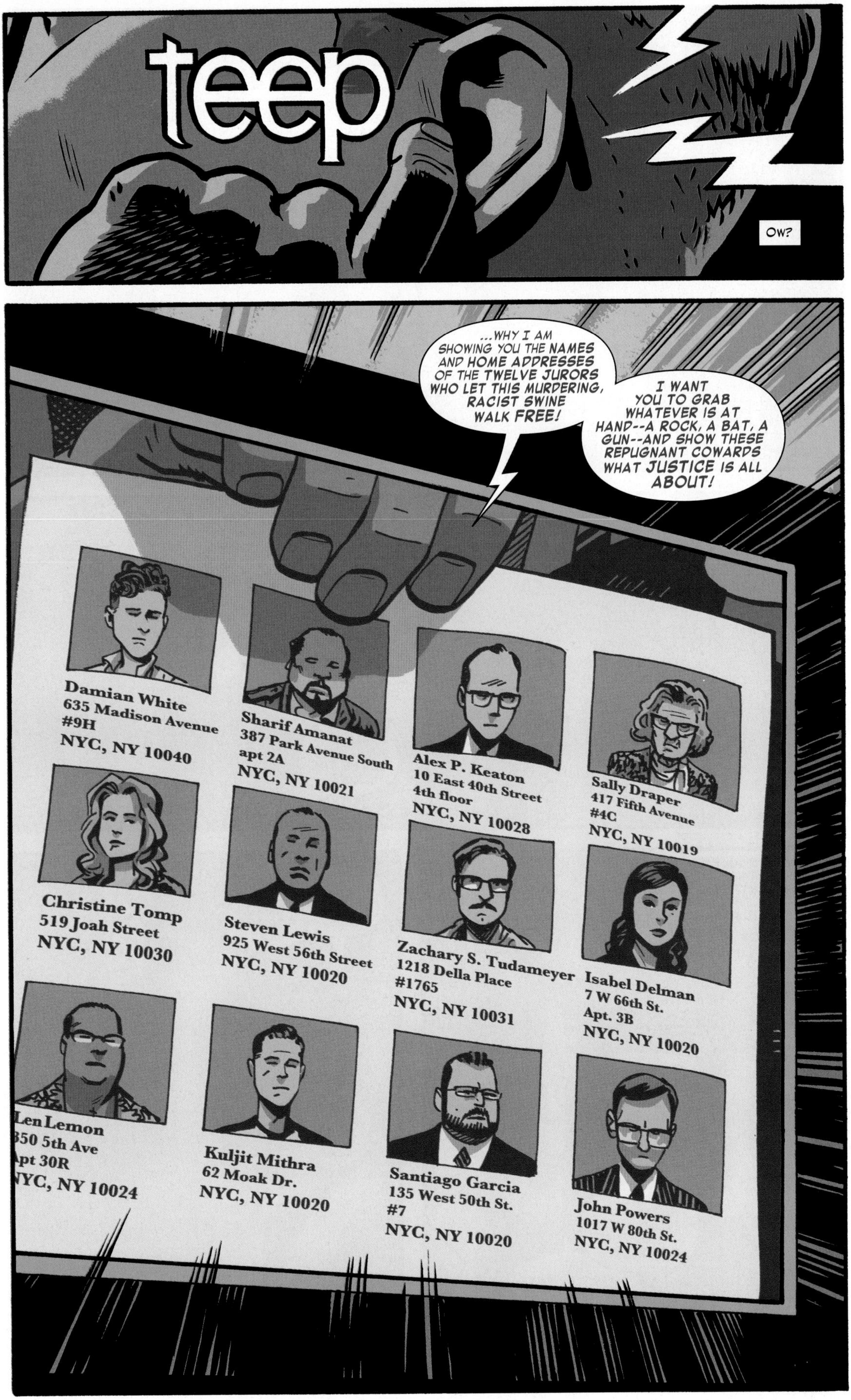
teep
OW?
...WHY I AM SHOWING YOU THE NAMES AND HOME ADDRESSES OF THE TWELVE JURORS WHO LET THIS MURDERING, RACIST SWINE WALK FREE!
I WANT YOU TO GRAB WHATEVER IS AT HAND--A ROCK, A BAT, A GUN--AND SHOW THESE REPUGNANT COWARDS WHAT JUSTICE IS ALL ABOUT!
Damian White 635 Madison Avenue #9H NYC, NY 10040
Sharif Amanat 387 Park Avenue South apt 2A NYC, NY 10021
Alex P. Keaton 10 East 40th Street 4th floor NYC, NY 10028
Sally Draper 417 Fifth Avenue #4C NYC, NY 10019
Christine Tomp 519 Joah Street NYC, NY 10030
Steven Lewis 925 West 56th Street NYC, NY 10020
Zachary S. Tudameyer 1218 Della Place #1765 NYC, NY 10031
Isabel Delman 7 W 66th St. Apt. 3B NYC, NY 10020
Len Lemon 350 5th Ave Apt 30R NYC, NY 10024
Kuljit Mithra 62 Moak Dr. NYC, NY 10020
Santiago Garcia 135 West 50th St. #7 NYC, NY 10020
John Powers 1017 W 80th St. NYC, NY 10024

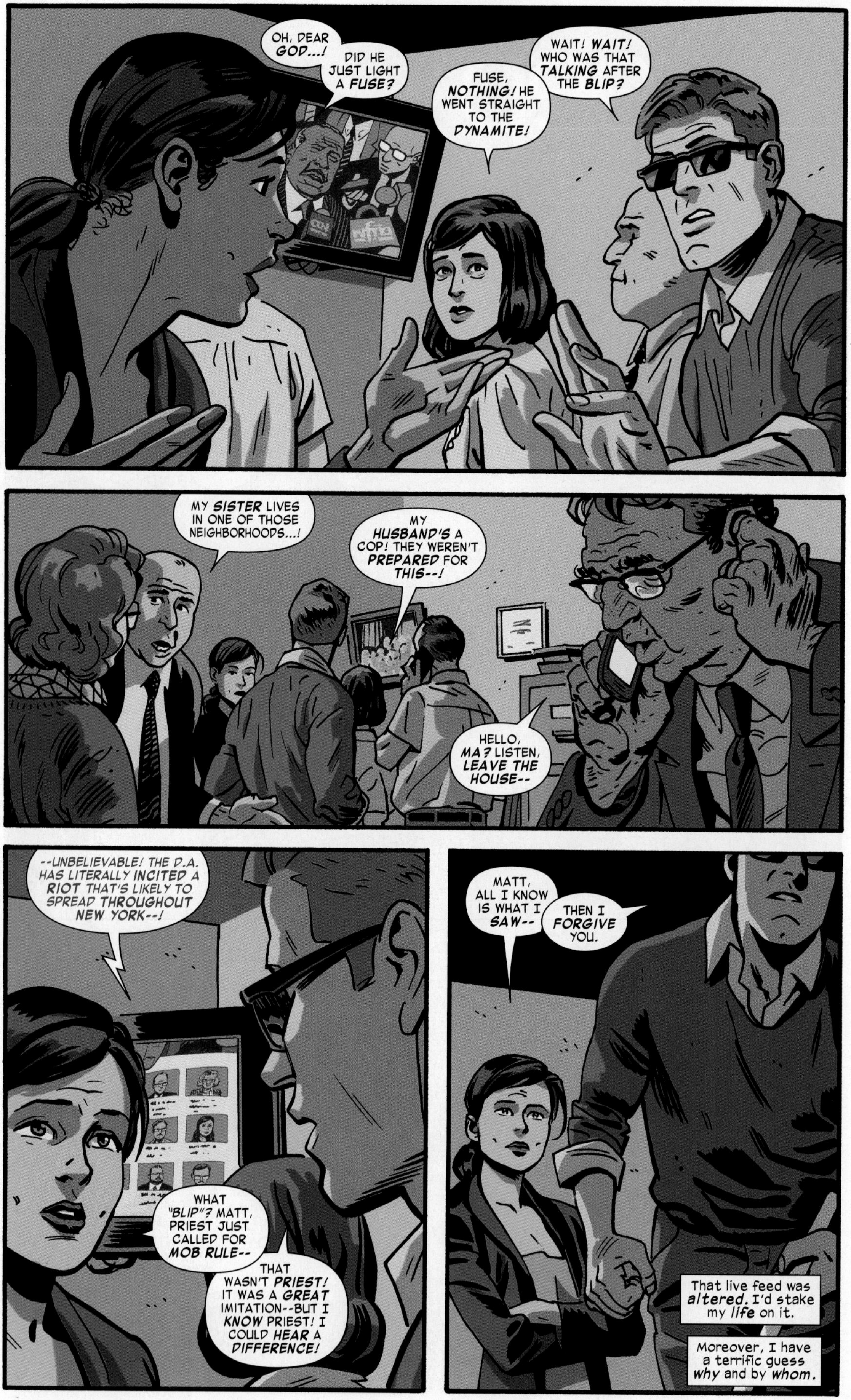
OH, DEAR GOD...!
DID HE JUST LIGHT A FUSE?
FUSE, NOTHING! HE WENT STRAIGHT TO THE DYNAMITE!
WAIT! WAIT! WHO WAS THAT TALKING AFTER THE BLIP?
MY SISTER LIVES IN ONE OF THOSE NEIGHBORHOODS...!
MY HUSBAND'S A COP! THEY WEREN'T PREPARED FOR THIS--!
HELLO, MA? LISTEN, LEAVE THE HOUSE--
--UNBELIEVABLE! THE D.A. HAS LITERALLY INCITED A RIOT THAT'S LIKELY TO SPREAD THROUGHOUT NEW YORK--!
WHAT "BLIP"? MATT, PRIEST JUST CALLED FOR MOB RULE--
THAT WASN'T PRIEST! IT WAS A GREAT IMITATION--BUT I KNOW PRIEST! I COULD HEAR A DIFFERENCE!
MATT, ALL I KNOW IS WHAT I SAW--
THEN I FORGIVE YOU.
That live feed was altered. I'd stake my life on it.
Moreover, I have a terrific guess why and by whom.

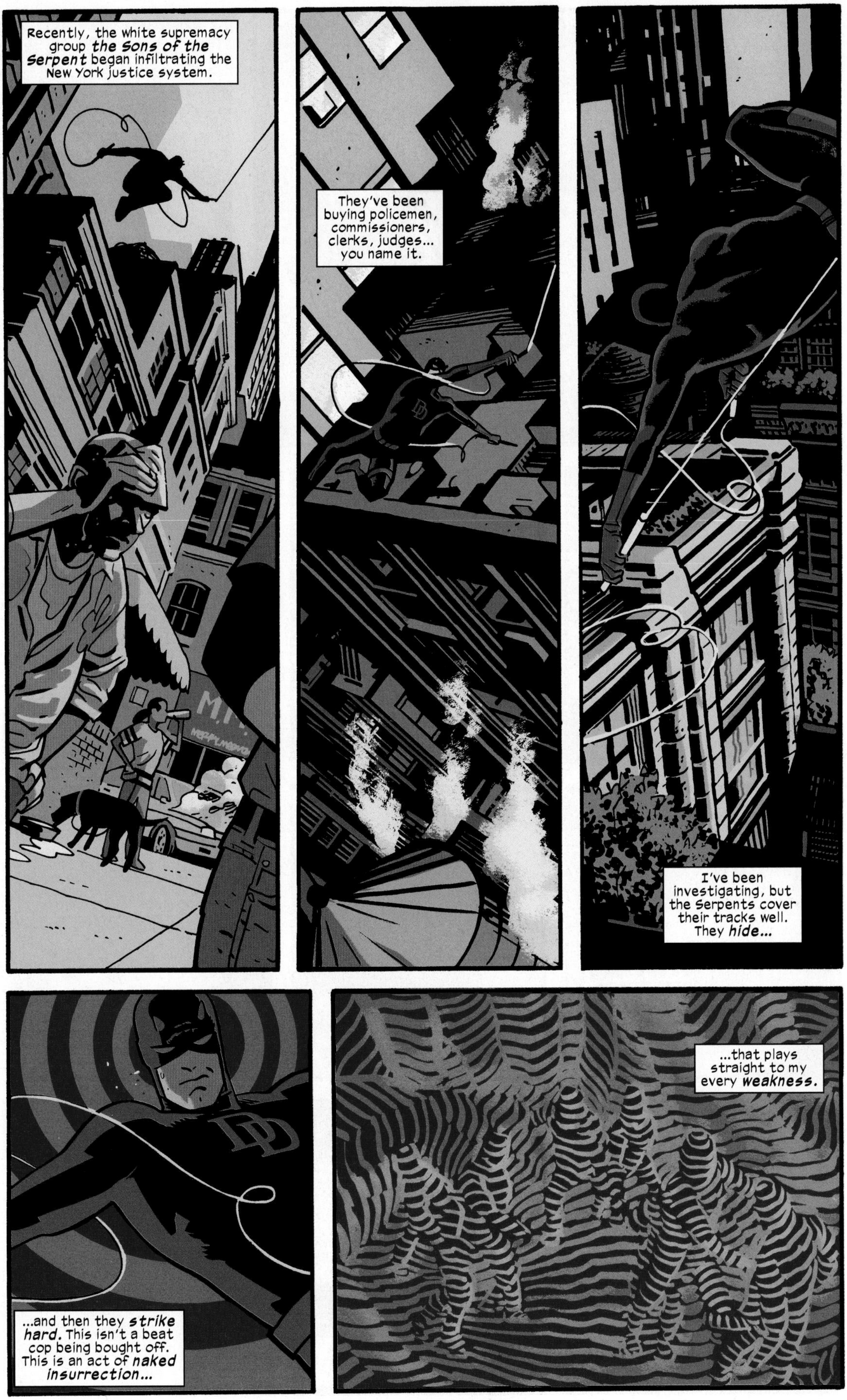
Recently, the white supremacy group *the Sons of the Serpent* began infiltrating the New York justice system.
They've been buying policemen, commissioners, clerks, judges... you name it.
I've been investigating, but the Serpents cover their tracks well. They *hide*...
...and then they *strike hard.* This isn't a beat cop being bought off. This is an act of *naked insurrection*...
...that plays straight to my every *weakness.*

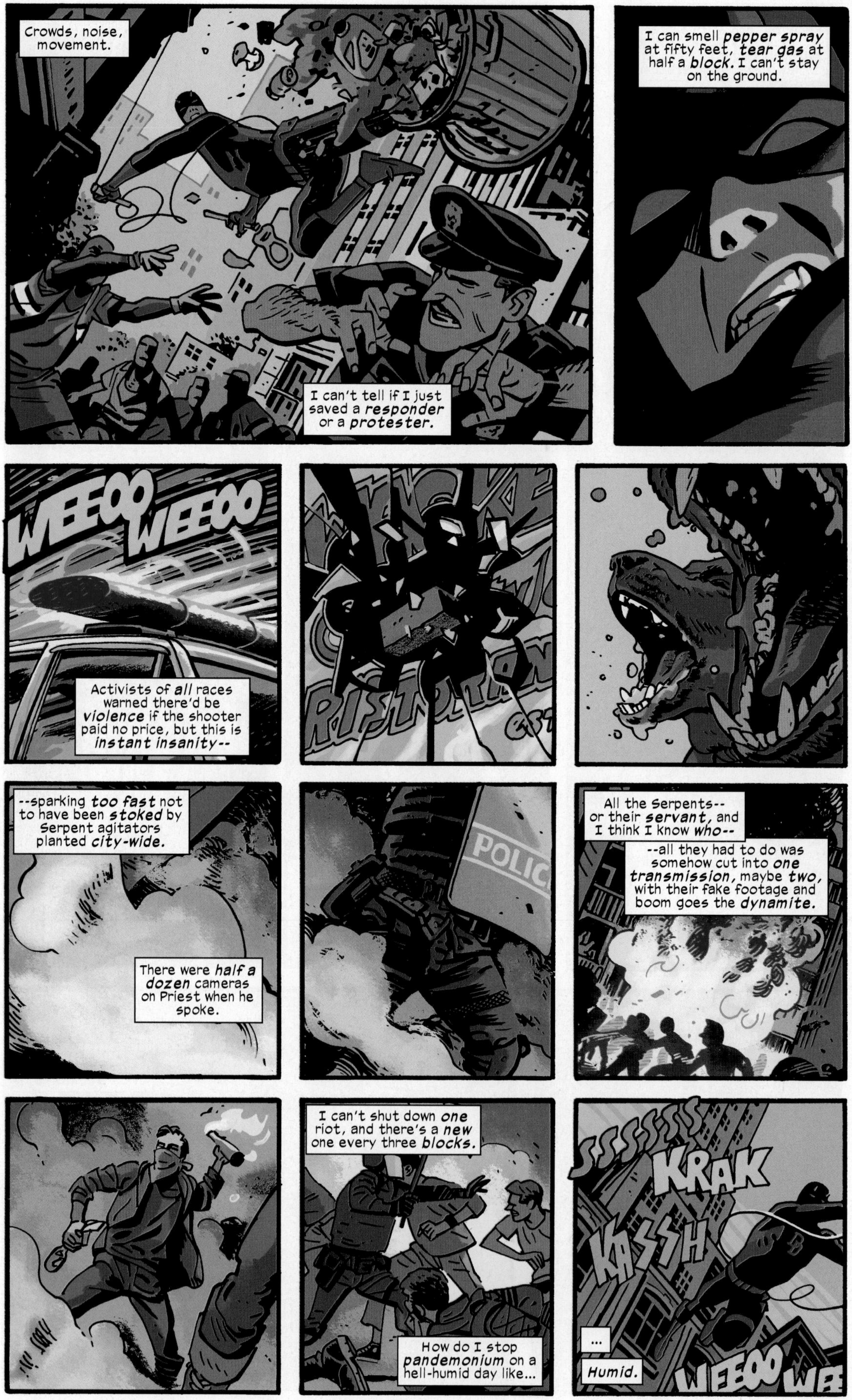
Crowds, noise, movement.
I can't tell if I just saved a *responder* or a *protester.*
I can smell *pepper spray* at fifty feet, *tear gas* at half a *block.* I can't stay on the ground.
WEEOO WEEOO
Activists of *all* races warned there'd be *violence* if the shooter paid no price, but this is *instant insanity*--
--sparking *too fast* not to have been *stoked* by Serpent agitators planted *city-wide.*
There were *half a dozen* cameras on Priest when he spoke.
POLIC
All the Serpents-- or their *servant,* and I think I know *who*--
--all they had to do was somehow cut into *one transmission,* maybe *two,* with their fake footage and boom goes the *dynamite.*
I can't shut down *one* riot, and there's a *new* one every three *blocks.*
How do I stop *pandemonium* on a hell-humid day like...
SSSSSSS
KRAK
KASSH
...
Humid.
WEEOO

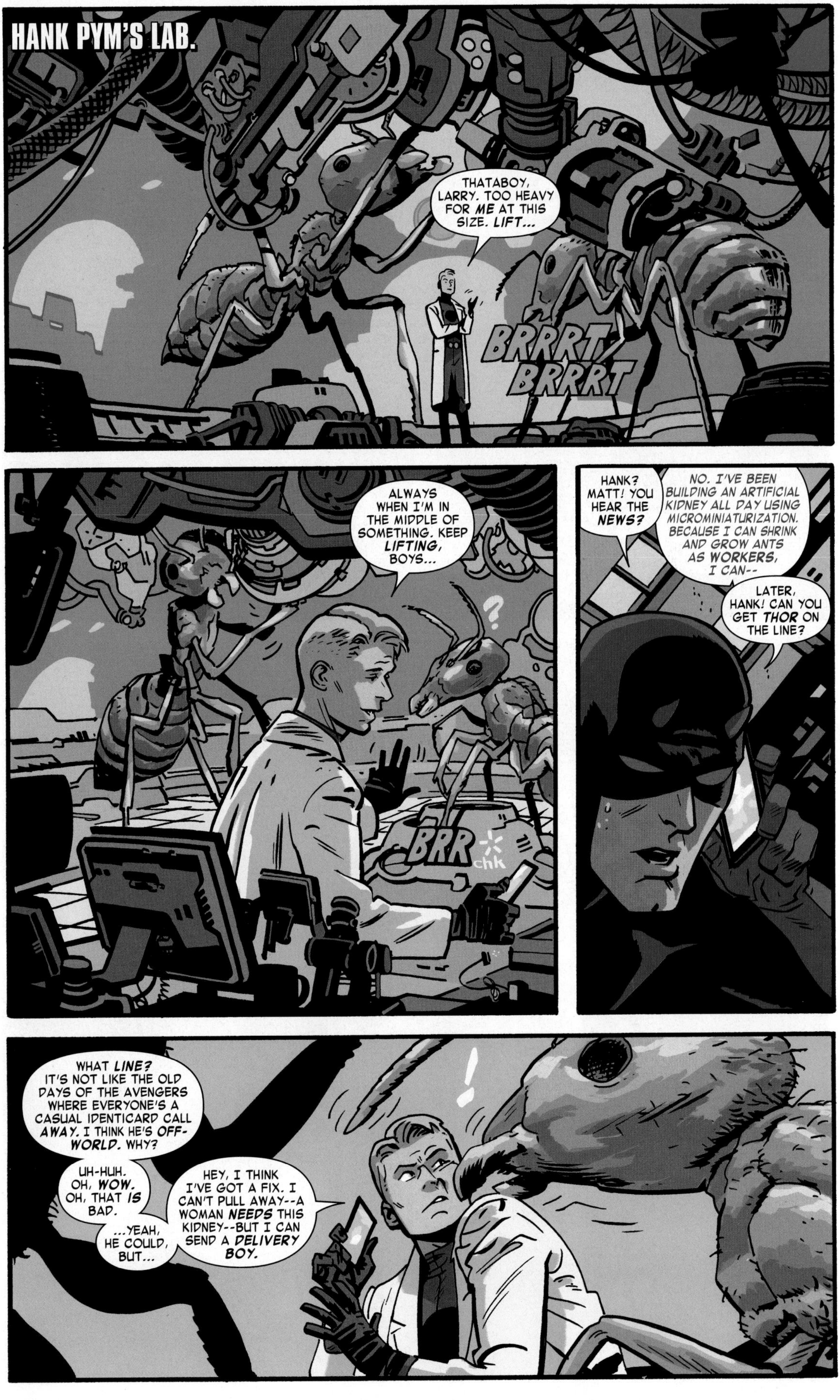
HANK PYM'S LAB.
THATABOY, LARRY. TOO HEAVY FOR ME AT THIS SIZE. LIFT...
BRRRT BRRRT
ALWAYS WHEN I'M IN THE MIDDLE OF SOMETHING. KEEP LIFTING, BOYS...
?
BRR
chk
HANK? MATT! YOU HEAR THE NEWS?
NO. I'VE BEEN BUILDING AN ARTIFICIAL KIDNEY ALL DAY USING MICROMINIATURIZATION. BECAUSE I CAN SHRINK AND GROW ANTS AS WORKERS, I CAN--
LATER, HANK! CAN YOU GET THOR ON THE LINE?
WHAT LINE? IT'S NOT LIKE THE OLD DAYS OF THE AVENGERS WHERE EVERYONE'S A CASUAL IDENTICARD CALL AWAY. I THINK HE'S OFF-WORLD. WHY?
UH-HUH. OH, WOW. OH, THAT IS BAD.
...YEAH, HE COULD, BUT...
HEY, I THINK I'VE GOT A FIX. I CAN'T PULL AWAY--A WOMAN NEEDS THIS KIDNEY--BUT I CAN SEND A DELIVERY BOY.
!

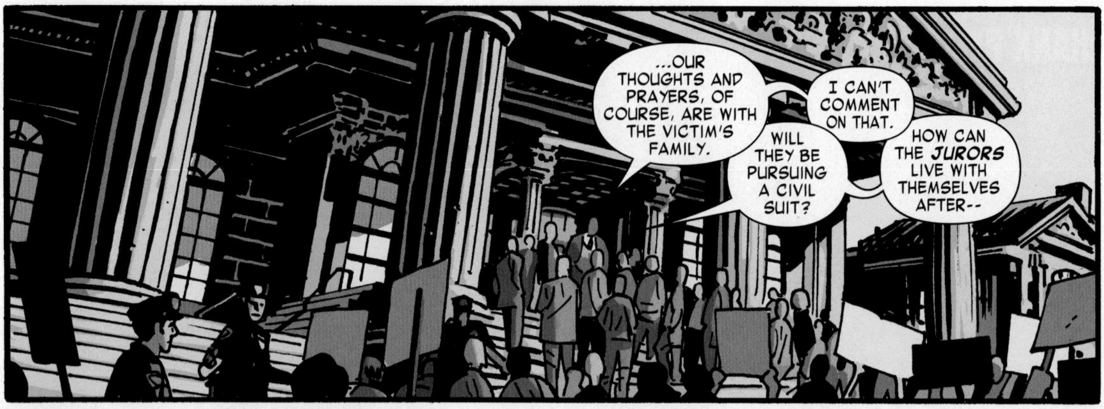
...OUR THOUGHTS AND PRAYERS, OF COURSE, ARE WITH THE VICTIM'S FAMILY.
I CAN'T COMMENT ON THAT.
WILL THEY BE PURSUING A CIVIL SUIT?
HOW CAN THE JURORS LIVE WITH THEMSELVES AFTER--

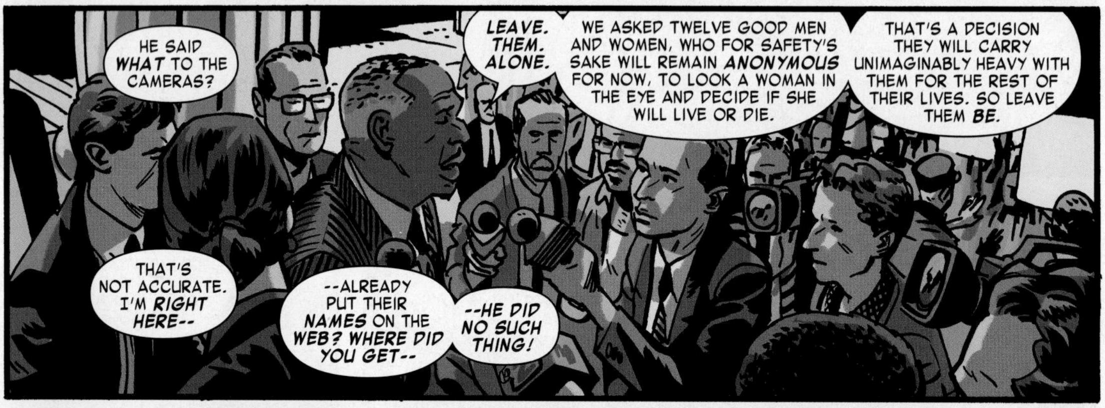
HE SAID WHAT TO THE CAMERAS?
LEAVE. THEM. ALONE.
WE ASKED TWELVE GOOD MEN AND WOMEN, WHO FOR SAFETY'S SAKE WILL REMAIN ANONYMOUS FOR NOW, TO LOOK A WOMAN IN THE EYE AND DECIDE IF SHE WILL LIVE OR DIE.
THAT'S A DECISION THEY WILL CARRY UNIMAGINABLY HEAVY WITH THEM FOR THE REST OF THEIR LIVES. SO LEAVE THEM BE.
THAT'S NOT ACCURATE. I'M RIGHT HERE--
--ALREADY PUT THEIR NAMES ON THE WEB? WHERE DID YOU GET--
--HE DID NO SUCH THING!

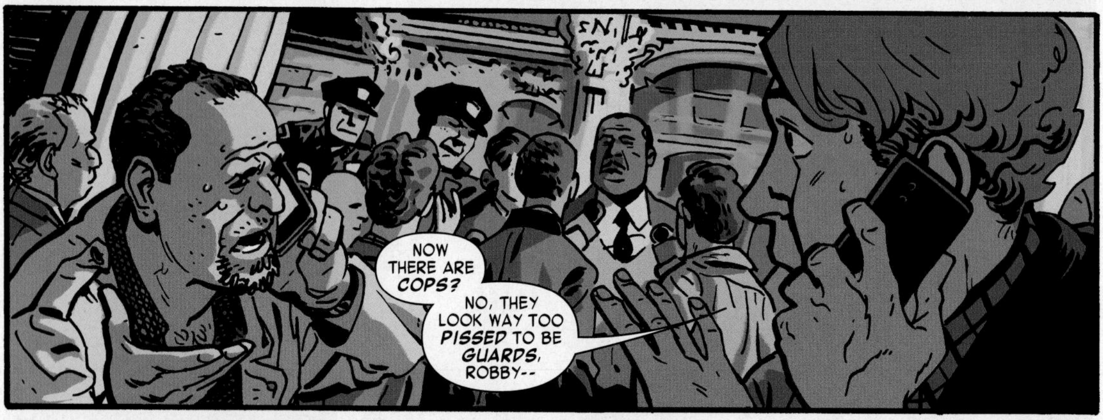
NOW THERE ARE COPS?
NO, THEY LOOK WAY TOO PISSED TO BE GUARDS, ROBBY--

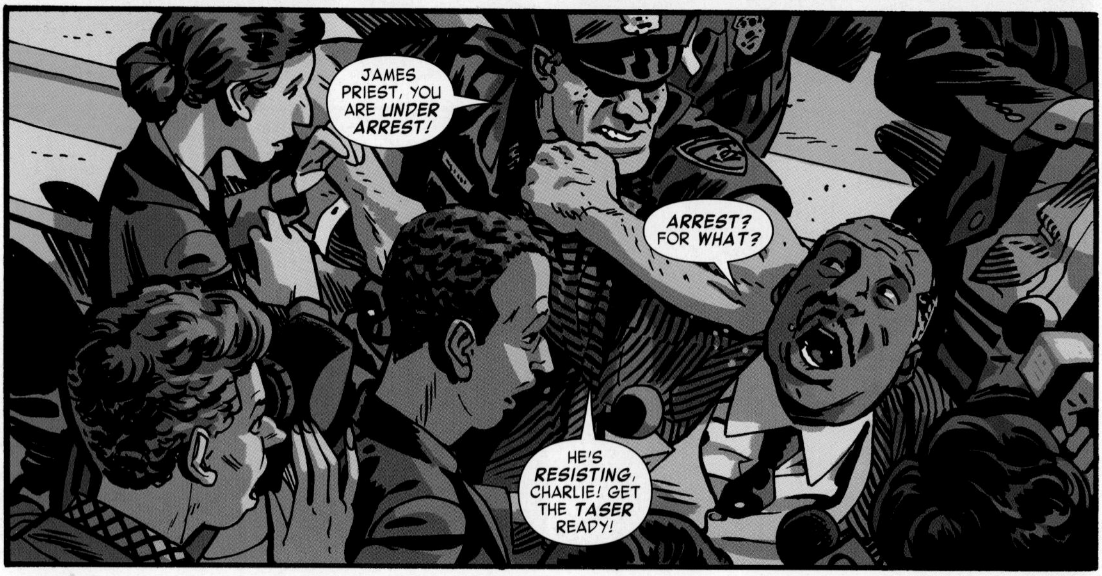
JAMES PRIEST, YOU ARE UNDER ARREST!
ARREST? FOR WHAT?
HE'S RESISTING, CHARLIE! GET THE TASER READY!

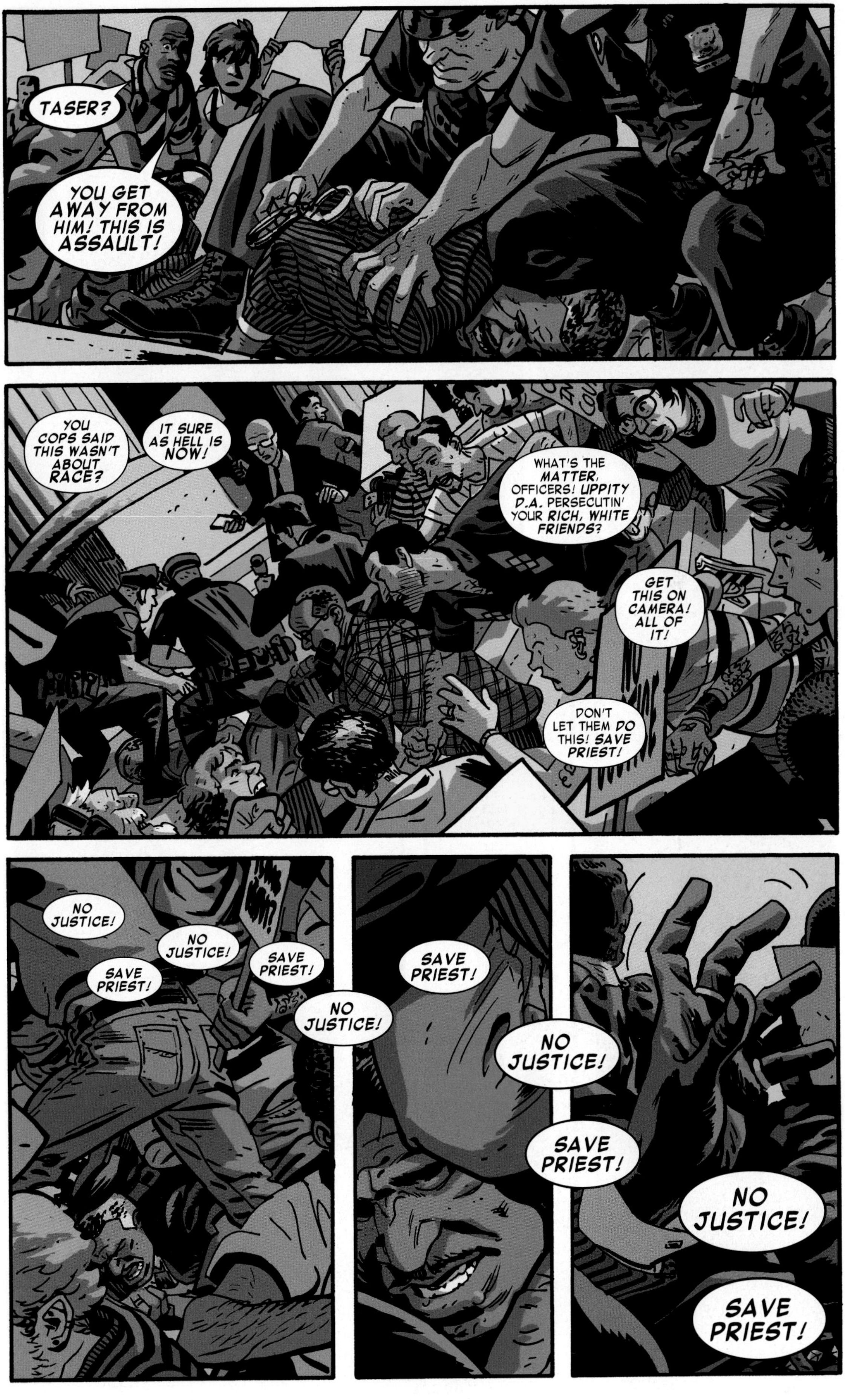
TASER?
YOU GET AWAY FROM HIM! THIS IS ASSAULT!
YOU COPS SAID THIS WASN'T ABOUT RACE?
IT SURE AS HELL IS NOW!
WHAT'S THE MATTER, OFFICERS! UPPITY D.A. PERSECUTIN' YOUR RICH, WHITE FRIENDS?
GET THIS ON CAMERA! ALL OF IT!
DON'T LET THEM DO THIS! SAVE PRIEST!
NO JUSTICE!
SAVE PRIEST!
NO JUSTICE!
SAVE PRIEST!
NO JUSTICE!
SAVE PRIEST!
NO JUSTICE!
SAVE PRIEST!
NO JUSTICE!
SAVE PRIEST!

SAVE PRIEST!

SAVE PRIES

SAVE PRIEST.

MY PLEASURE.

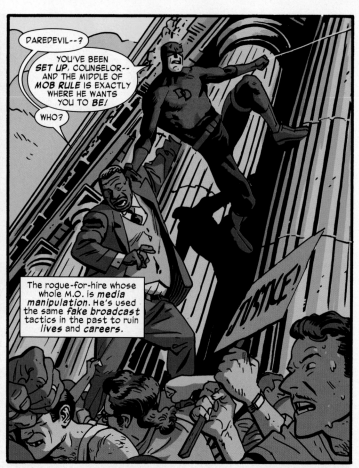

DAREDEVIL--?

YOU'VE BEEN *SET UP*, COUNSELOR-- AND THE MIDDLE OF *MOB RULE* IS EXACTLY WHERE HE WANTS YOU TO *BE!*

WHO?

The rogue-for-hire whose whole M.O. is *media manipulation.* He's used the same *fake broadcast* tactics in the past to ruin *lives* and *careers.*

His name is the *Jester*--but there's not one thing *funny* about him.

God, it's sweltering. Hank, if you're good with your *word*--

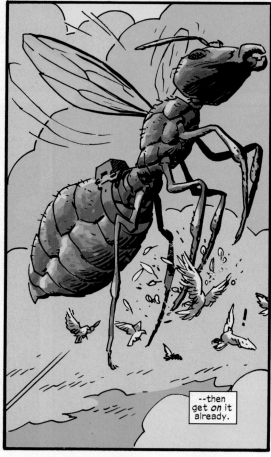

--then get *on* it already.

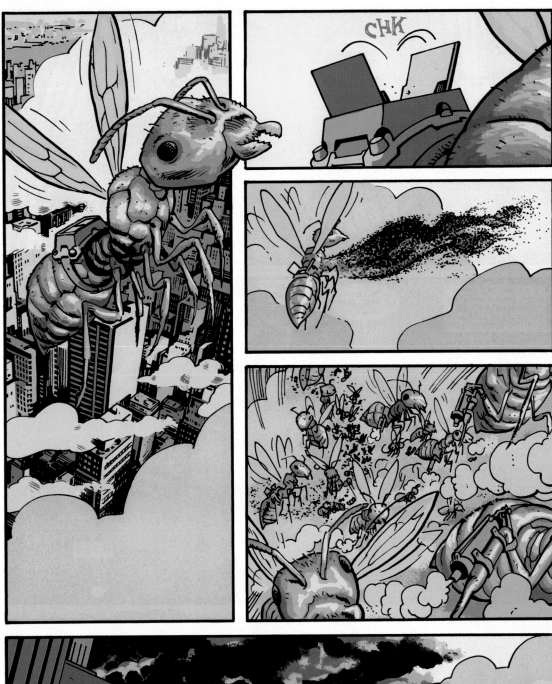

CHK

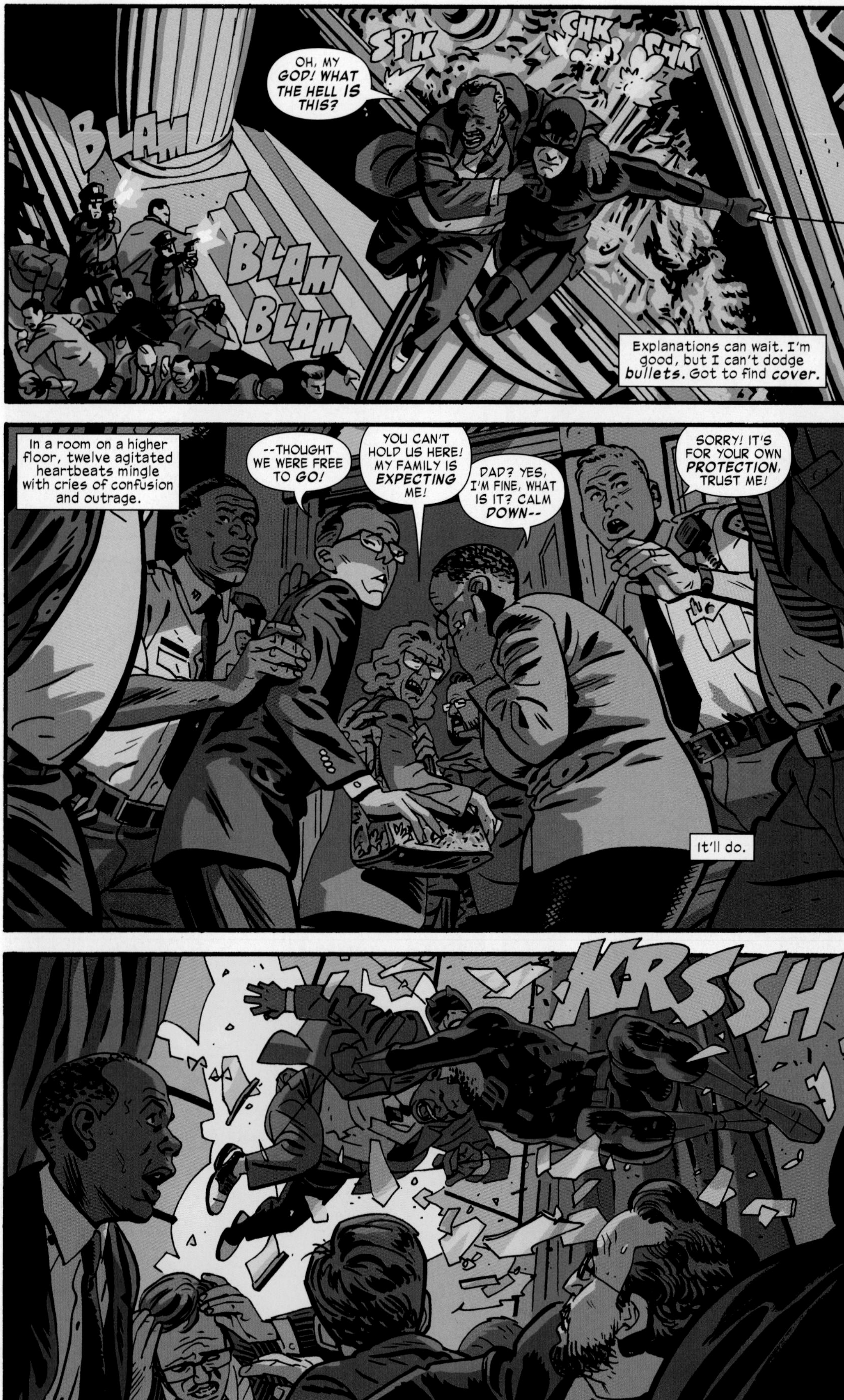
SPK
CHK
CHK
OH, MY GOD! WHAT THE HELL IS THIS?
BLAM
BLAM BLAM
Explanations can wait. I'm good, but I can't dodge bullets. Got to find cover.
In a room on a higher floor, twelve agitated heartbeats mingle with cries of confusion and outrage.
--THOUGHT WE WERE FREE TO GO!
YOU CAN'T HOLD US HERE! MY FAMILY IS EXPECTING ME!
DAD? YES, I'M FINE, WHAT IS IT? CALM DOWN--
SORRY! IT'S FOR YOUR OWN PROTECTION, TRUST ME!
It'll do.
KRSSH

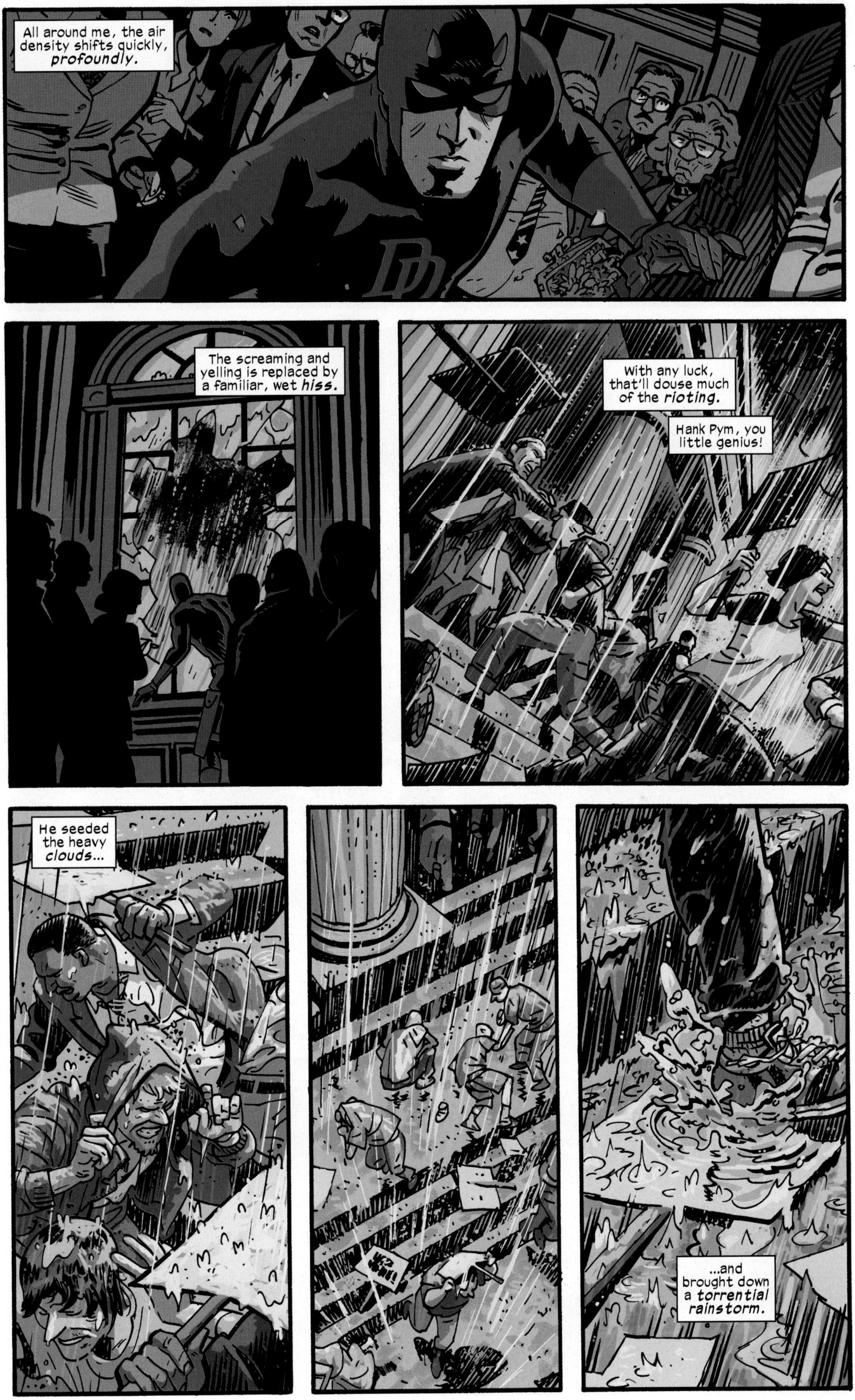
All around me, the air density shifts quickly, profoundly.
The screaming and yelling is replaced by a familiar, wet hiss.
With any luck, that'll douse much of the rioting.
Hank Pym, you little genius!
He seeded the heavy clouds...
...and brought down a torrential rainstorm.

EVERYONE *SHUT UP, LISTEN,* AND ABOVE ALL, *DO NOT MOVE!*

YOUR LIVES *DEPEND* ON STAYING *RIGHT WHERE YOU ARE!*

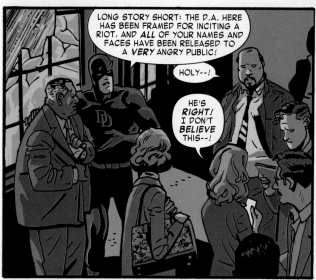

LONG STORY SHORT: THE D.A. HERE HAS BEEN FRAMED FOR INCITING A RIOT, AND *ALL* OF YOUR NAMES AND FACES HAVE BEEN RELEASED TO A *VERY* ANGRY PUBLIC!

HOLY--!

HE'S *RIGHT!* I DON'T *BELIEVE* THIS--!

ALL OF US! THEY'RE CALLING FOR *BLOOD!* SEE?

HOW COULD THIS HAVE *HAPPENED?*

WE'LL GET *COPS* TO YOUR *HOMES!* YOU'LL BE SAFE *HERE,* ALL OF YOU!

EXCEPT *THIS GUY!* HE'S NOT ONE OF *US!*

What?

I'M NOT ON THE LIST, BUT HE *IS!* SEE? WHO *IS* HE?

John Powers
1017 W 80th St
NYC, NY 100[ ]

DO YOU *RECOGNIZE* HIM?

Ummm...

JOHN POWERS. DOES ANYBODY HERE KNOW THAT NAME?

Jonathan Powers. The *Jester.* Thank God for super villain *egos.*

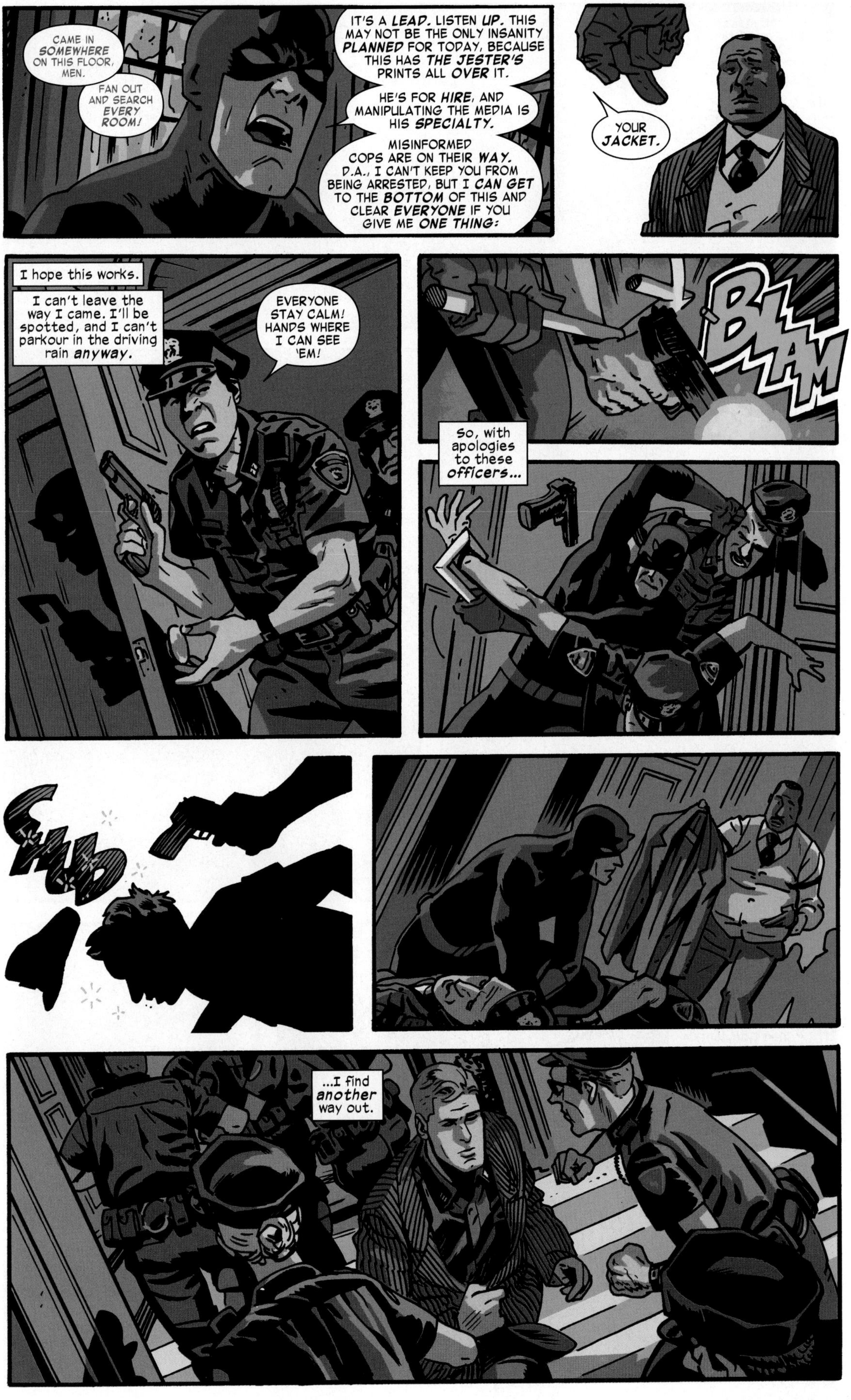

CAME IN SOMEWHERE ON THIS FLOOR, MEN.
FAN OUT AND SEARCH EVERY ROOM!
IT'S A LEAD. LISTEN UP. THIS MAY NOT BE THE ONLY INSANITY PLANNED FOR TODAY, BECAUSE THIS HAS THE JESTER'S PRINTS ALL OVER IT.
HE'S FOR HIRE, AND MANIPULATING THE MEDIA IS HIS SPECIALTY.
MISINFORMED COPS ARE ON THEIR WAY. D.A., I CAN'T KEEP YOU FROM BEING ARRESTED, BUT I CAN GET TO THE BOTTOM OF THIS AND CLEAR EVERYONE IF YOU GIVE ME ONE THING:
YOUR JACKET.
I hope this works.
I can't leave the way I came. I'll be spotted, and I can't parkour in the driving rain anyway.
EVERYONE STAY CALM! HANDS WHERE I CAN SEE 'EM!
BLAM
So, with apologies to these officers...
...I find another way out.

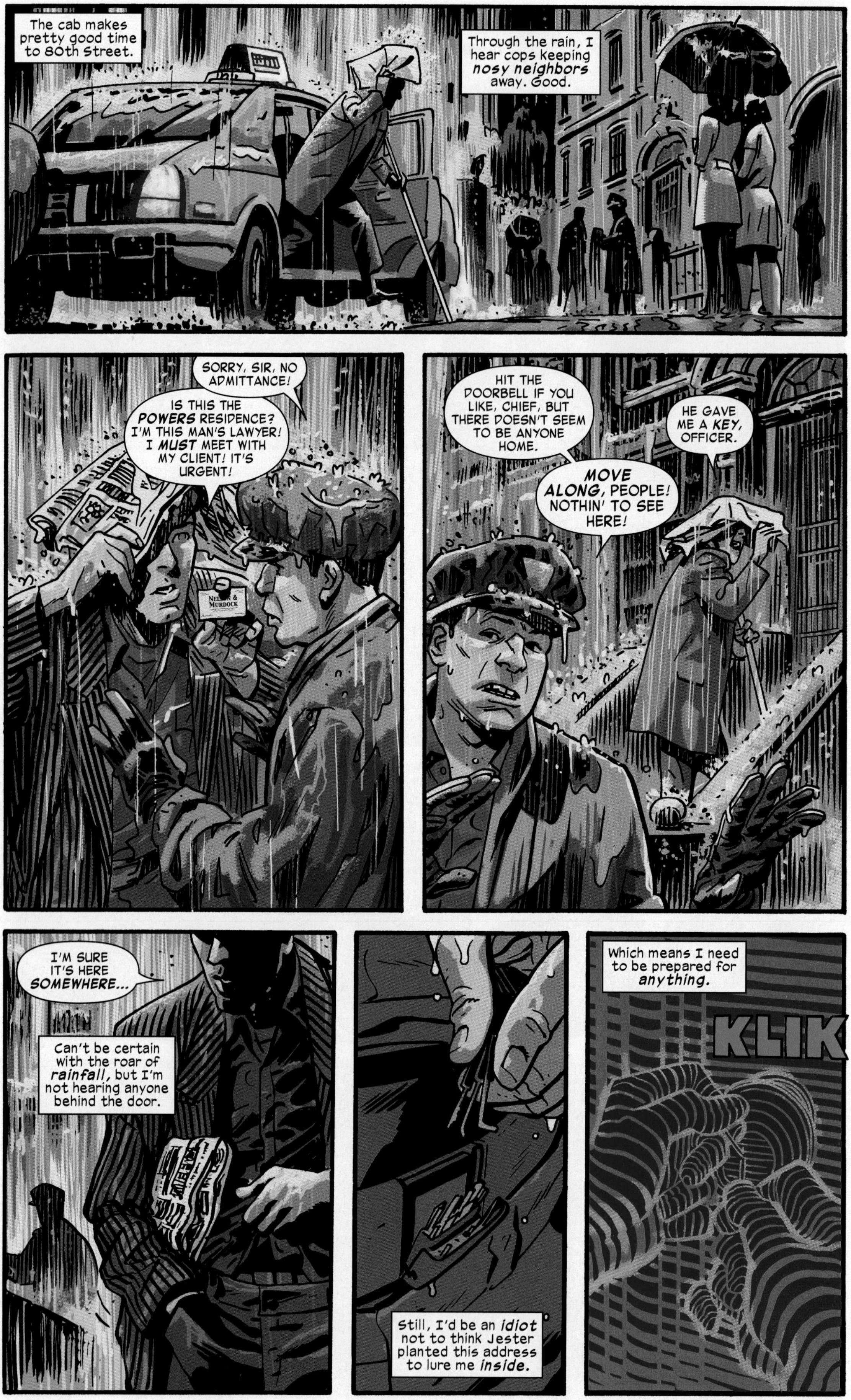
The cab makes pretty good time to 80th Street.
Through the rain, I hear cops keeping nosy neighbors away. Good.
SORRY, SIR, NO ADMITTANCE!
IS THIS THE POWERS RESIDENCE? I'M THIS MAN'S LAWYER! I MUST MEET WITH MY CLIENT! IT'S URGENT!
NELSON & MURDOCK
HIT THE DOORBELL IF YOU LIKE, CHIEF, BUT THERE DOESN'T SEEM TO BE ANYONE HOME.
HE GAVE ME A KEY, OFFICER.
MOVE ALONG, PEOPLE! NOTHIN' TO SEE HERE!
I'M SURE IT'S HERE SOMEWHERE...
Can't be certain with the roar of rainfall, but I'm not hearing anyone behind the door.
Still, I'd be an idiot not to think Jester planted this address to lure me inside.
Which means I need to be prepared for anything.
KLIK

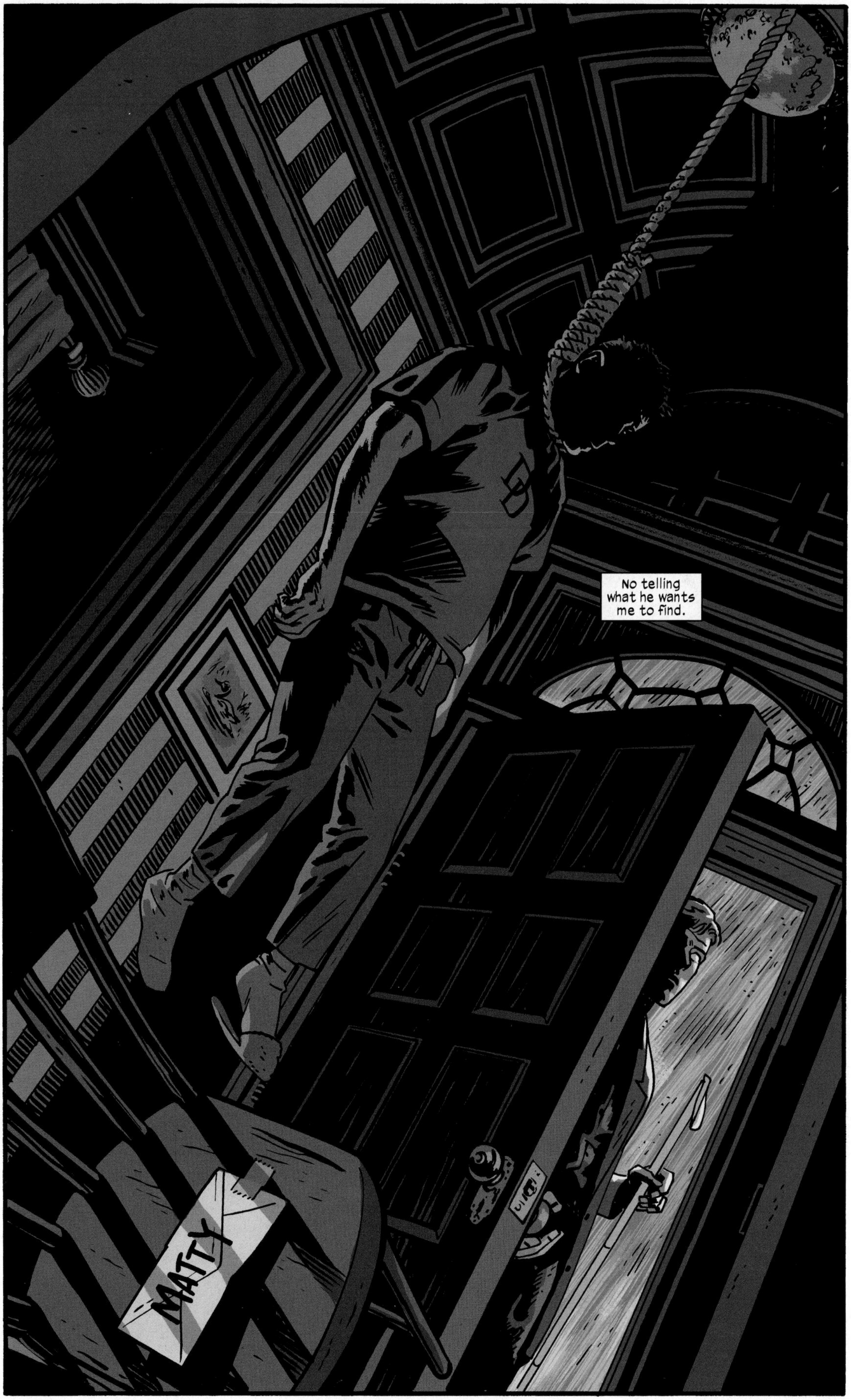
No telling what he wants me to find.
MATTY

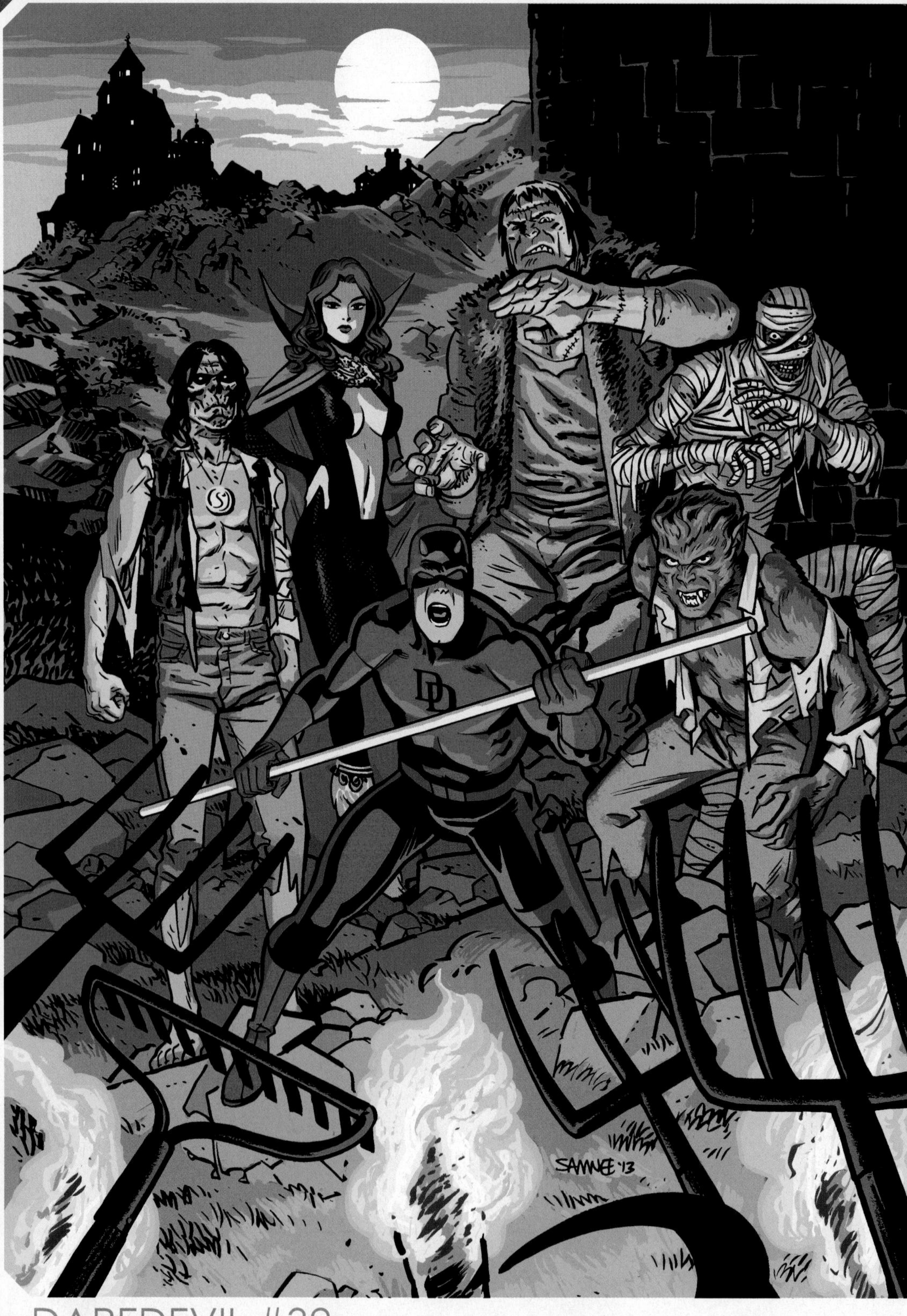
SAMNEE '13

DAREDEVIL #32

WHEN MOST DULLARDS HEAR THE WORDS "THE THEATER," THEY ENVISION A TWELVE-SCREEN MULTIPLEX WHERE DISASTER PORN ENTERTAINS THE CULTURALLY *WITLESS* FOR 90 MINUTES AT A TIME.

PFAUGH.

THE WORD "THEATER" HAS GRANDEUR. *POWER.* BACK TO ITS ANCIENT GRECIAN ORIGINS, IT MEANS "THE *SEEING* PLACE."

A *STAGE* UPON WHICH *LIVE ACTORS* AND *ACTRESSES* USE *FICTION* TO SHOW US *TRUTHS.*

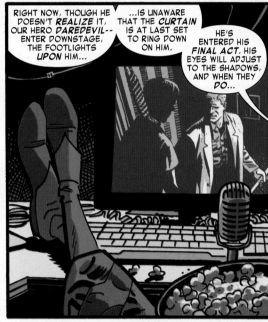

RIGHT NOW, THOUGH HE DOESN'T *REALIZE* IT, OUR HERO *DAREDEVIL*-- ENTER DOWNSTAGE, THE FOOTLIGHTS *UPON* HIM...

...IS UNAWARE THAT THE *CURTAIN* IS AT LAST SET TO RING DOWN ON HIM.

HE'S ENTERED HIS *FINAL ACT.* HIS EYES WILL ADJUST TO THE SHADOWS, AND WHEN THEY *DO*...

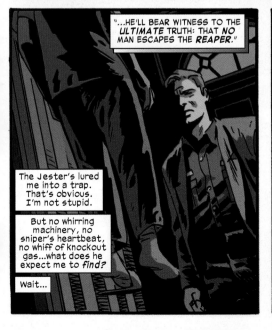

"...HE'LL BEAR WITNESS TO THE *ULTIMATE* TRUTH: THAT *NO* MAN ESCAPES THE *REAPER.*"

The Jester's lured me into a trap. That's obvious. I'm not stupid.

But no whirring machinery, no sniper's heartbeat, no whiff of knockout gas...what does he expect me to find?

Wait...

ANNND *CUE* THE SHOCKED REACTION FROM THE BARRISTER!

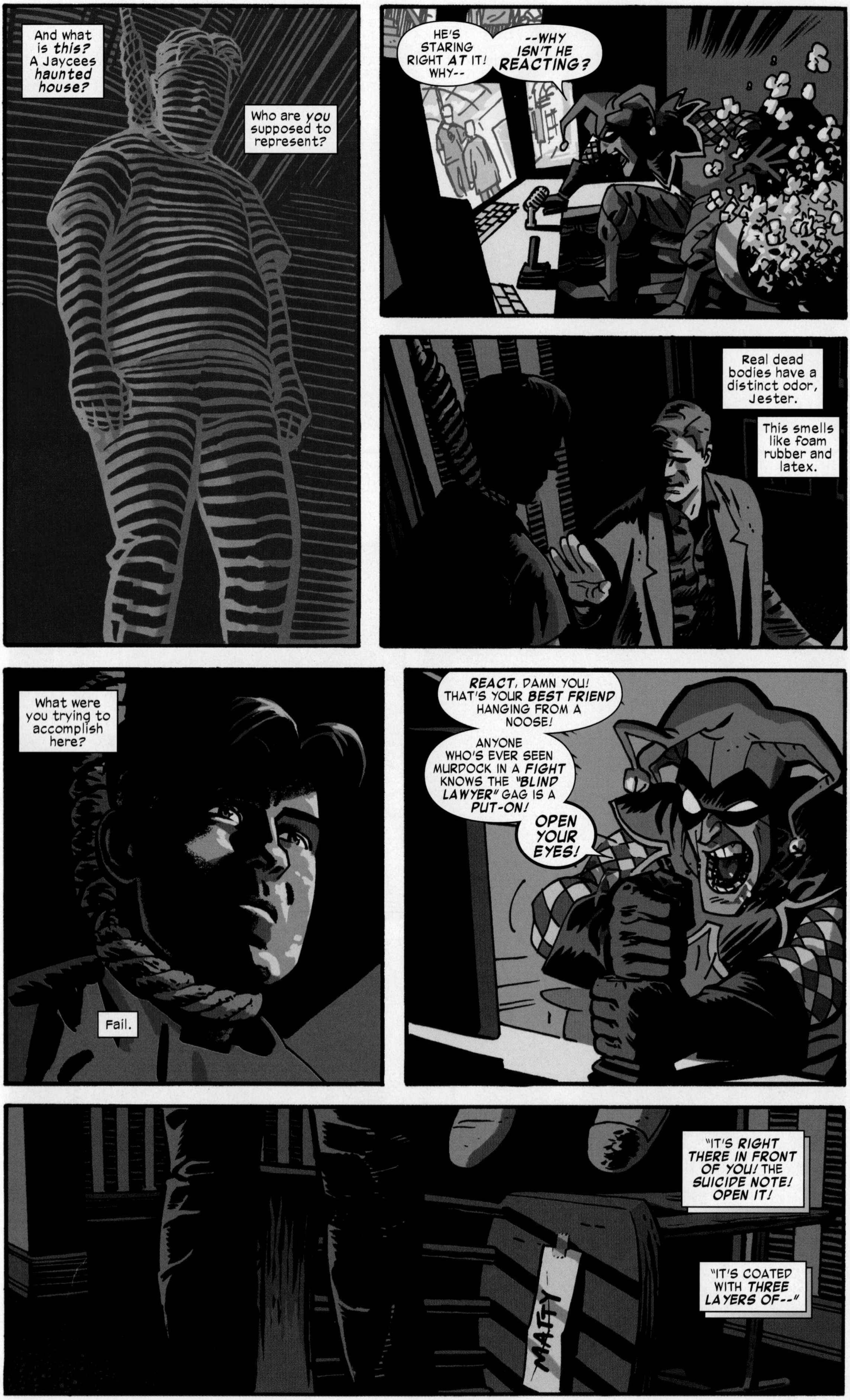
And what is *this?* A Jaycees *haunted house?*
Who are *you* supposed to represent?
HE'S STARING RIGHT *AT* IT! WHY--
--WHY *ISN'T* HE *REACTING?*
Real dead bodies have a distinct odor, Jester.
This smells like foam rubber and latex.
What were you trying to accomplish here?
Fail.
REACT, DAMN YOU! THAT'S YOUR *BEST FRIEND* HANGING FROM A NOOSE!
ANYONE WHO'S EVER SEEN MURDOCK IN A *FIGHT* KNOWS THE *"BLIND LAWYER"* GAG IS A *PUT-ON!*
OPEN YOUR EYES!
"IT'S *RIGHT THERE IN FRONT OF YOU!* THE *SUICIDE NOTE! OPEN IT!*
"IT'S COATED WITH *THREE LAYERS OF--"*
MATTY

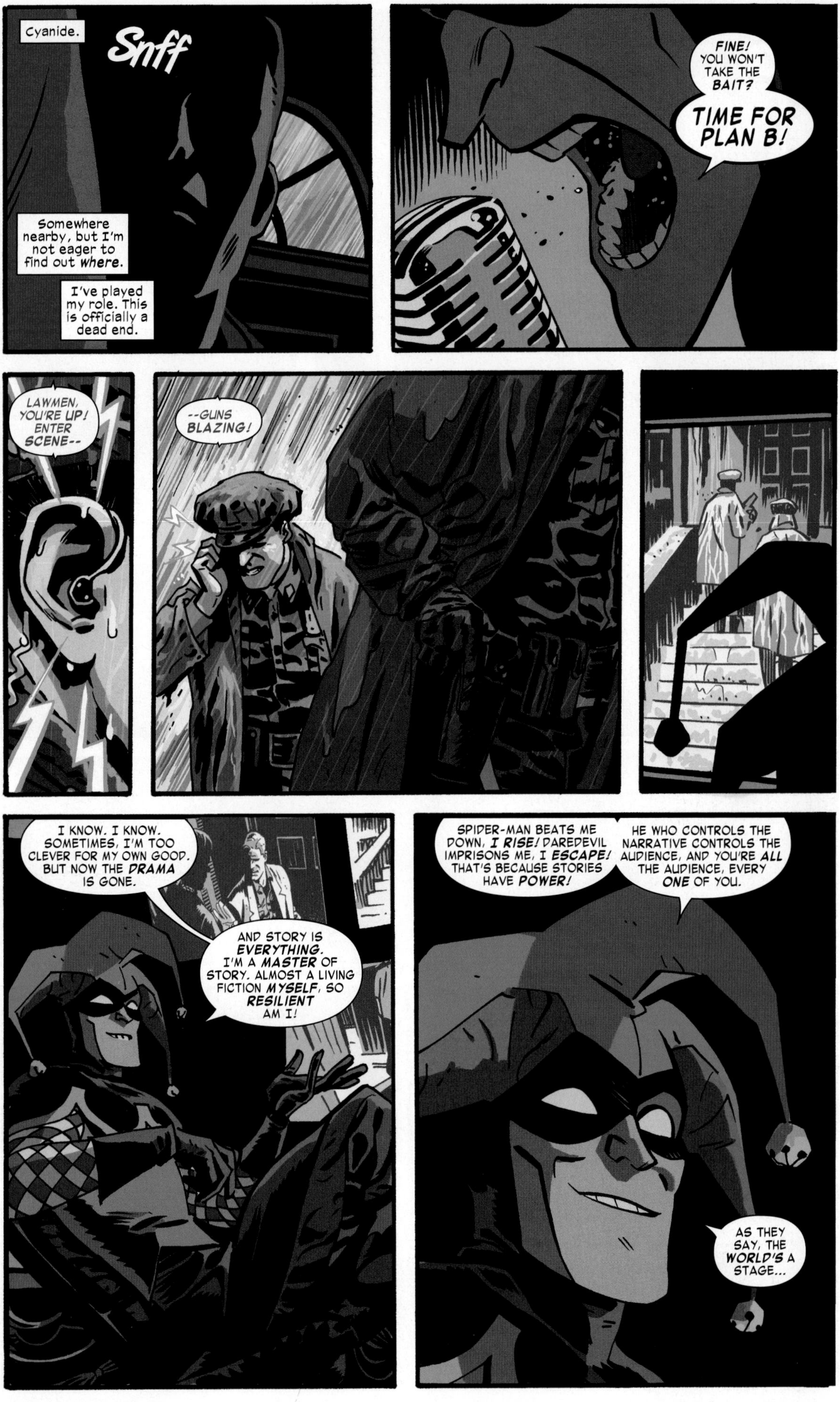
Cyanide.
Snff
Somewhere nearby, but I'm not eager to find out where.
I've played my role. This is officially a dead end.
FINE! YOU WON'T TAKE THE BAIT?
TIME FOR PLAN B!
LAWMEN, YOU'RE UP! ENTER SCENE--
--GUNS BLAZING!
I KNOW. I KNOW. SOMETIMES, I'M TOO CLEVER FOR MY OWN GOOD. BUT NOW THE DRAMA IS GONE.
AND STORY IS EVERYTHING. I'M A MASTER OF STORY. ALMOST A LIVING FICTION MYSELF, SO RESILIENT AM I!
SPIDER-MAN BEATS ME DOWN, I RISE! DAREDEVIL IMPRISONS ME, I ESCAPE! THAT'S BECAUSE STORIES HAVE POWER!
HE WHO CONTROLS THE NARRATIVE CONTROLS THE AUDIENCE, AND YOU'RE ALL THE AUDIENCE, EVERY ONE OF YOU.
AS THEY SAY, THE WORLD'S A STAGE...

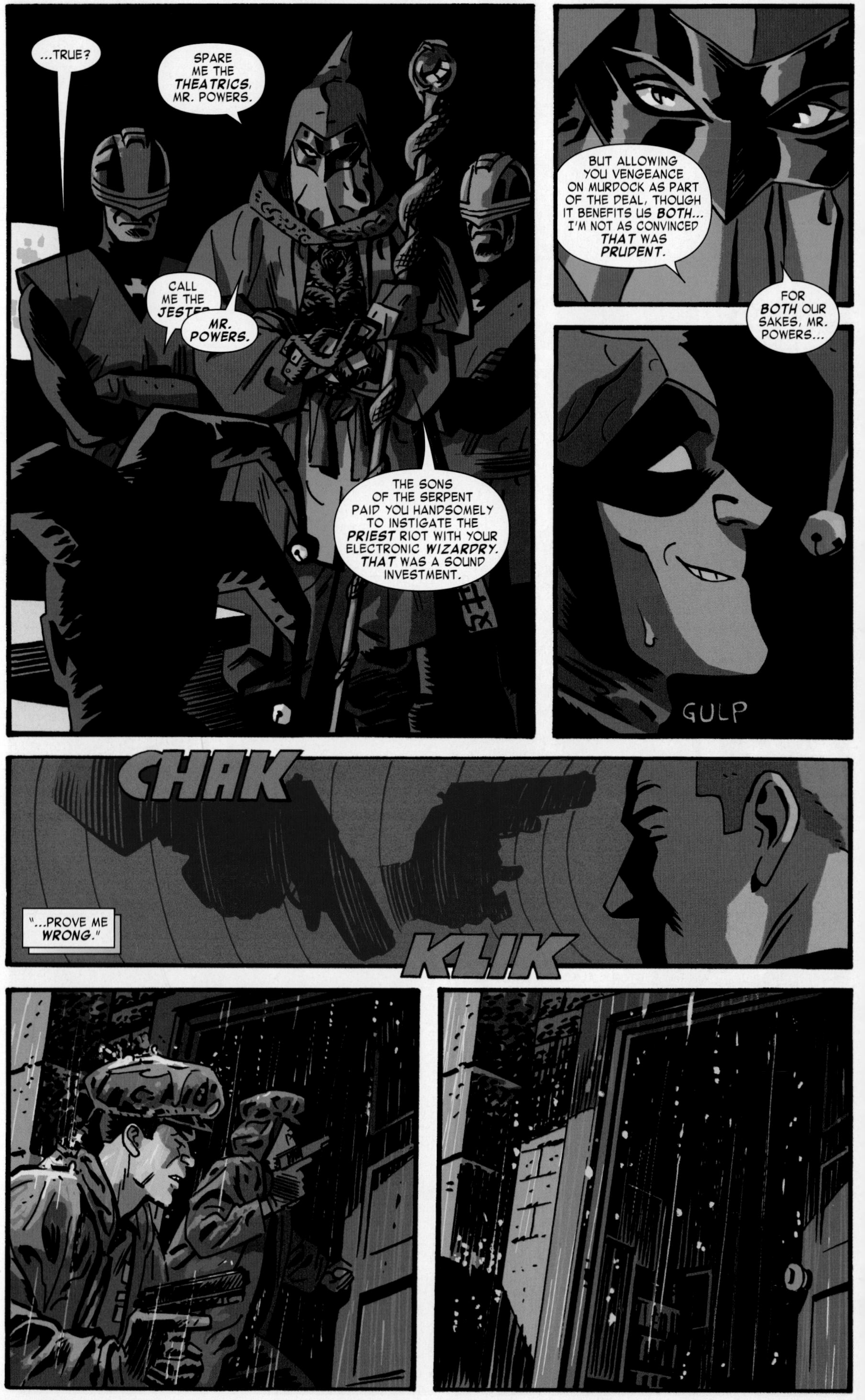
...TRUE?
SPARE ME THE THEATRICS, MR. POWERS.
CALL ME THE JESTER,
MR. POWERS.
THE SONS OF THE SERPENT PAID YOU HANDSOMELY TO INSTIGATE THE PRIEST RIOT WITH YOUR ELECTRONIC WIZARDRY. THAT WAS A SOUND INVESTMENT.
BUT ALLOWING YOU VENGEANCE ON MURDOCK AS PART OF THE DEAL, THOUGH IT BENEFITS US BOTH... I'M NOT AS CONVINCED THAT WAS PRUDENT.
FOR BOTH OUR SAKES, MR. POWERS...
GULP
CHAK
"...PROVE ME WRONG."
KLIK

I REALLY HATE GUNS, YOU LUMBERING *OX*.

BUT I REALLY, *REALLY* HATE COPS ON THE *TAKE* FROM THE SONS OF THE SERPENT...

...AND I WOULD REALLY, *REALLY LIKE* ONE OR BOTH OF YOU TO *TELL ME WHERE THE JESTER IS,* AND FAST.

WE DON'T KNOW! I SWEAR! OH GOD PLEASE DON'T KILL ME PLEASE PLEASE DON'T I'M *BEGGING* YOU WE DON'T KNOW!

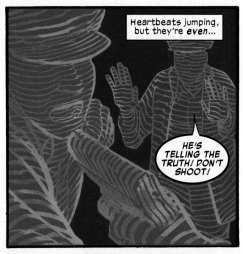

Heartbeats jumping, but they're *even*...

HE'S TELLING THE *TRUTH! DON'T* SHOOT!

...damn it.

I WASN'T GOING TO.

NOT MY STYLE.

CHAK

WUMP

YOU'RE ABOUT TO BE SOMEONE ELSE'S PROBLEM...

...ONCE THE D.A. HAS YOUR *NAMES.*

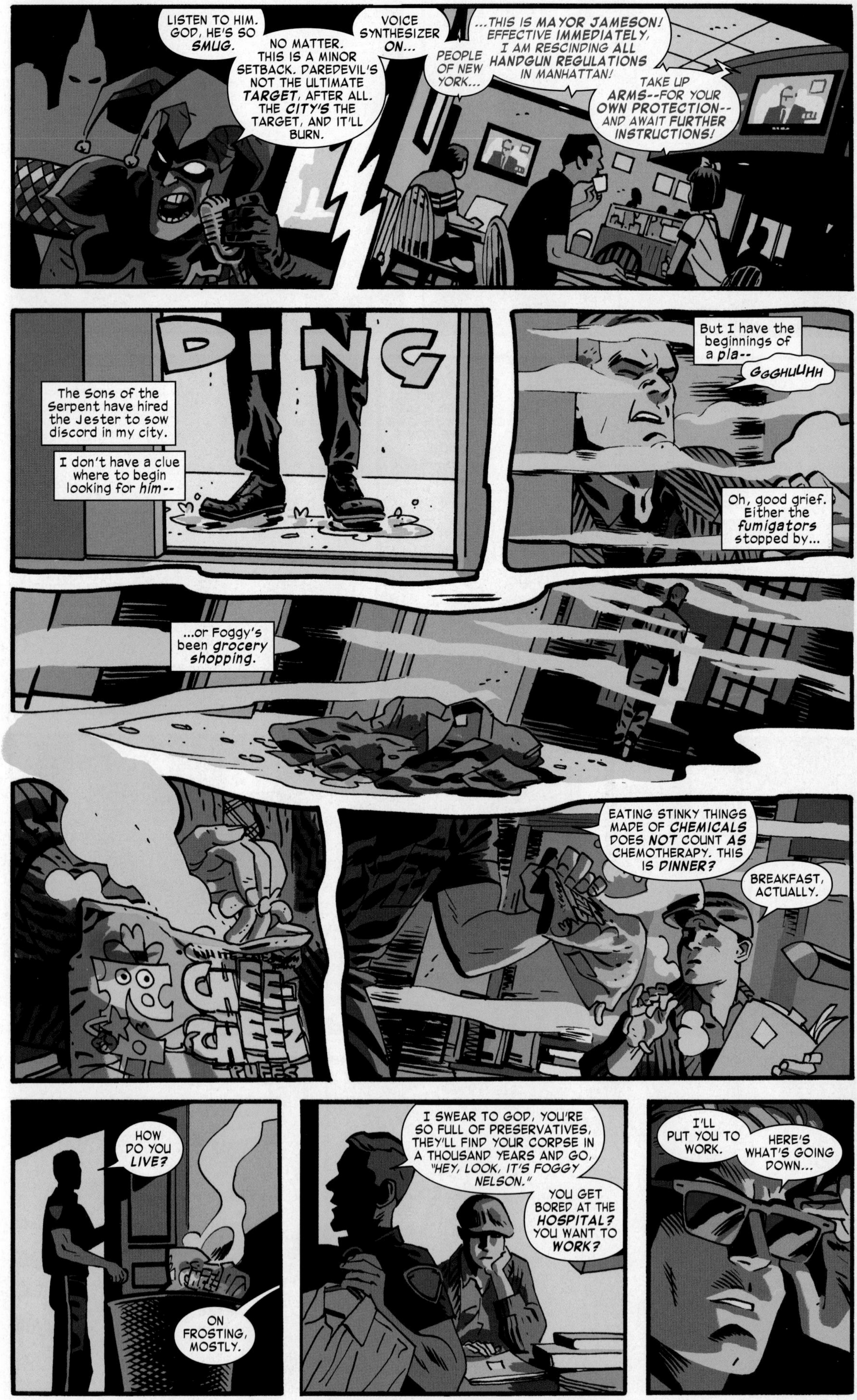
LISTEN TO HIM. GOD, HE'S SO SMUG.
NO MATTER. THIS IS A MINOR SETBACK. DAREDEVIL'S NOT THE ULTIMATE TARGET, AFTER ALL. THE CITY'S THE TARGET, AND IT'LL BURN.
VOICE SYNTHESIZER ON...
PEOPLE OF NEW YORK...
...THIS IS MAYOR JAMESON! EFFECTIVE IMMEDIATELY, I AM RESCINDING ALL HANDGUN REGULATIONS IN MANHATTAN!
TAKE UP ARMS--FOR YOUR OWN PROTECTION--AND AWAIT FURTHER INSTRUCTIONS!
DING
The Sons of the Serpent have hired the Jester to sow discord in my city.
I don't have a clue where to begin looking for him--
But I have the beginnings of a pla--
GGGHUUHH
Oh, good grief. Either the fumigators stopped by...
...or Foggy's been grocery shopping.
CHEEZ PUFFS
EATING STINKY THINGS MADE OF CHEMICALS DOES NOT COUNT AS CHEMOTHERAPY. THIS IS DINNER?
BREAKFAST, ACTUALLY.
HOW DO YOU LIVE?
ON FROSTING, MOSTLY.
I SWEAR TO GOD, YOU'RE SO FULL OF PRESERVATIVES, THEY'LL FIND YOUR CORPSE IN A THOUSAND YEARS AND GO, "HEY, LOOK, IT'S FOGGY NELSON."
YOU GET BORED AT THE HOSPITAL? YOU WANT TO WORK?
I'LL PUT YOU TO WORK.
HERE'S WHAT'S GOING DOWN...

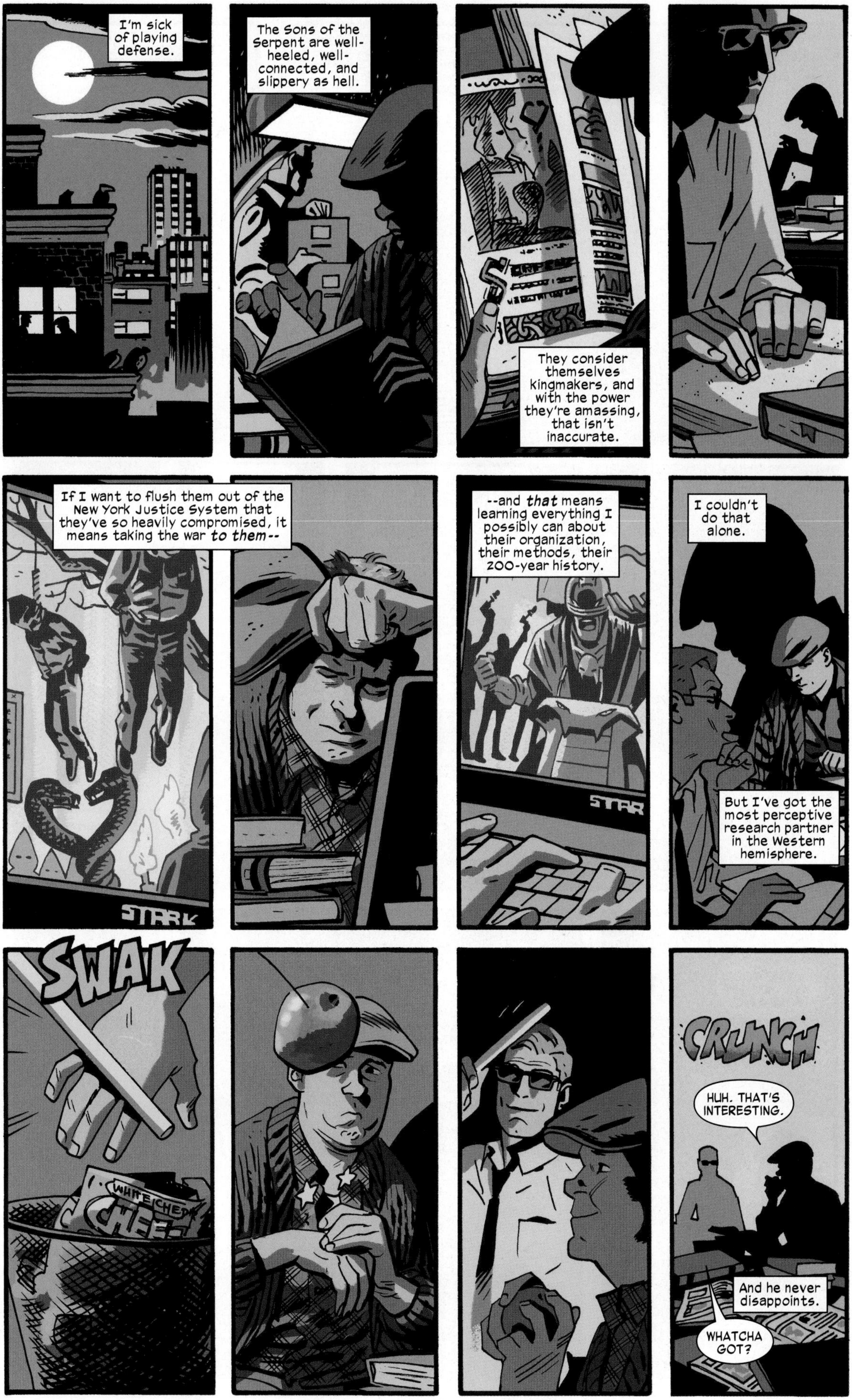
I'm sick of playing defense.
The Sons of the Serpent are well-heeled, well-connected, and slippery as hell.
They consider themselves kingmakers, and with the power they're amassing, that isn't inaccurate.
If I want to flush them out of the New York Justice System that they've so heavily compromised, it means taking the war *to them*--
STARK
--and *that* means learning everything I possibly can about their organization, their methods, their 200-year history.
STARK
I couldn't do that alone.
But I've got the most perceptive research partner in the Western hemisphere.
SWAK
CRUNCH
HUH. THAT'S INTERESTING.
And he never disappoints.
WHATCHA GOT?

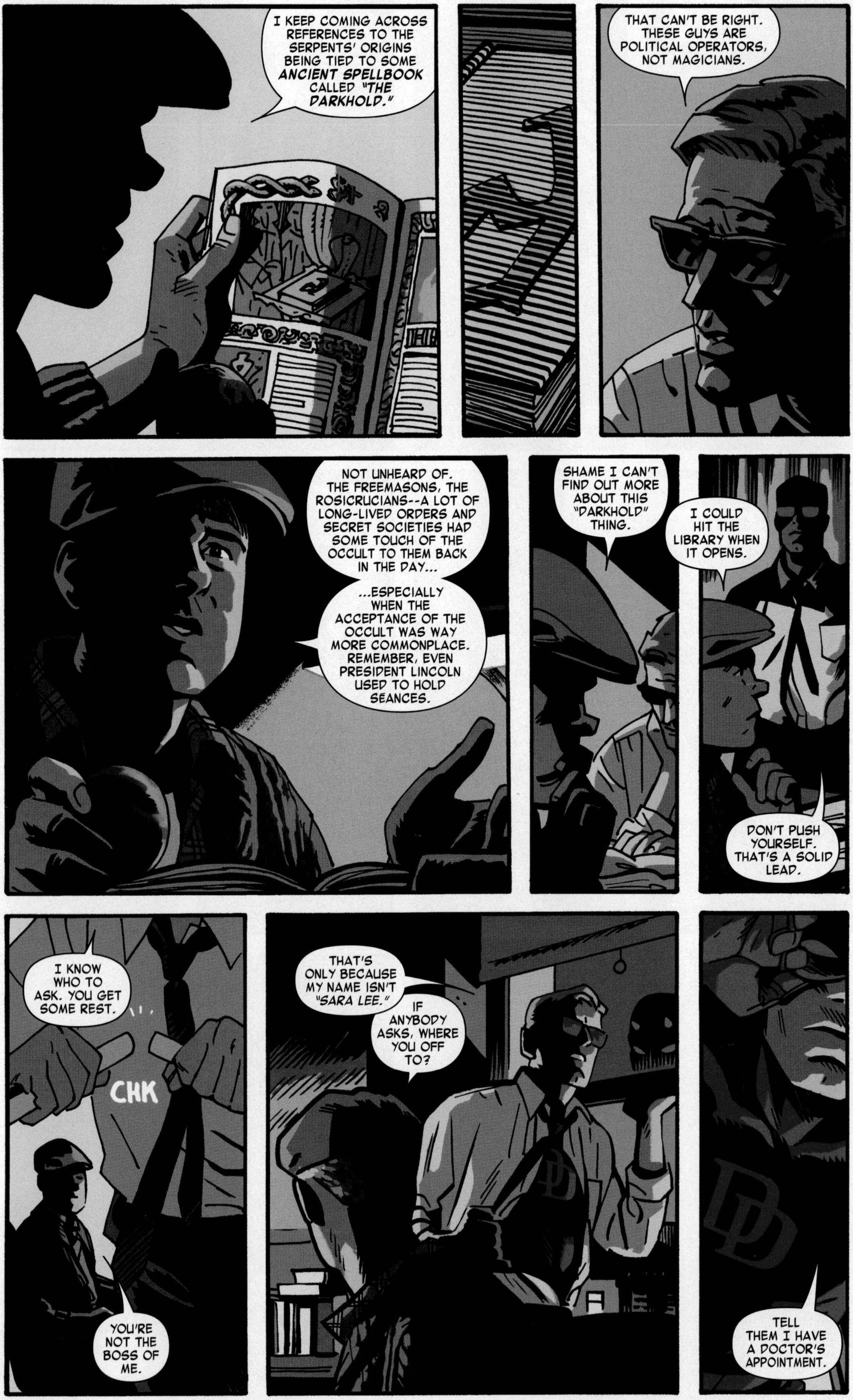
I KEEP COMING ACROSS REFERENCES TO THE SERPENTS' ORIGINS BEING TIED TO SOME ANCIENT SPELLBOOK CALLED "THE DARKHOLD."
THAT CAN'T BE RIGHT. THESE GUYS ARE POLITICAL OPERATORS, NOT MAGICIANS.
NOT UNHEARD OF. THE FREEMASONS, THE ROSICRUCIANS--A LOT OF LONG-LIVED ORDERS AND SECRET SOCIETIES HAD SOME TOUCH OF THE OCCULT TO THEM BACK IN THE DAY...
...ESPECIALLY WHEN THE ACCEPTANCE OF THE OCCULT WAS WAY MORE COMMONPLACE. REMEMBER, EVEN PRESIDENT LINCOLN USED TO HOLD SEANCES.
SHAME I CAN'T FIND OUT MORE ABOUT THIS "DARKHOLD" THING.
I COULD HIT THE LIBRARY WHEN IT OPENS.
DON'T PUSH YOURSELF. THAT'S A SOLID LEAD.
I KNOW WHO TO ASK. YOU GET SOME REST.
CHK
YOU'RE NOT THE BOSS OF ME.
THAT'S ONLY BECAUSE MY NAME ISN'T "SARA LEE."
IF ANYBODY ASKS, WHERE YOU OFF TO?
TELL THEM I HAVE A DOCTOR'S APPOINTMENT.

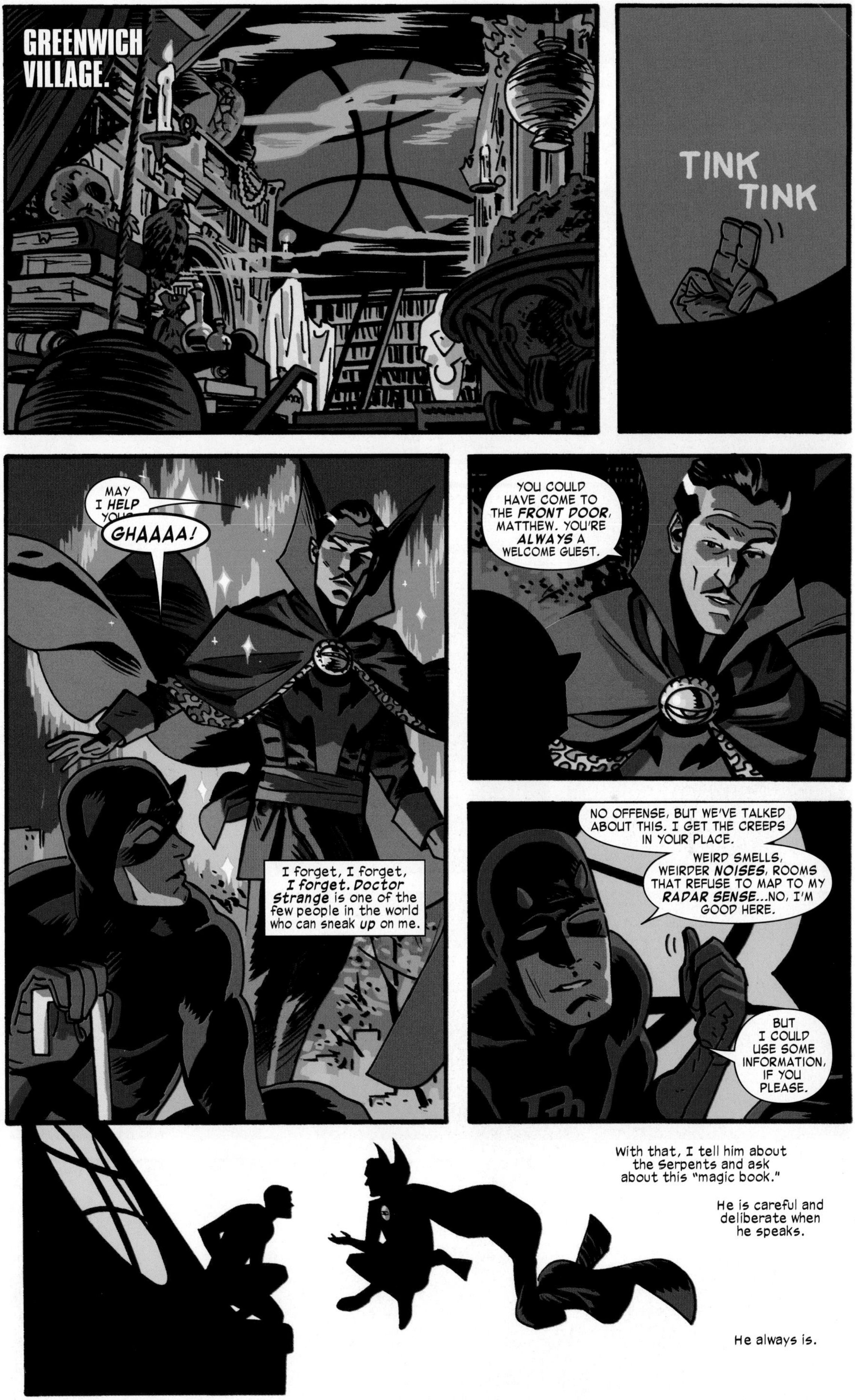
GREENWICH VILLAGE.
TINK TINK
MAY I HELP YOU--
GHAAAA!
I forget, I forget, I forget. Doctor Strange is one of the few people in the world who can sneak up on me.
YOU COULD HAVE COME TO THE FRONT DOOR, MATTHEW. YOU'RE ALWAYS A WELCOME GUEST.
NO OFFENSE, BUT WE'VE TALKED ABOUT THIS. I GET THE CREEPS IN YOUR PLACE.
WEIRD SMELLS, WEIRDER NOISES, ROOMS THAT REFUSE TO MAP TO MY RADAR SENSE...NO, I'M GOOD HERE.
BUT I COULD USE SOME INFORMATION, IF YOU PLEASE.
With that, I tell him about the Serpents and ask about this "magic book."
He is careful and deliberate when he speaks.
He always is.

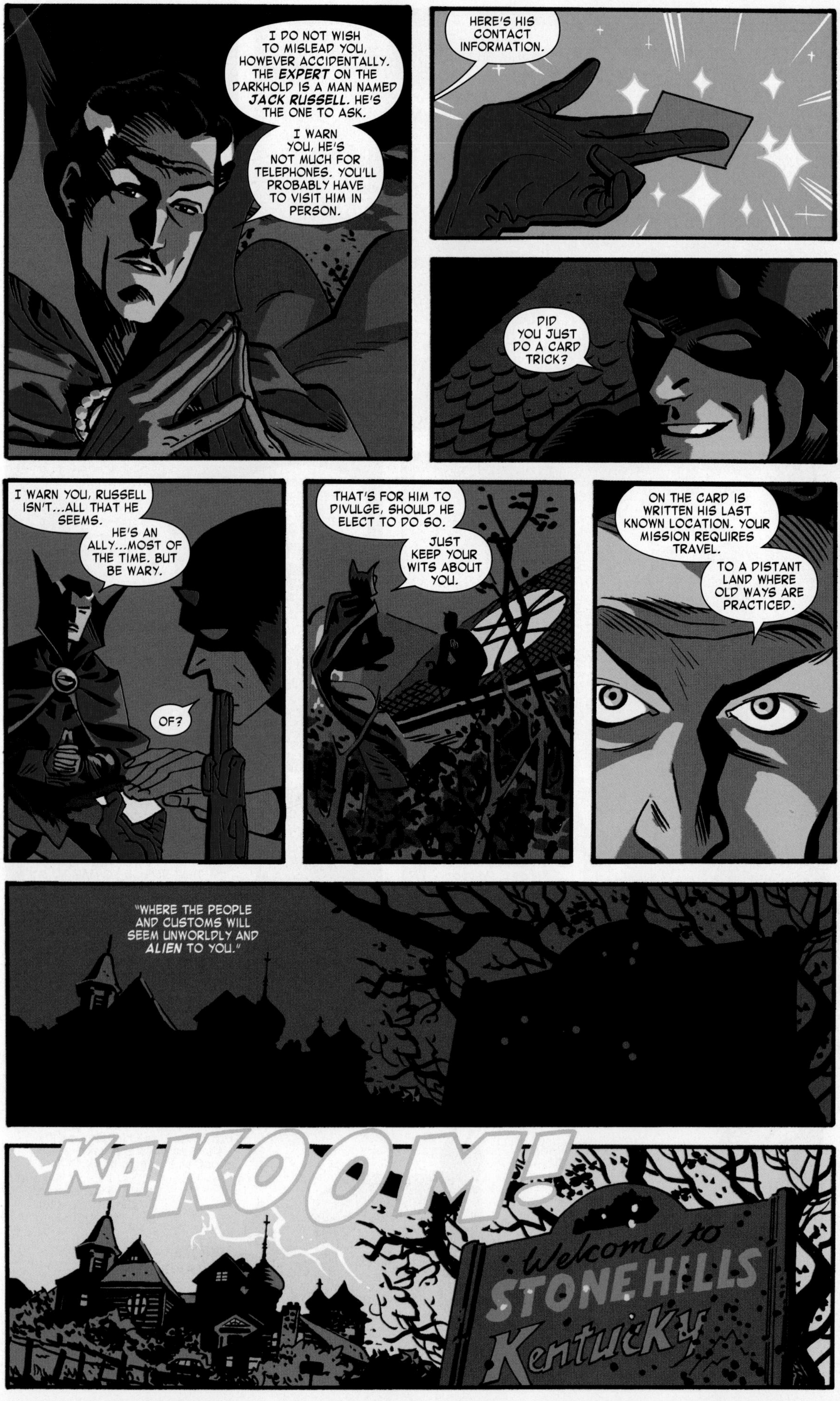
I DO NOT WISH TO MISLEAD YOU, HOWEVER ACCIDENTALLY. THE EXPERT ON THE DARKHOLD IS A MAN NAMED JACK RUSSELL. HE'S THE ONE TO ASK.
I WARN YOU, HE'S NOT MUCH FOR TELEPHONES. YOU'LL PROBABLY HAVE TO VISIT HIM IN PERSON.
HERE'S HIS CONTACT INFORMATION.
DID YOU JUST DO A CARD TRICK?
I WARN YOU, RUSSELL ISN'T...ALL THAT HE SEEMS.
HE'S AN ALLY...MOST OF THE TIME. BUT BE WARY.
OF?
THAT'S FOR HIM TO DIVULGE, SHOULD HE ELECT TO DO SO.
JUST KEEP YOUR WITS ABOUT YOU.
ON THE CARD IS WRITTEN HIS LAST KNOWN LOCATION. YOUR MISSION REQUIRES TRAVEL.
TO A DISTANT LAND WHERE OLD WAYS ARE PRACTICED.
"WHERE THE PEOPLE AND CUSTOMS WILL SEEM UNWORLDLY AND ALIEN TO YOU."
KAKOOM!
Welcome to STONE HILLS Kentucky

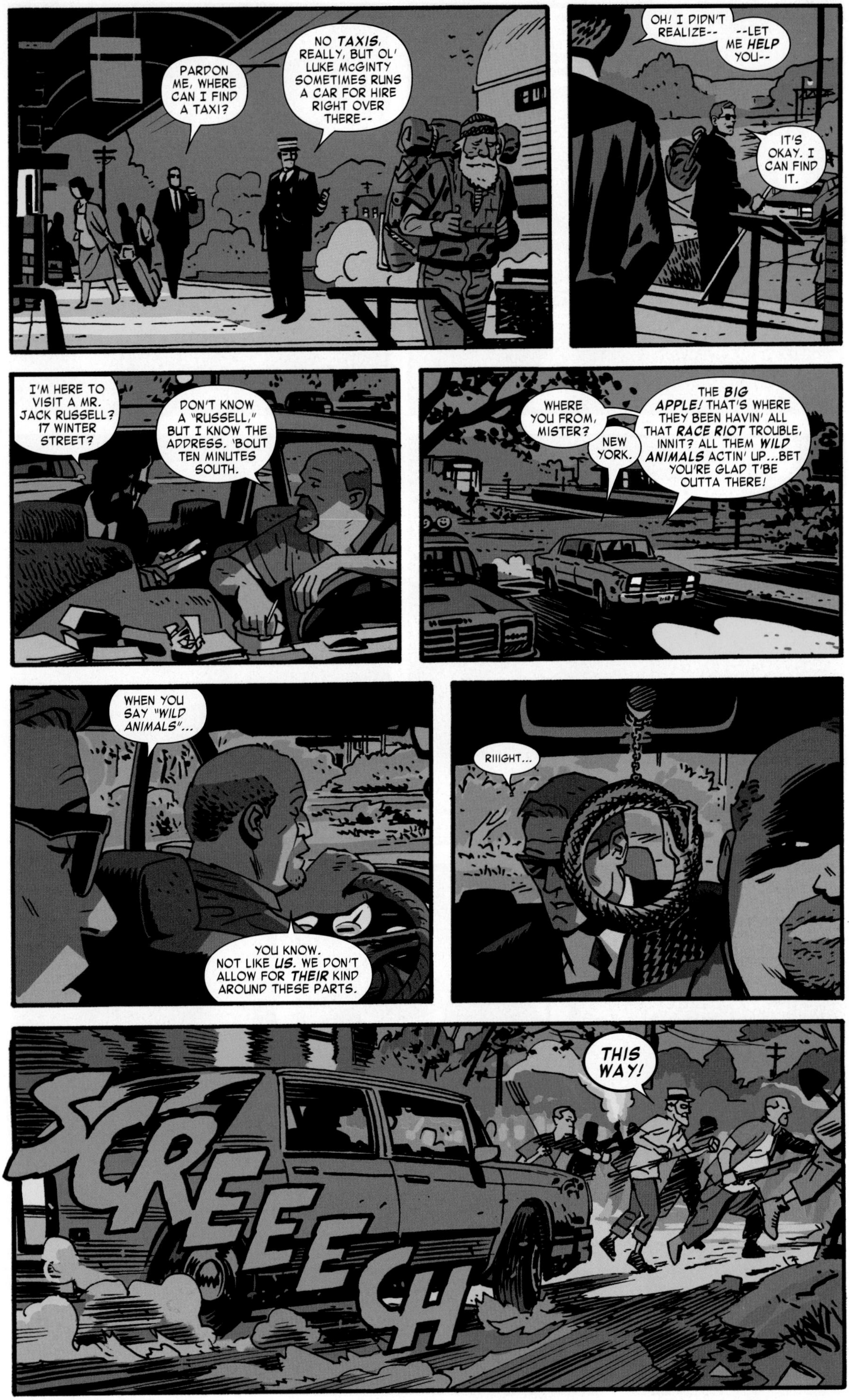
PARDON ME, WHERE CAN I FIND A TAXI?
NO TAXIS, REALLY, BUT OL' LUKE McGINTY SOMETIMES RUNS A CAR FOR HIRE RIGHT OVER THERE--
OH! I DIDN'T REALIZE--
--LET ME HELP YOU--
IT'S OKAY. I CAN FIND IT.
I'M HERE TO VISIT A MR. JACK RUSSELL? 17 WINTER STREET?
DON'T KNOW A "RUSSELL," BUT I KNOW THE ADDRESS. 'BOUT TEN MINUTES SOUTH.
WHERE YOU FROM, MISTER?
NEW YORK.
THE BIG APPLE! THAT'S WHERE THEY BEEN HAVIN' ALL THAT RACE RIOT TROUBLE, INNIT? ALL THEM WILD ANIMALS ACTIN' UP...BET YOU'RE GLAD T'BE OUTTA THERE!
WHEN YOU SAY "WILD ANIMALS"...
YOU KNOW. NOT LIKE US. WE DON'T ALLOW FOR THEIR KIND AROUND THESE PARTS.
RIIIGHT...
SCREEECH
THIS WAY!

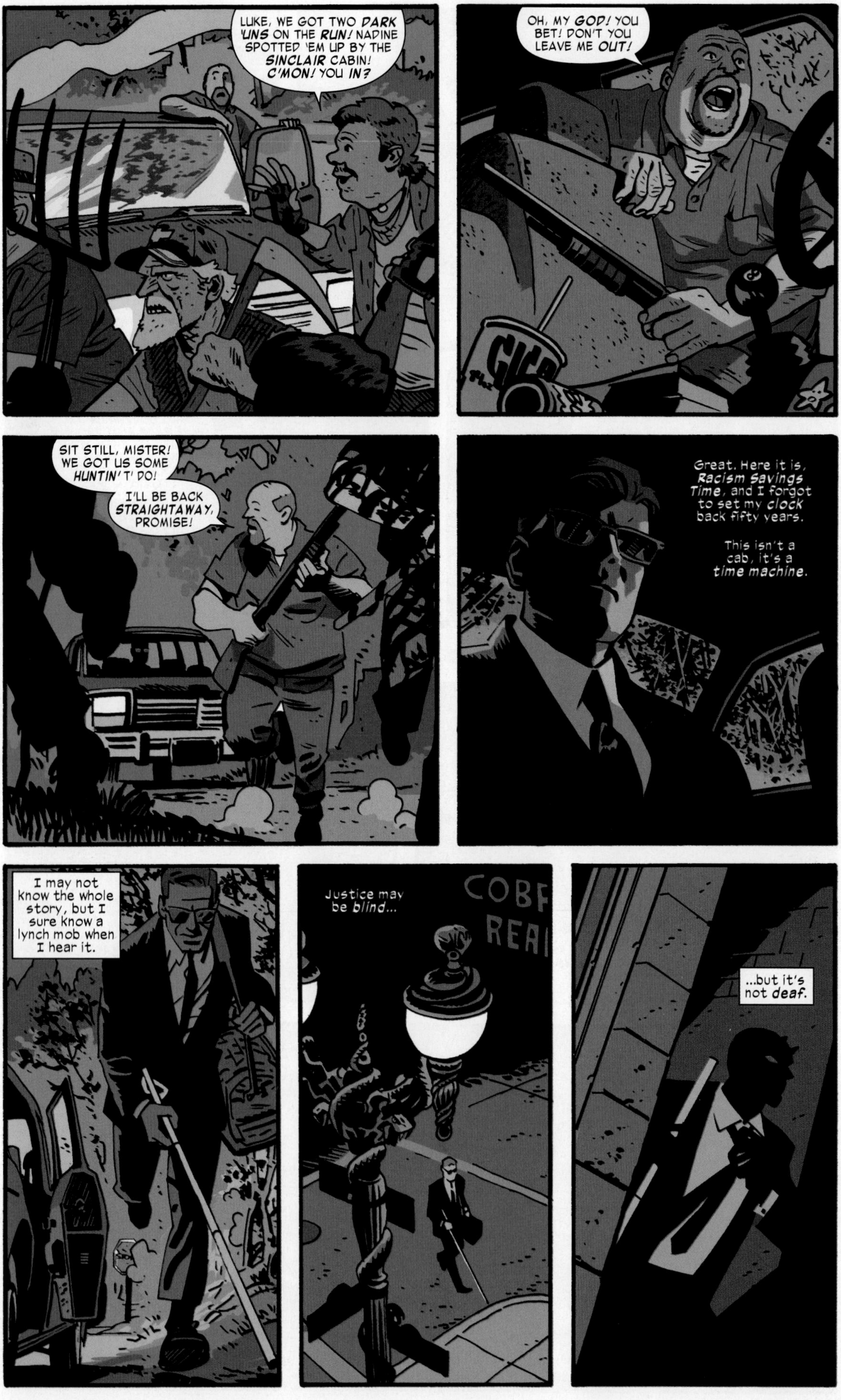
LUKE, WE GOT TWO DARK 'UNS ON THE RUN! NADINE SPOTTED 'EM UP BY THE SINCLAIR CABIN! C'MON! YOU IN?
OH, MY GOD! YOU BET! DON'T YOU LEAVE ME OUT!
SIT STILL, MISTER! WE GOT US SOME HUNTIN' T' DO!
I'LL BE BACK STRAIGHTAWAY, PROMISE!
Great. Here it is, Racism Savings Time, and I forgot to set my clock back fifty years.
This isn't a cab, it's a time machine.
I may not know the whole story, but I sure know a lynch mob when I hear it.
Justice may be blind...
COBR
REA
...but it's not deaf.

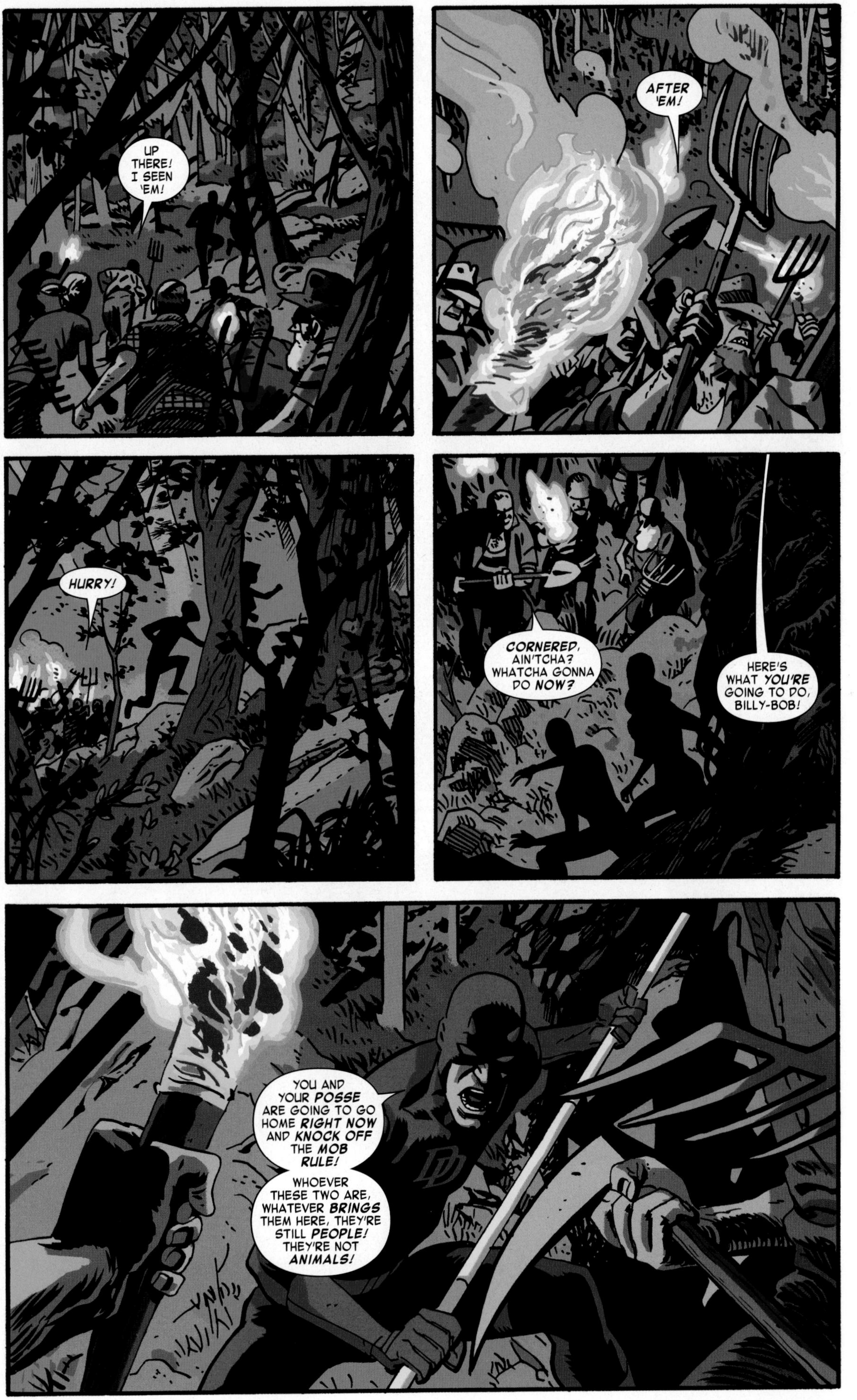
UP THERE! I SEEN 'EM!
AFTER 'EM!
HURRY!
CORNERED, AIN'TCHA? WHATCHA GONNA DO NOW?
HERE'S WHAT YOU'RE GOING TO DO, BILLY-BOB!
YOU AND YOUR POSSE ARE GOING TO GO HOME RIGHT NOW AND KNOCK OFF THE MOB RULE!
WHOEVER THESE TWO ARE, WHATEVER BRINGS THEM HERE, THEY'RE STILL PEOPLE! THEY'RE NOT ANIMALS!

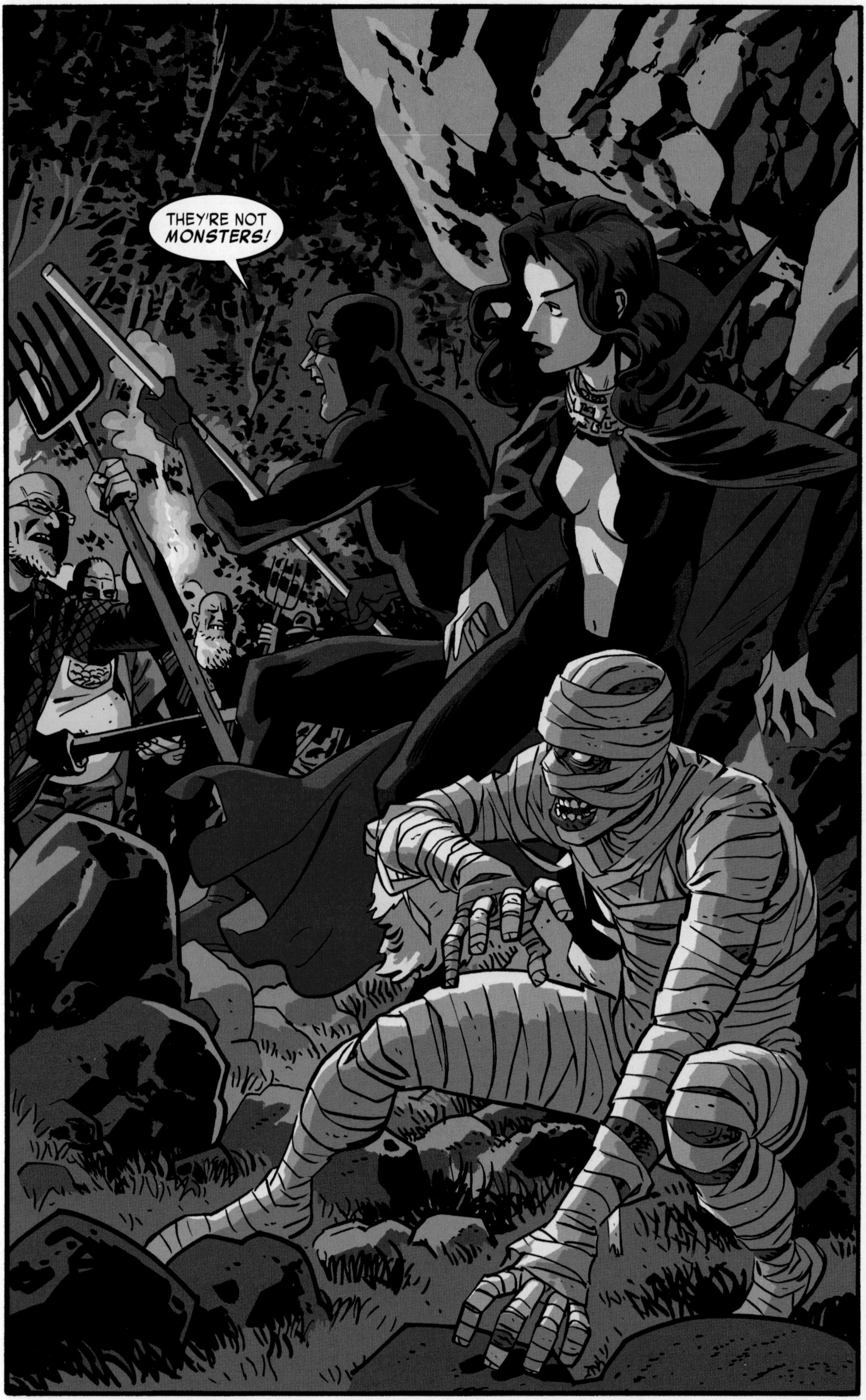
THEY'RE NOT *MONSTERS!*

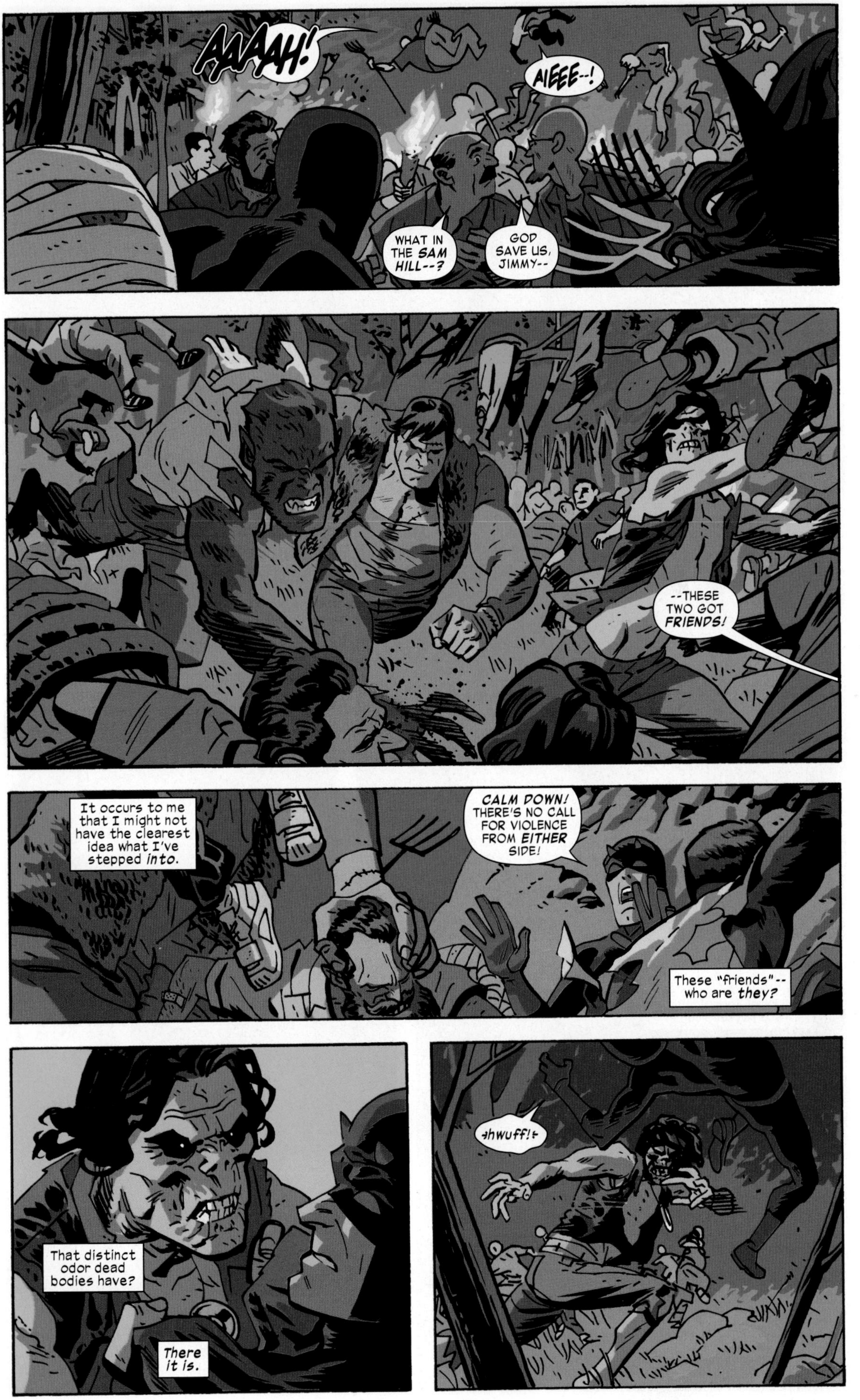
AAAAH!
AIEEE--!
WHAT IN THE SAM HILL--?
GOD SAVE US, JIMMY--
--THESE TWO GOT FRIENDS!
It occurs to me that I might not have the clearest idea what I've stepped into.
CALM DOWN! THERE'S NO CALL FOR VIOLENCE FROM EITHER SIDE!
These "friends"-- who are they?
That distinct odor dead bodies have?
There it is.
+hwuff!+

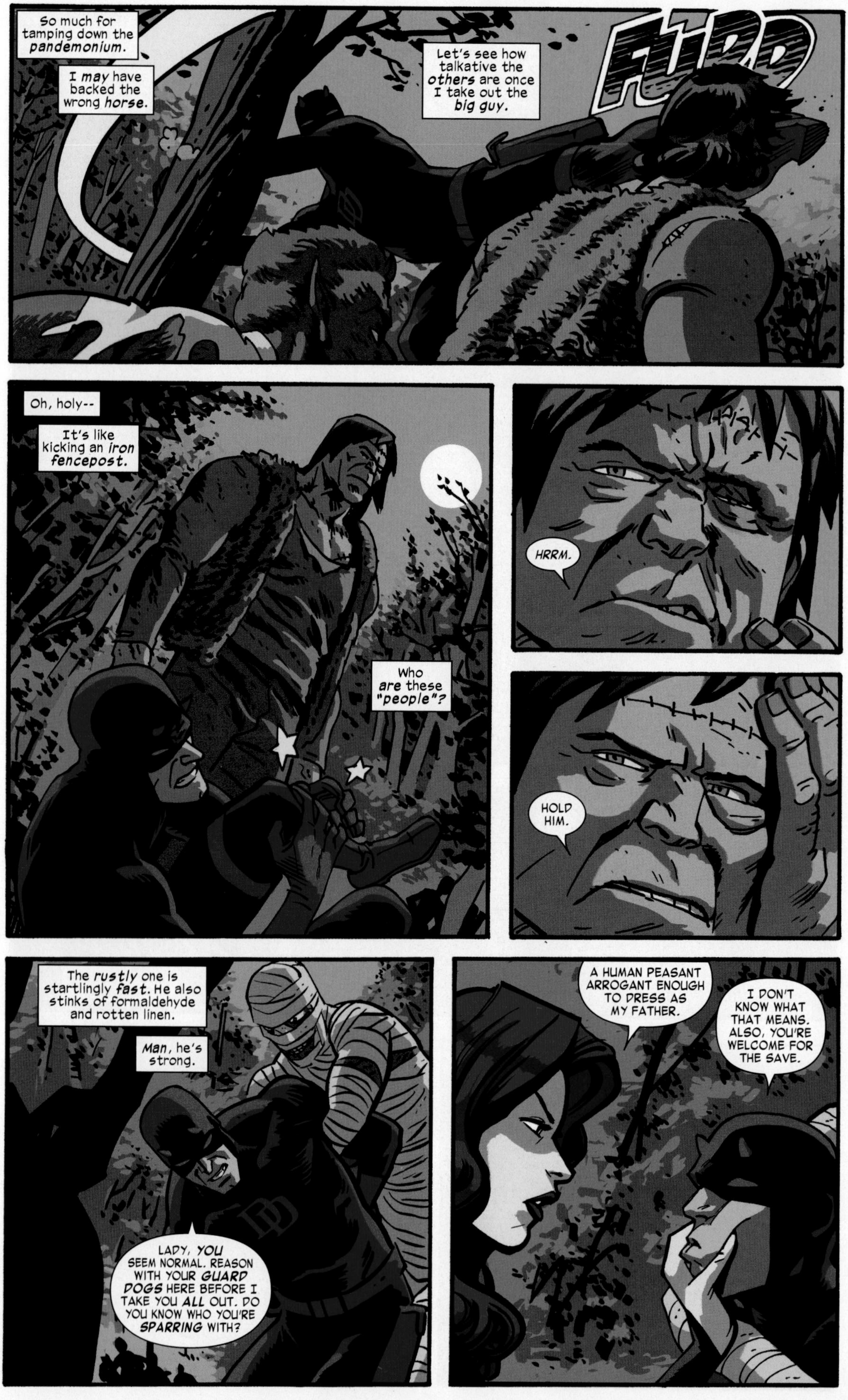
So much for tamping down the *pandemonium*.
I *may* have backed the wrong *horse*.
Let's see how talkative the *others* are once I take out the *big guy*.
FUDD
Oh, holy--
It's like kicking an *iron fencepost*.
Who *are* these *"people"*?
HRRM.
HOLD HIM.
The *rusty* one is startlingly *fast*. He also stinks of formaldehyde and rotten linen.
Man, he's strong.
LADY, ***YOU*** SEEM NORMAL. REASON WITH YOUR ***GUARD DOGS*** HERE BEFORE I TAKE YOU ***ALL*** OUT. DO YOU KNOW WHO YOU'RE ***SPARRING*** WITH?
A HUMAN PEASANT ARROGANT ENOUGH TO DRESS AS MY FATHER.
I DON'T KNOW WHAT THAT MEANS. ALSO, YOU'RE WELCOME FOR THE SAVE.

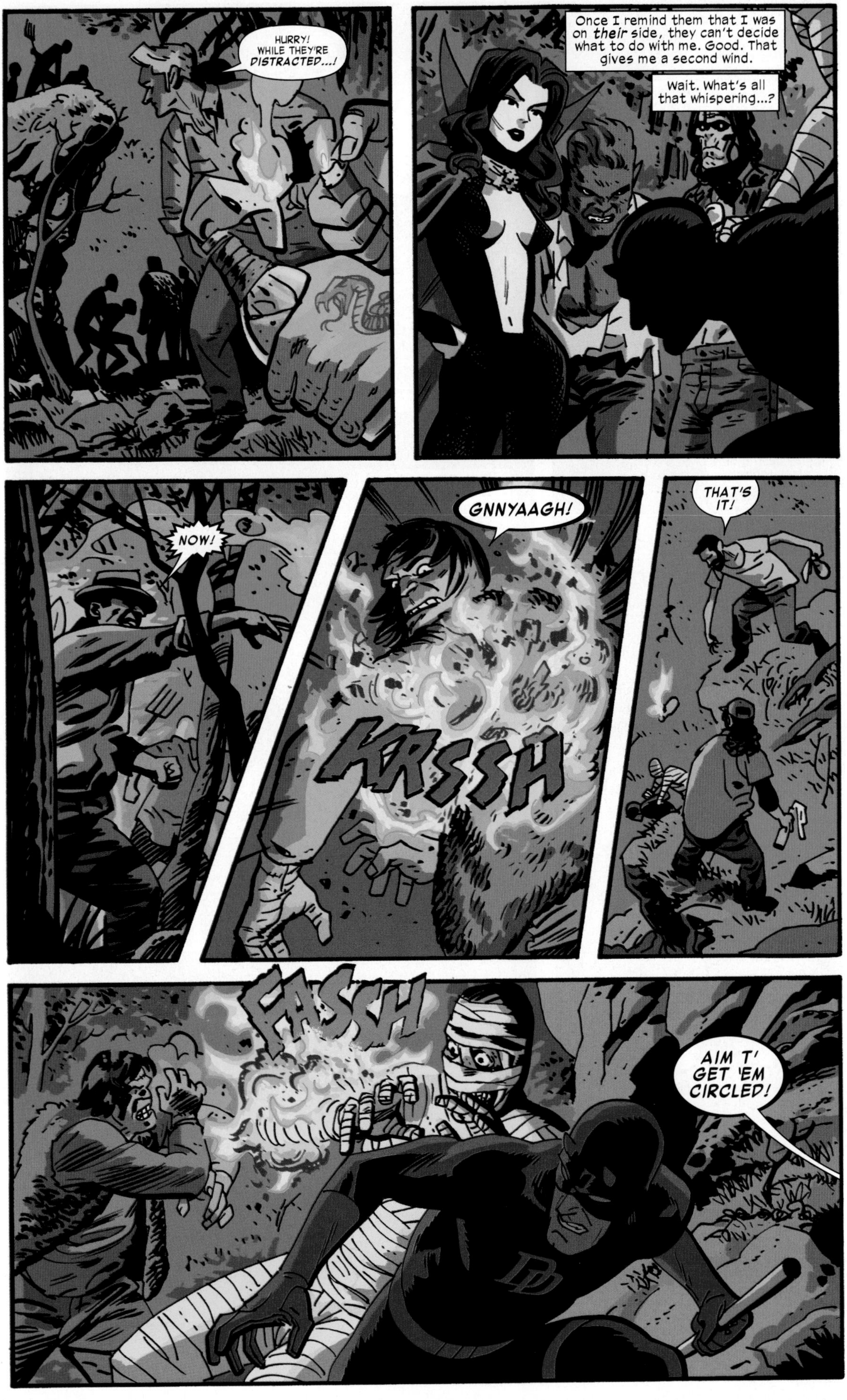
HURRY! WHILE THEY'RE DISTRACTED...!
Once I remind them that I was on their side, they can't decide what to do with me. Good. That gives me a second wind.
Wait. What's all that whispering...?
NOW!
GNNYAAGH!
KRSSH
THAT'S IT!
FASCH
AIM T' GET 'EM CIRCLED!

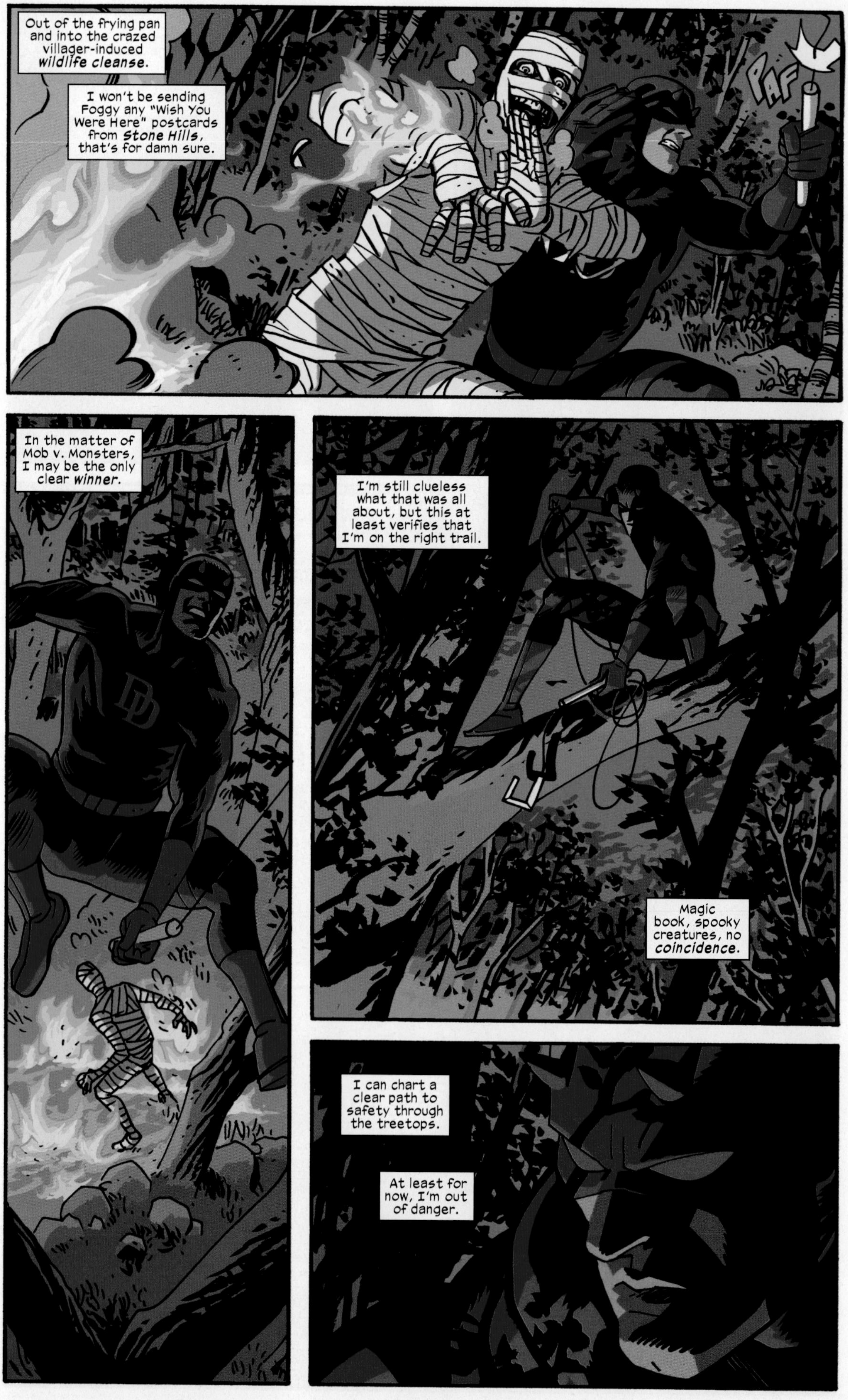
Out of the frying pan and into the crazed villager-induced *wildlife cleanse*.
I won't be sending Foggy any "Wish You Were Here" postcards from *Stone Hills*, that's for damn sure.
PAF
In the matter of Mob v. Monsters, I may be the only clear *winner*.
I'm still clueless what that was all about, but this at least verifies that I'm on the right trail.
Magic book, spooky creatures, no *coincidence*.
I can chart a clear path to safety through the treetops.
At least for now, I'm out of danger.

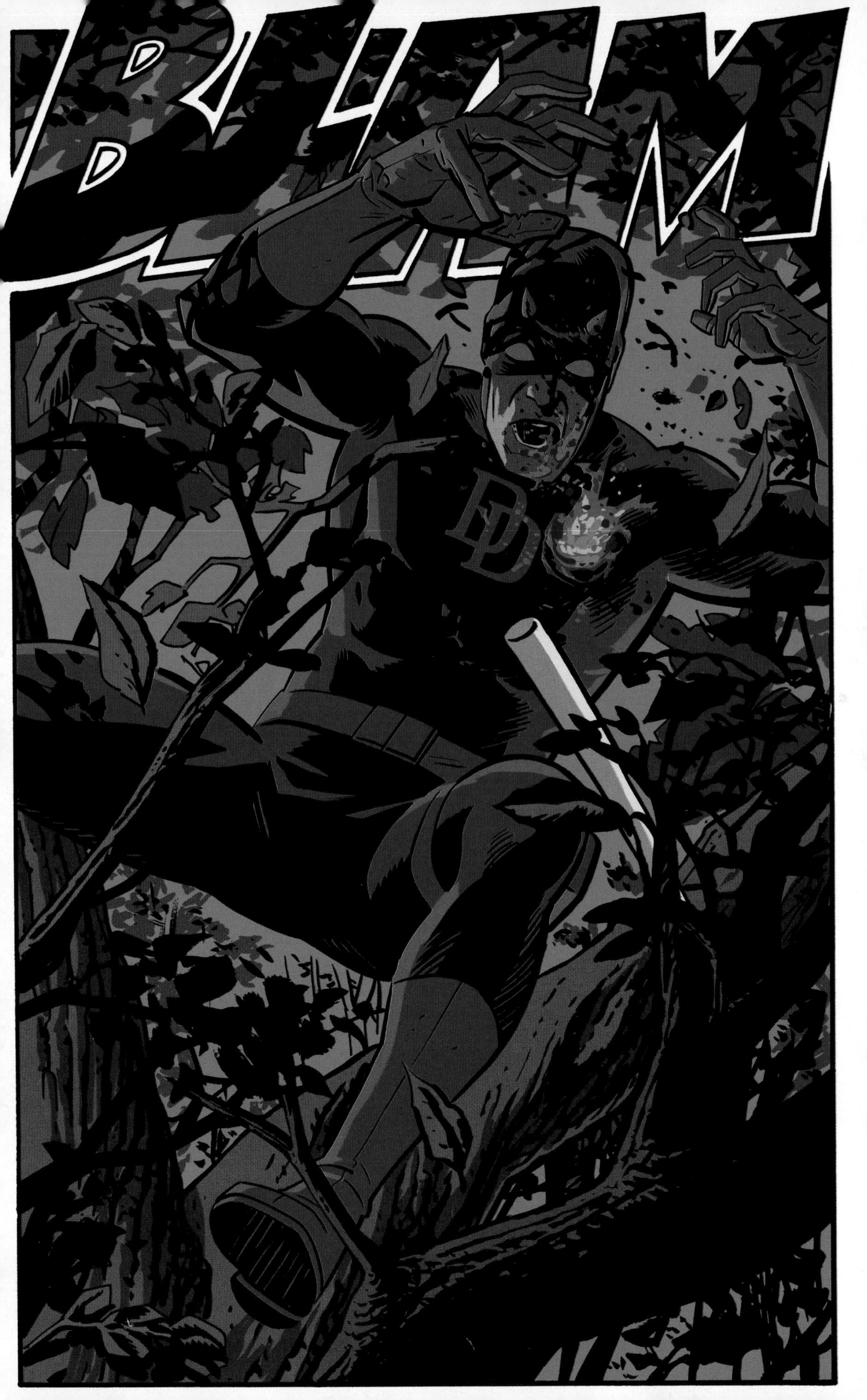
BLAM

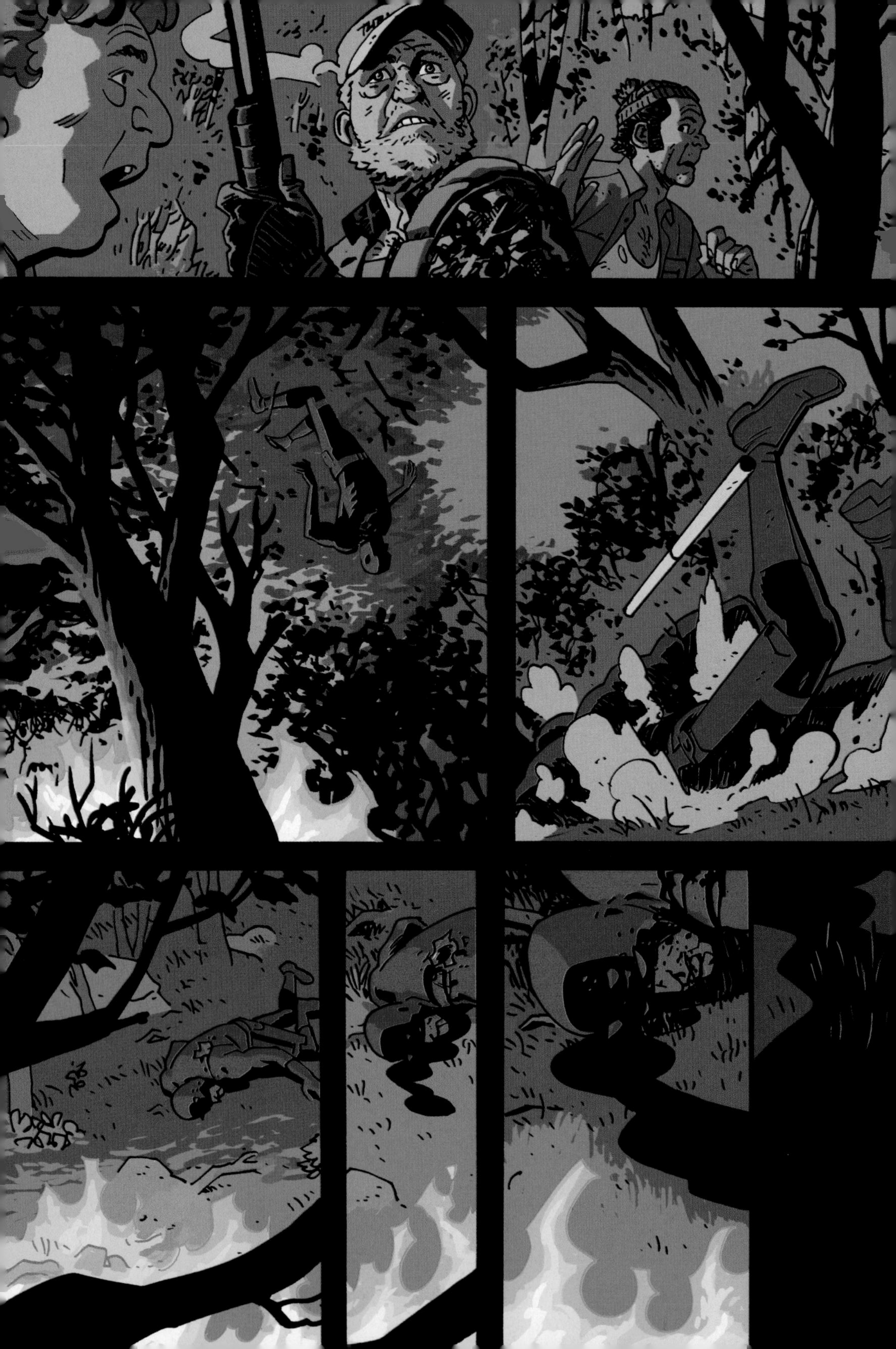

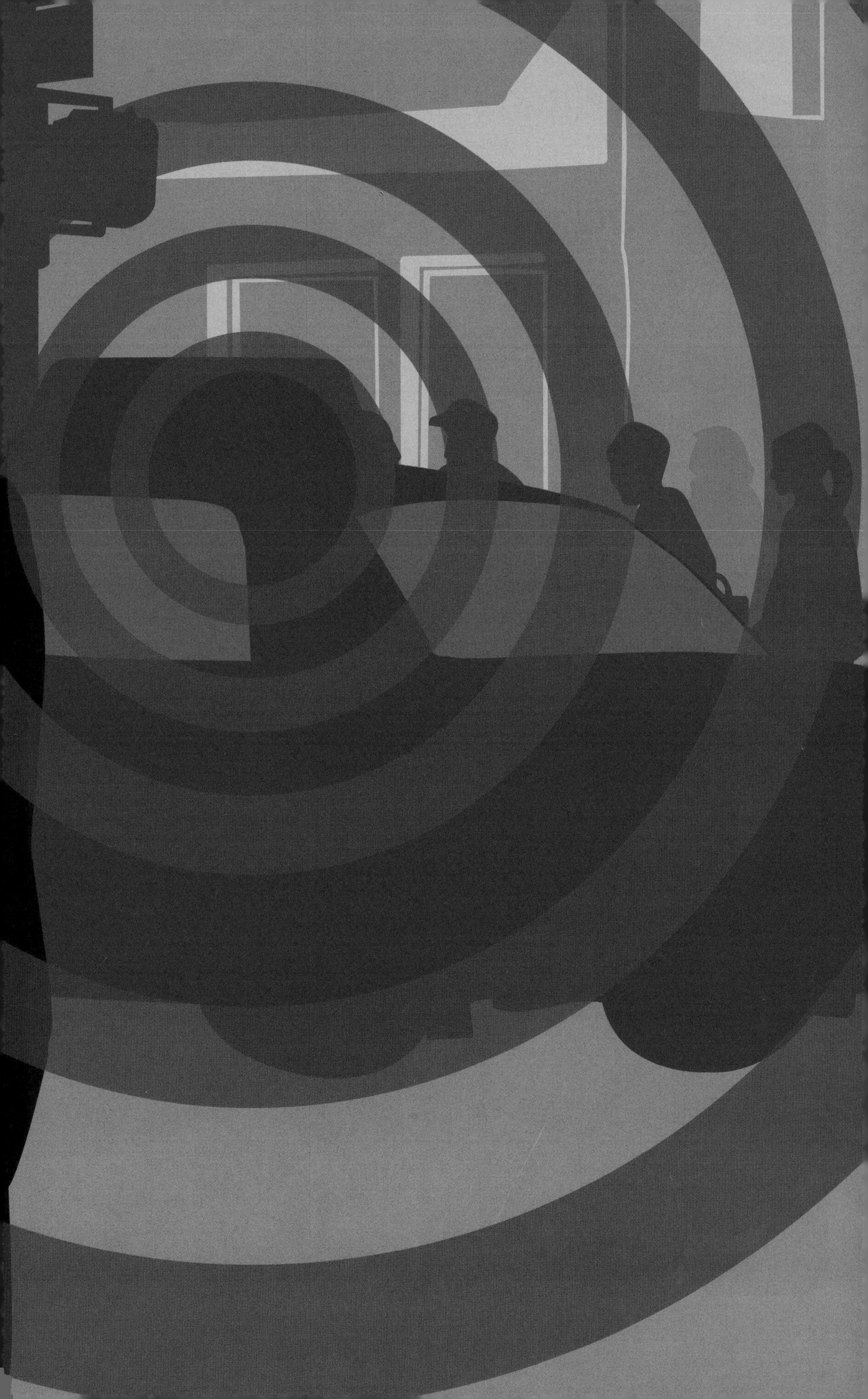

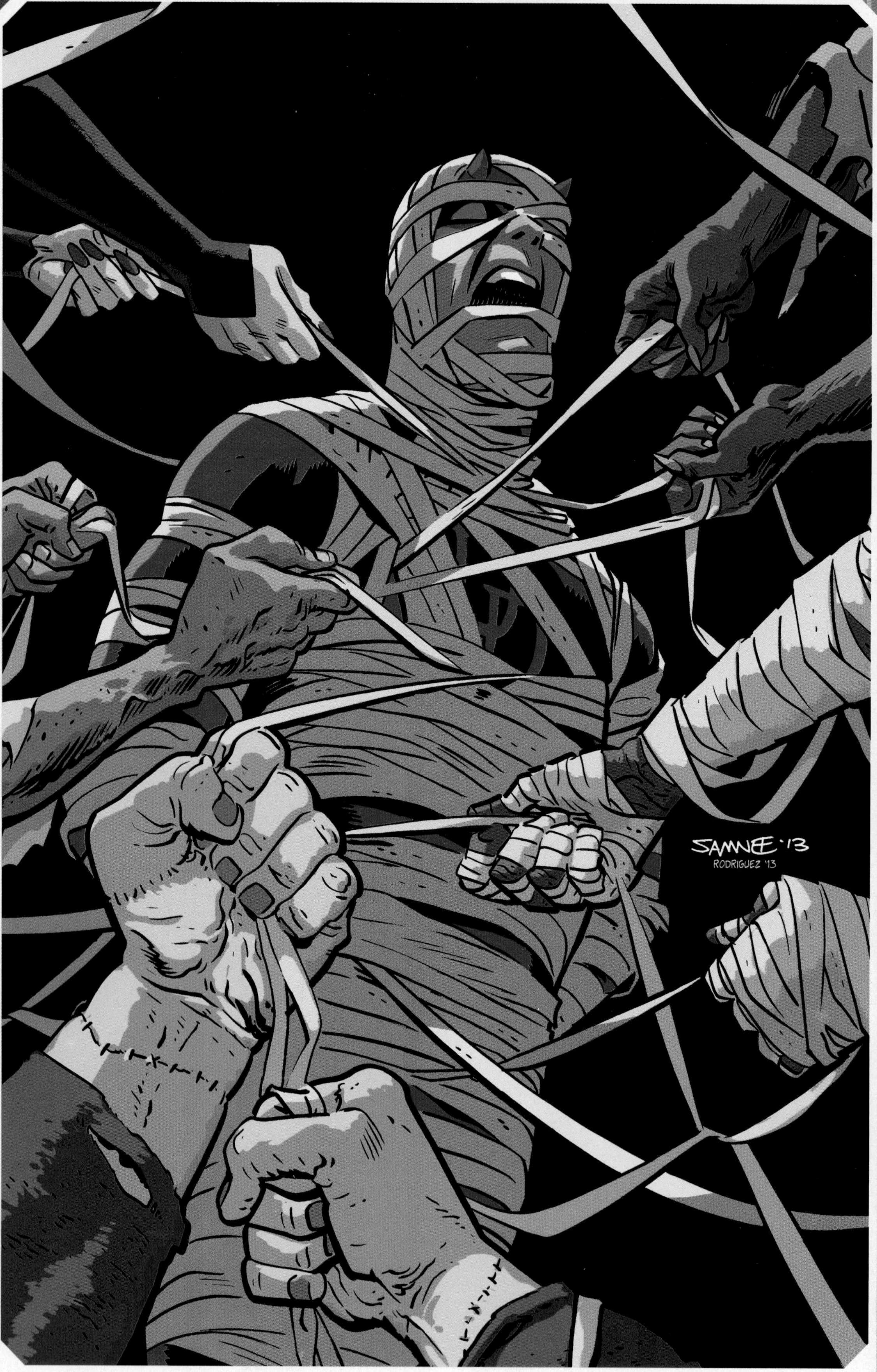
SAMNEE '13
RODRIGUEZ '13

DAREDEVIL #33

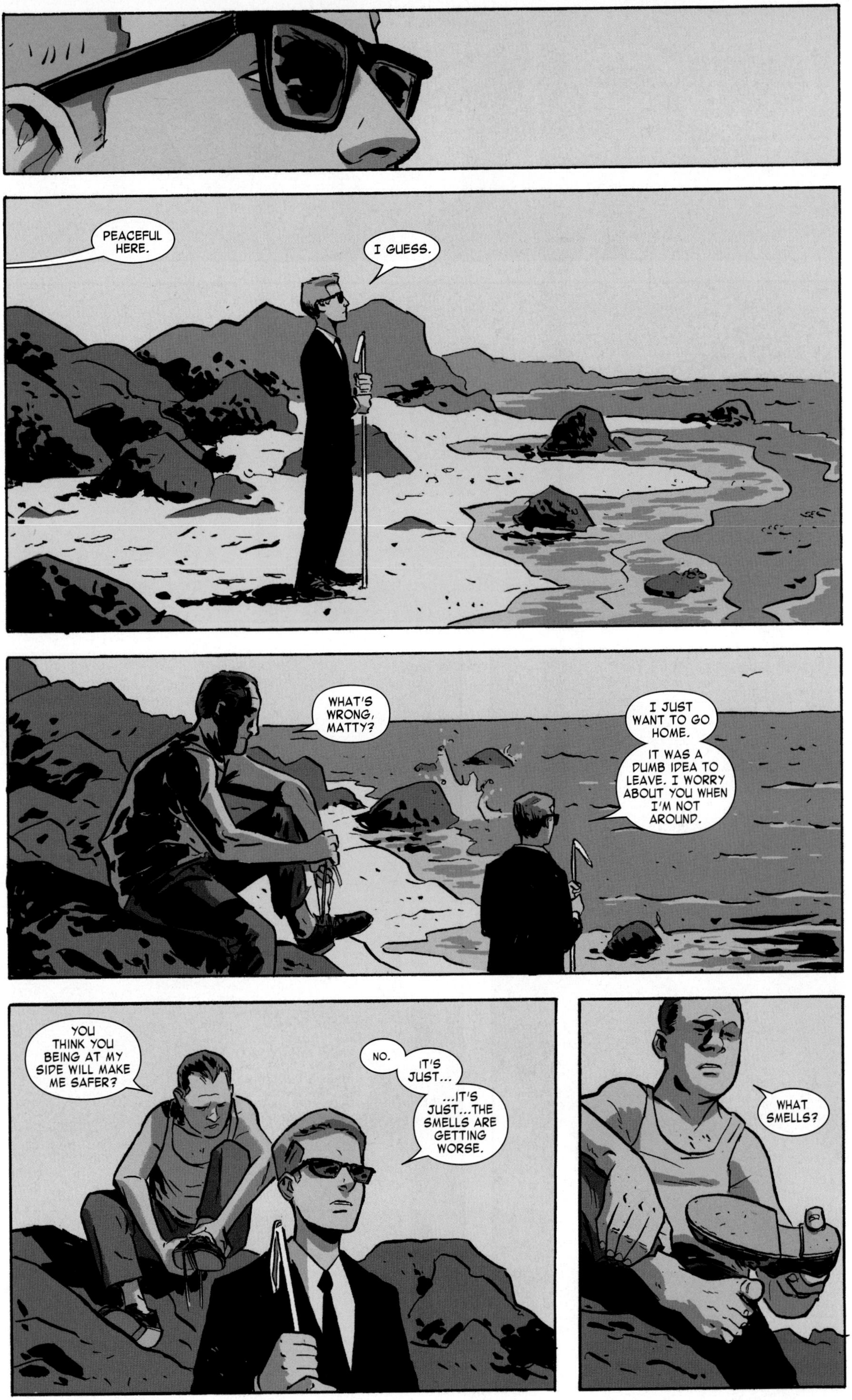
PEACEFUL HERE.
I GUESS.
WHAT'S WRONG, MATTY?
I JUST WANT TO GO HOME.
IT WAS A DUMB IDEA TO LEAVE. I WORRY ABOUT YOU WHEN I'M NOT AROUND.
YOU THINK YOU BEING AT MY SIDE WILL MAKE ME SAFER?
NO.
IT'S JUST...
...IT'S JUST...THE SMELLS ARE GETTING WORSE.
WHAT SMELLS?

THE SMELLS OF DEATH. THE DIN OF LINEN BANDAGES SCRAPING YOUR SKIN. THE TASTE OF *ROT* IN THE AIR AROUND YOU.

IT'S GROWING *UNBEARABLE*, FOGGY.

EVEN HERE?

ESPECIALLY HERE.

EVEN THOUGH YOU KNOW I'M NOT REALLY FOGGY NELSON?

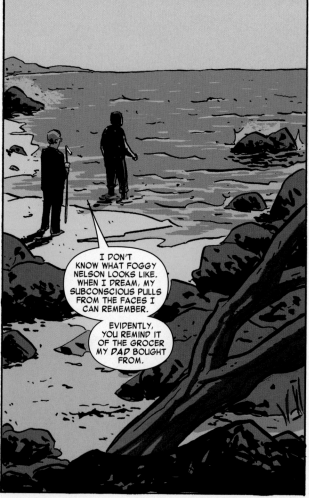

I DON'T KNOW WHAT FOGGY NELSON LOOKS LIKE. WHEN I DREAM, MY SUBCONSCIOUS PULLS FROM THE FACES I CAN REMEMBER.

EVIDENTLY, YOU REMIND IT OF THE GROCER MY *DAD* BOUGHT FROM.

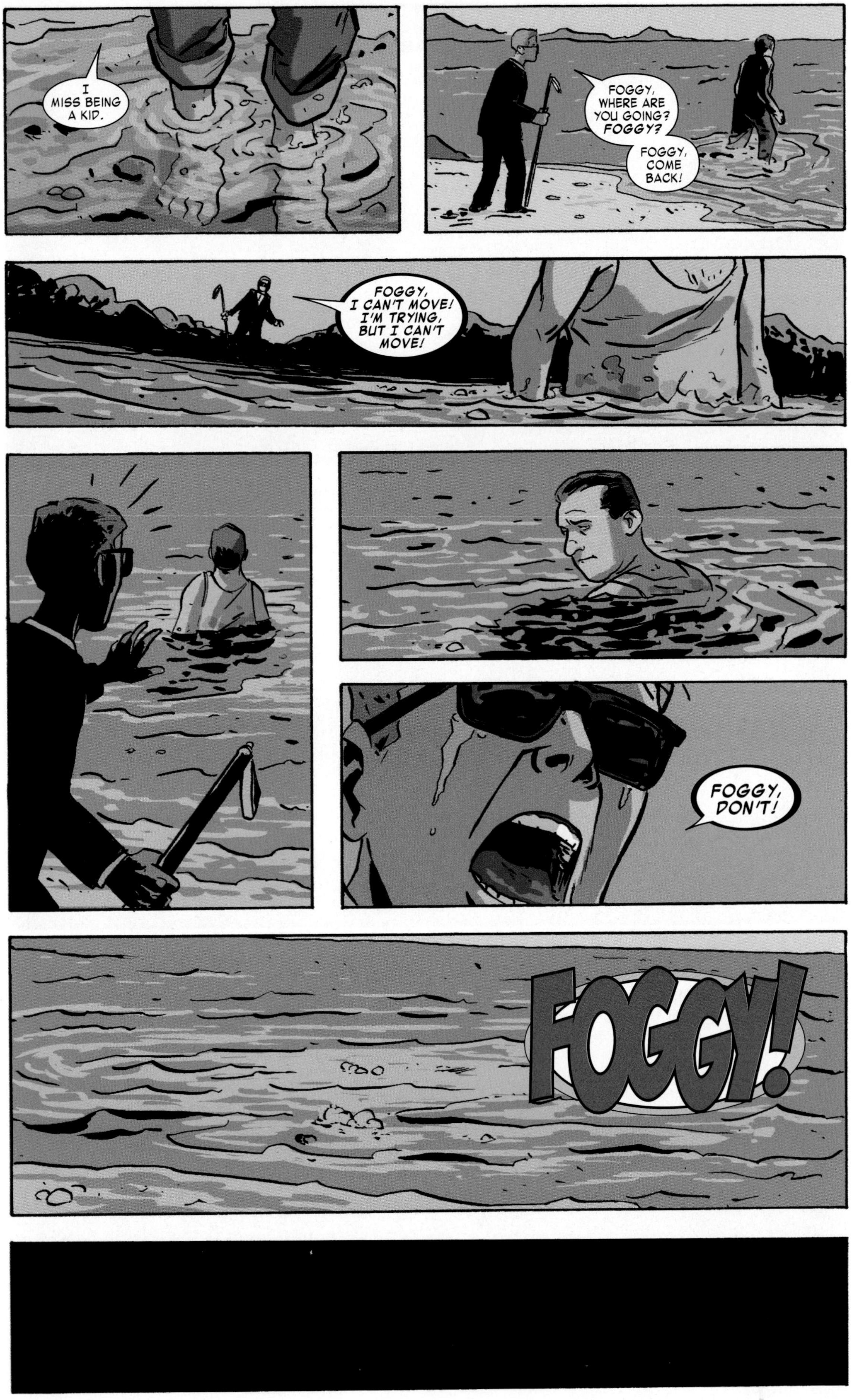
I MISS BEING A KID.
FOGGY, WHERE ARE YOU GOING? FOGGY?
FOGGY, COME BACK!
FOGGY, I CAN'T MOVE! I'M TRYING, BUT I CAN'T MOVE!
FOGGY, DON'T!
FOGGY!

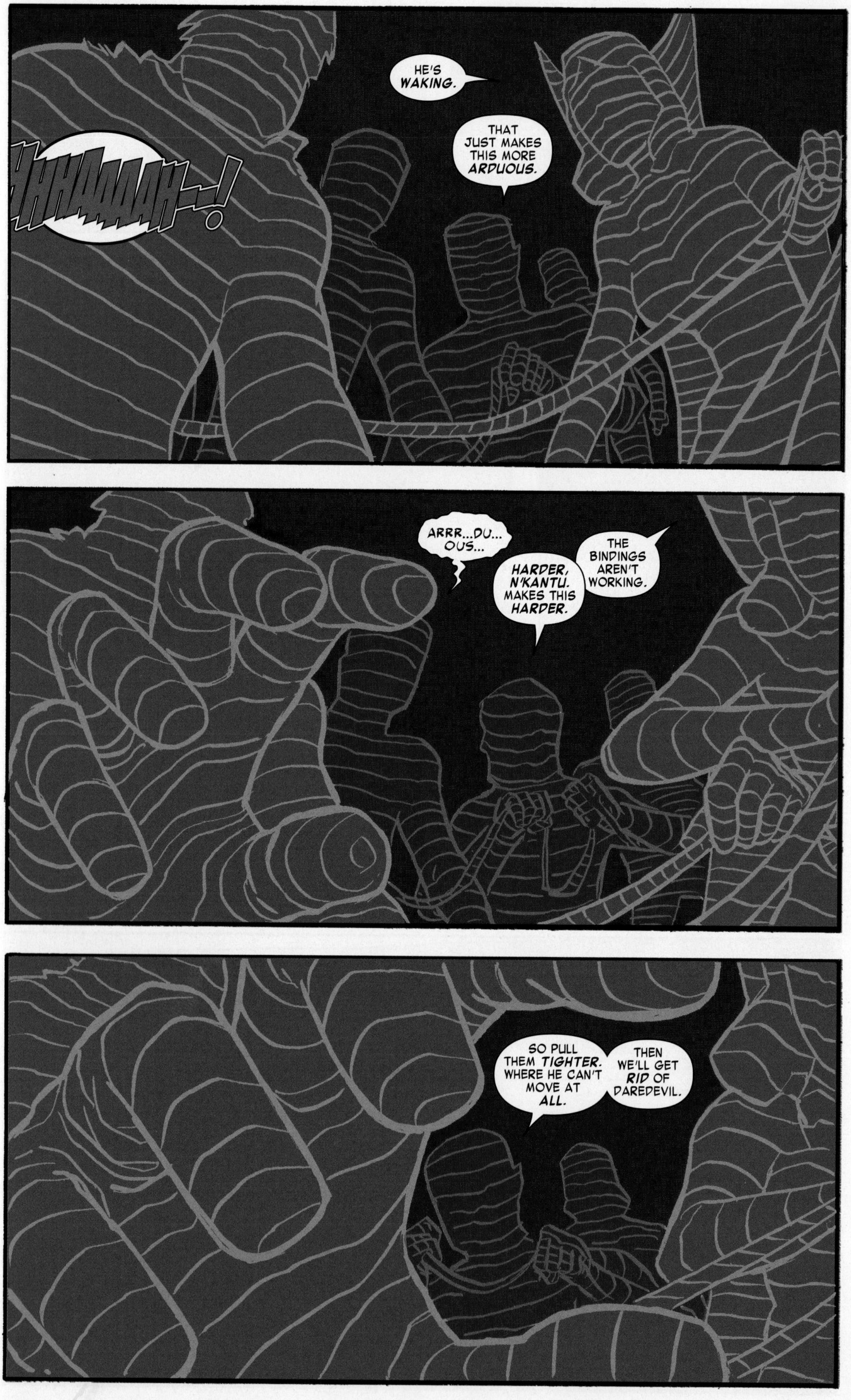
HE'S WAKING.
THAT JUST MAKES THIS MORE ARDUOUS.
HHHAAAAH--!
ARRR...DU... OUS...
HARDER, N'KANTU. MAKES THIS HARDER.
THE BINDINGS AREN'T WORKING.
SO PULL THEM TIGHTER. WHERE HE CAN'T MOVE AT ALL.
THEN WE'LL GET RID OF DAREDEVIL.

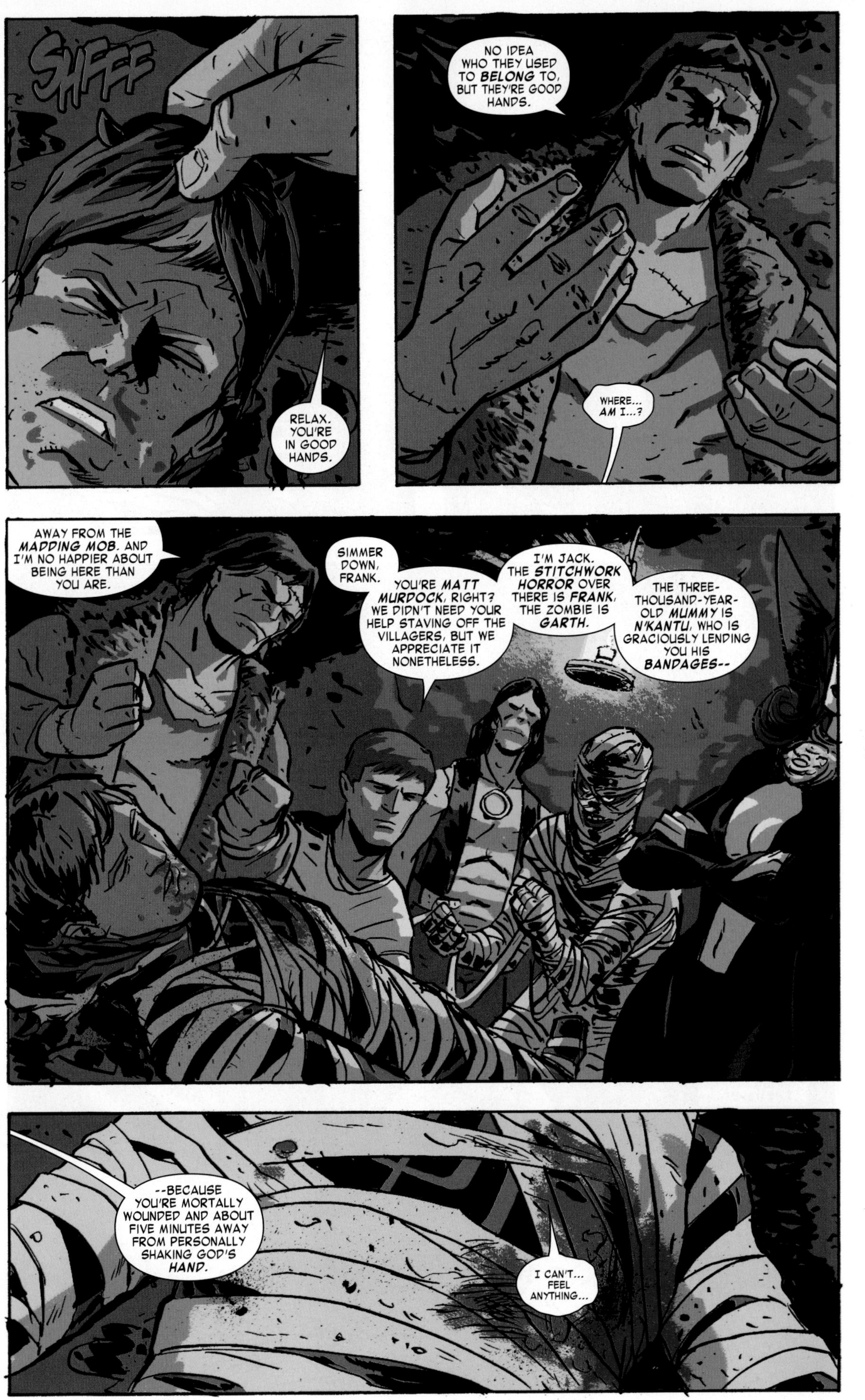
SHFFF
RELAX. YOU'RE IN GOOD HANDS.
NO IDEA WHO THEY USED TO BELONG TO, BUT THEY'RE GOOD HANDS.
WHERE... AM I...?
AWAY FROM THE MADDING MOB. AND I'M NO HAPPIER ABOUT BEING HERE THAN YOU ARE.
SIMMER DOWN, FRANK.
YOU'RE MATT MURDOCK, RIGHT? WE DIDN'T NEED YOUR HELP STAVING OFF THE VILLAGERS, BUT WE APPRECIATE IT NONETHELESS.
I'M JACK. THE STITCHWORK HORROR OVER THERE IS FRANK, THE ZOMBIE IS GARTH.
THE THREE-THOUSAND-YEAR-OLD MUMMY IS N'KANTU, WHO IS GRACIOUSLY LENDING YOU HIS BANDAGES--
--BECAUSE YOU'RE MORTALLY WOUNDED AND ABOUT FIVE MINUTES AWAY FROM PERSONALLY SHAKING GOD'S HAND.
I CAN'T... FEEL ANYTHING...

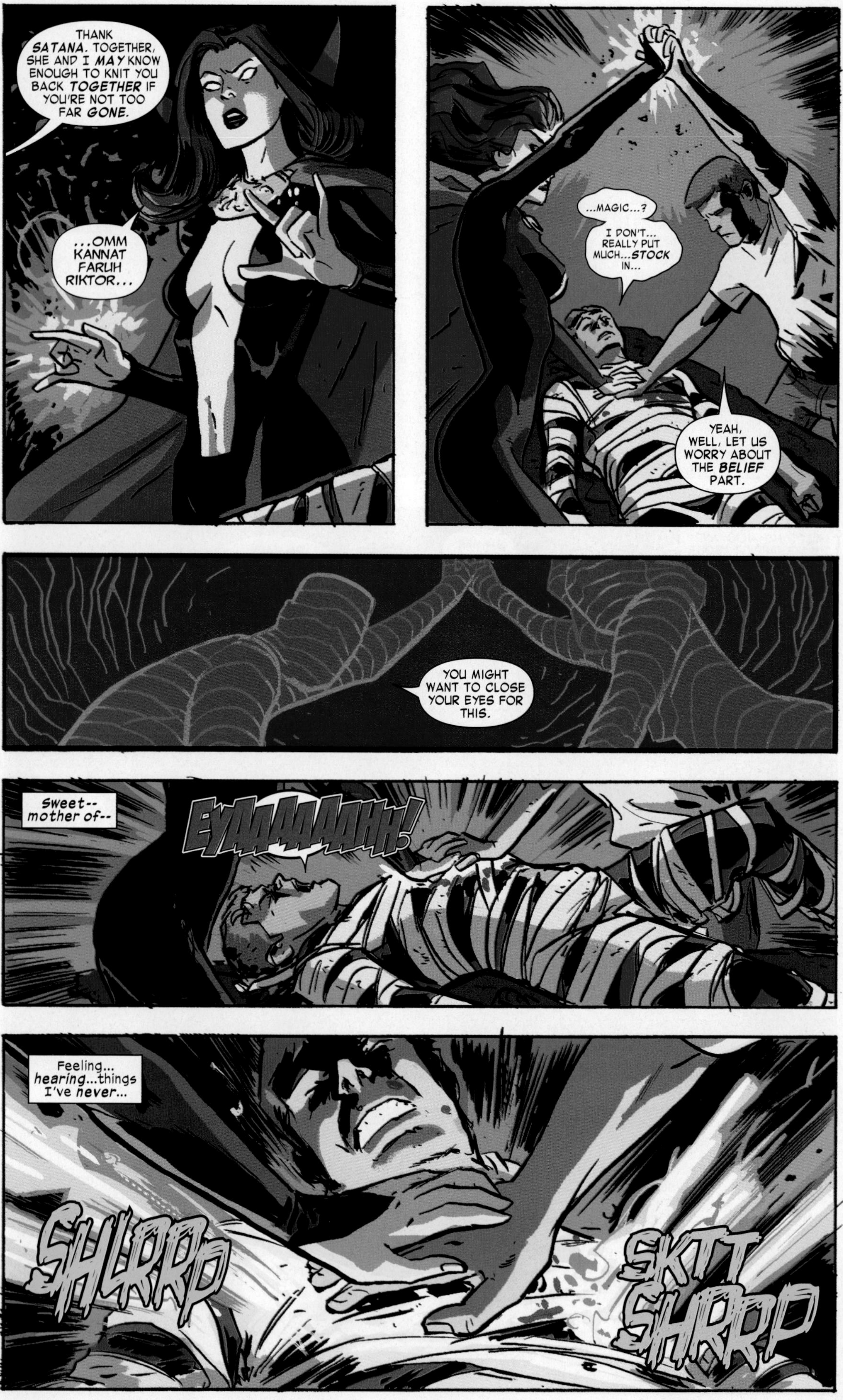
THANK SATANA. TOGETHER, SHE AND I MAY KNOW ENOUGH TO KNIT YOU BACK TOGETHER IF YOU'RE NOT TOO FAR GONE.
...OMM KANNAT FARUH RIKTOR...
...MAGIC...?
I DON'T... REALLY PUT MUCH...STOCK IN...
YEAH, WELL, LET US WORRY ABOUT THE BELIEF PART.
YOU MIGHT WANT TO CLOSE YOUR EYES FOR THIS.
Sweet-- mother of--
EYAAAAAAHH!
Feeling... hearing...things I've never...
SHRRP
SKTT SHRRP

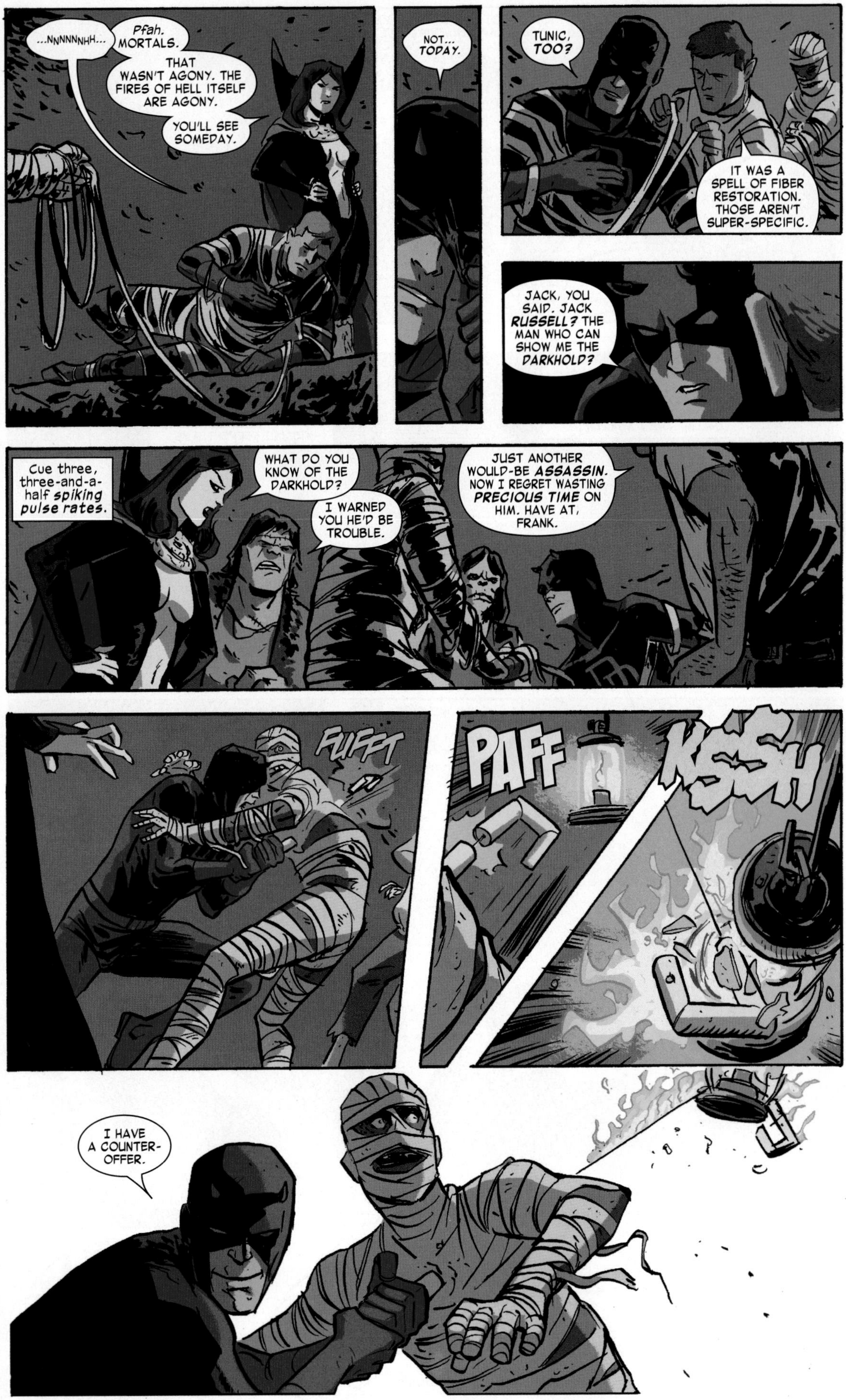
...NNNNNNNH...
Pfah. MORTALS.
THAT WASN'T AGONY. THE FIRES OF HELL ITSELF ARE AGONY.
YOU'LL SEE SOMEDAY.
NOT... TODAY.
TUNIC, TOO?
IT WAS A SPELL OF FIBER RESTORATION. THOSE AREN'T SUPER-SPECIFIC.
JACK, YOU SAID. JACK RUSSELL? THE MAN WHO CAN SHOW ME THE DARKHOLD?
Cue three, three-and-a-half spiking pulse rates.
WHAT DO YOU KNOW OF THE DARKHOLD?
I WARNED YOU HE'D BE TROUBLE.
JUST ANOTHER WOULD-BE ASSASSIN. NOW I REGRET WASTING PRECIOUS TIME ON HIM. HAVE AT, FRANK.
FUFFT
PAFF
KSSH
I HAVE A COUNTER-OFFER.

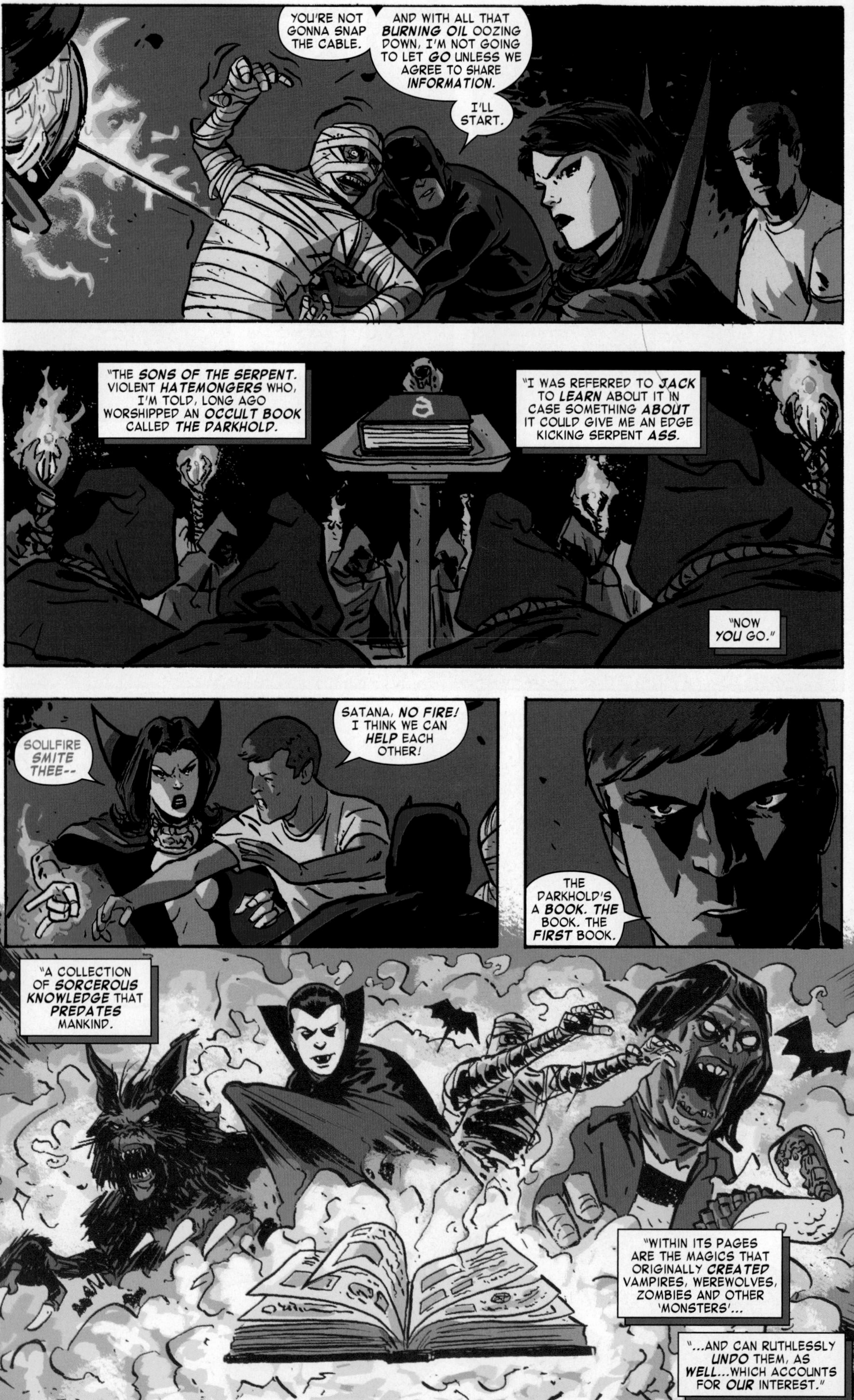

YOU'RE NOT GONNA SNAP THE CABLE.
AND WITH ALL THAT BURNING OIL OOZING DOWN, I'M NOT GOING TO LET GO UNLESS WE AGREE TO SHARE INFORMATION.
I'LL START.
"THE SONS OF THE SERPENT. VIOLENT HATEMONGERS WHO, I'M TOLD, LONG AGO WORSHIPPED AN OCCULT BOOK CALLED THE DARKHOLD.
"I WAS REFERRED TO JACK TO LEARN ABOUT IT IN CASE SOMETHING ABOUT IT COULD GIVE ME AN EDGE KICKING SERPENT ASS.
"NOW YOU GO."
SOULFIRE SMITE THEE--
SATANA, NO FIRE! I THINK WE CAN HELP EACH OTHER!
THE DARKHOLD'S A BOOK. THE BOOK. THE FIRST BOOK.
"A COLLECTION OF SORCEROUS KNOWLEDGE THAT PREDATES MANKIND.
"WITHIN ITS PAGES ARE THE MAGICS THAT ORIGINALLY CREATED VAMPIRES, WEREWOLVES, ZOMBIES AND OTHER 'MONSTERS'...
"...AND CAN RUTHLESSLY UNDO THEM, AS WELL...WHICH ACCOUNTS FOR OUR INTEREST."

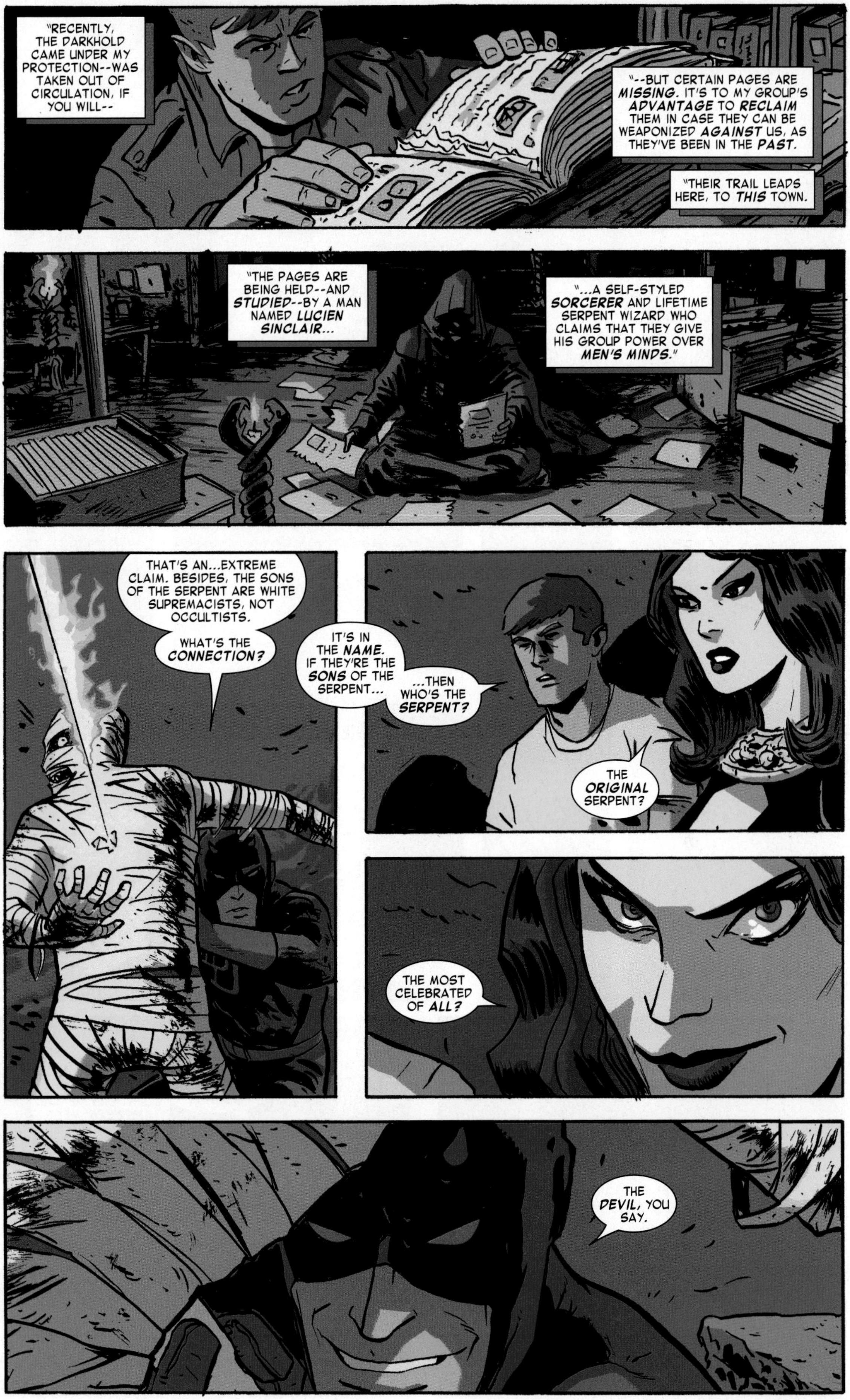
"RECENTLY, THE DARKHOLD CAME UNDER MY PROTECTION--WAS TAKEN OUT OF CIRCULATION, IF YOU WILL--
"--BUT CERTAIN PAGES ARE MISSING. IT'S TO MY GROUP'S ADVANTAGE TO RECLAIM THEM IN CASE THEY CAN BE WEAPONIZED AGAINST US, AS THEY'VE BEEN IN THE PAST.
"THEIR TRAIL LEADS HERE, TO THIS TOWN.
"THE PAGES ARE BEING HELD--AND STUDIED--BY A MAN NAMED LUCIEN SINCLAIR...
"...A SELF-STYLED SORCERER AND LIFETIME SERPENT WIZARD WHO CLAIMS THAT THEY GIVE HIS GROUP POWER OVER MEN'S MINDS."
THAT'S AN...EXTREME CLAIM. BESIDES, THE SONS OF THE SERPENT ARE WHITE SUPREMACISTS, NOT OCCULTISTS.
WHAT'S THE CONNECTION?
IT'S IN THE NAME. IF THEY'RE THE SONS OF THE SERPENT...
...THEN WHO'S THE SERPENT?
THE ORIGINAL SERPENT?
THE MOST CELEBRATED OF ALL?
THE DEVIL, YOU SAY.

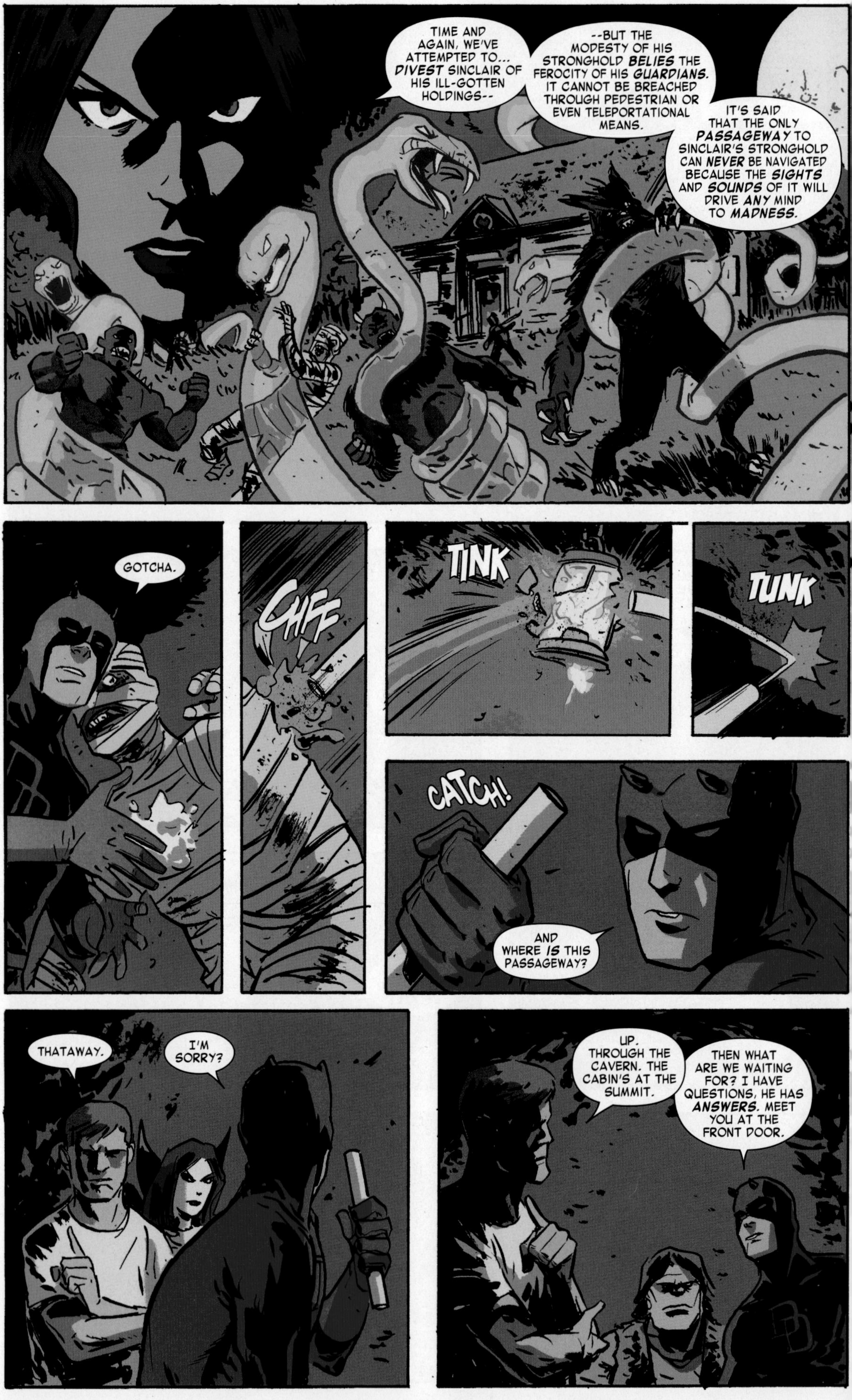
TIME AND AGAIN, WE'VE ATTEMPTED TO... DIVEST SINCLAIR OF HIS ILL-GOTTEN HOLDINGS--
--BUT THE MODESTY OF HIS STRONGHOLD BELIES THE FEROCITY OF HIS GUARDIANS. IT CANNOT BE BREACHED THROUGH PEDESTRIAN OR EVEN TELEPORTATIONAL MEANS.
IT'S SAID THAT THE ONLY PASSAGEWAY TO SINCLAIR'S STRONGHOLD CAN NEVER BE NAVIGATED BECAUSE THE SIGHTS AND SOUNDS OF IT WILL DRIVE ANY MIND TO MADNESS.
GOTCHA.
CHFF
TINK
TUNK
CATCH!
AND WHERE IS THIS PASSAGEWAY?
THATAWAY.
I'M SORRY?
UP. THROUGH THE CAVERN. THE CABIN'S AT THE SUMMIT.
THEN WHAT ARE WE WAITING FOR? I HAVE QUESTIONS, HE HAS ANSWERS. MEET YOU AT THE FRONT DOOR.

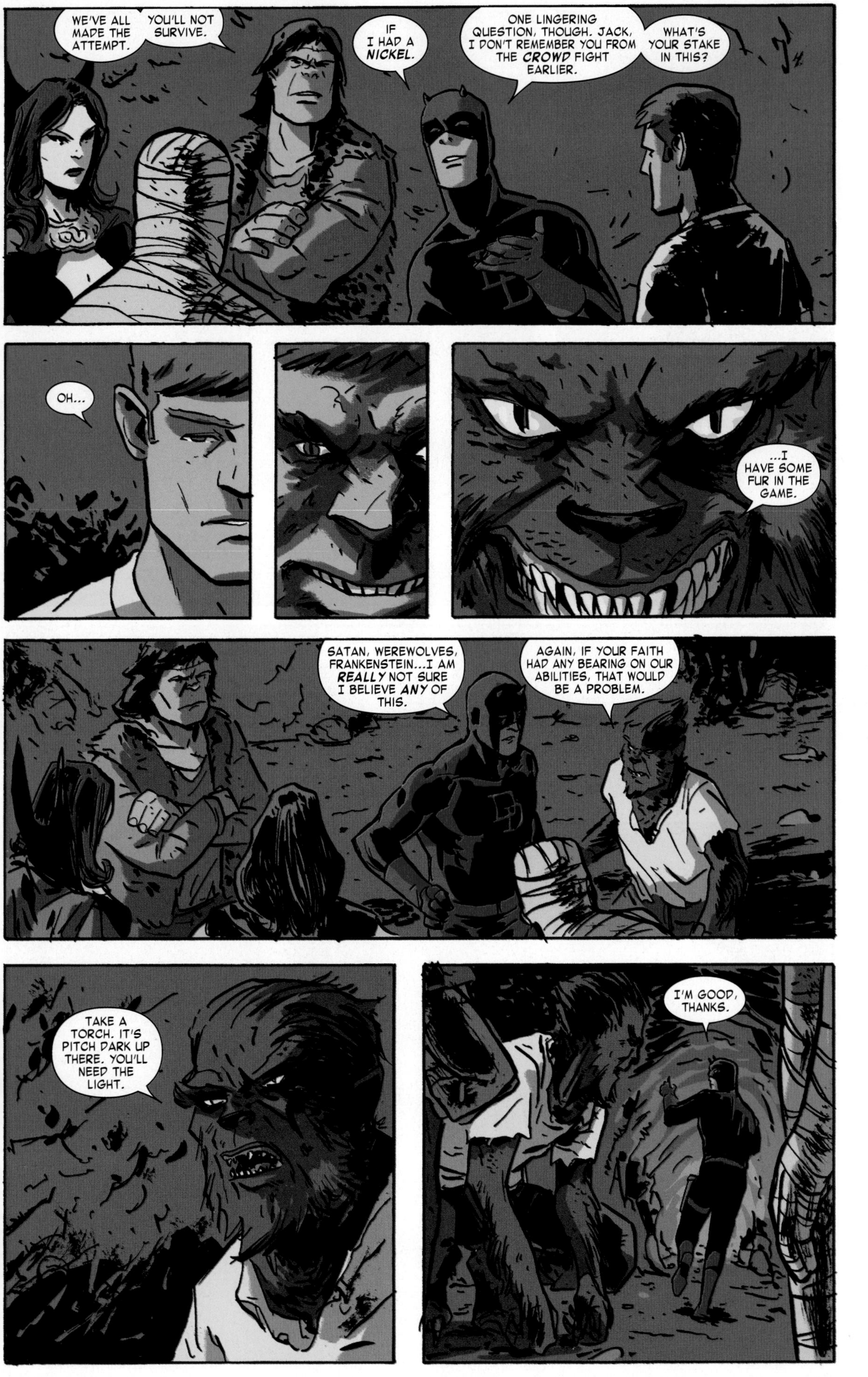

WE'VE ALL MADE THE ATTEMPT.
YOU'LL NOT SURVIVE.
IF I HAD A NICKEL.
ONE LINGERING QUESTION, THOUGH. JACK, I DON'T REMEMBER YOU FROM THE CROWD FIGHT EARLIER.
WHAT'S YOUR STAKE IN THIS?
OH...
...I HAVE SOME FUR IN THE GAME.
SATAN, WEREWOLVES, FRANKENSTEIN...I AM REALLY NOT SURE I BELIEVE ANY OF THIS.
AGAIN, IF YOUR FAITH HAD ANY BEARING ON OUR ABILITIES, THAT WOULD BE A PROBLEM.
TAKE A TORCH. IT'S PITCH DARK UP THERE. YOU'LL NEED THE LIGHT.
I'M GOOD, THANKS.

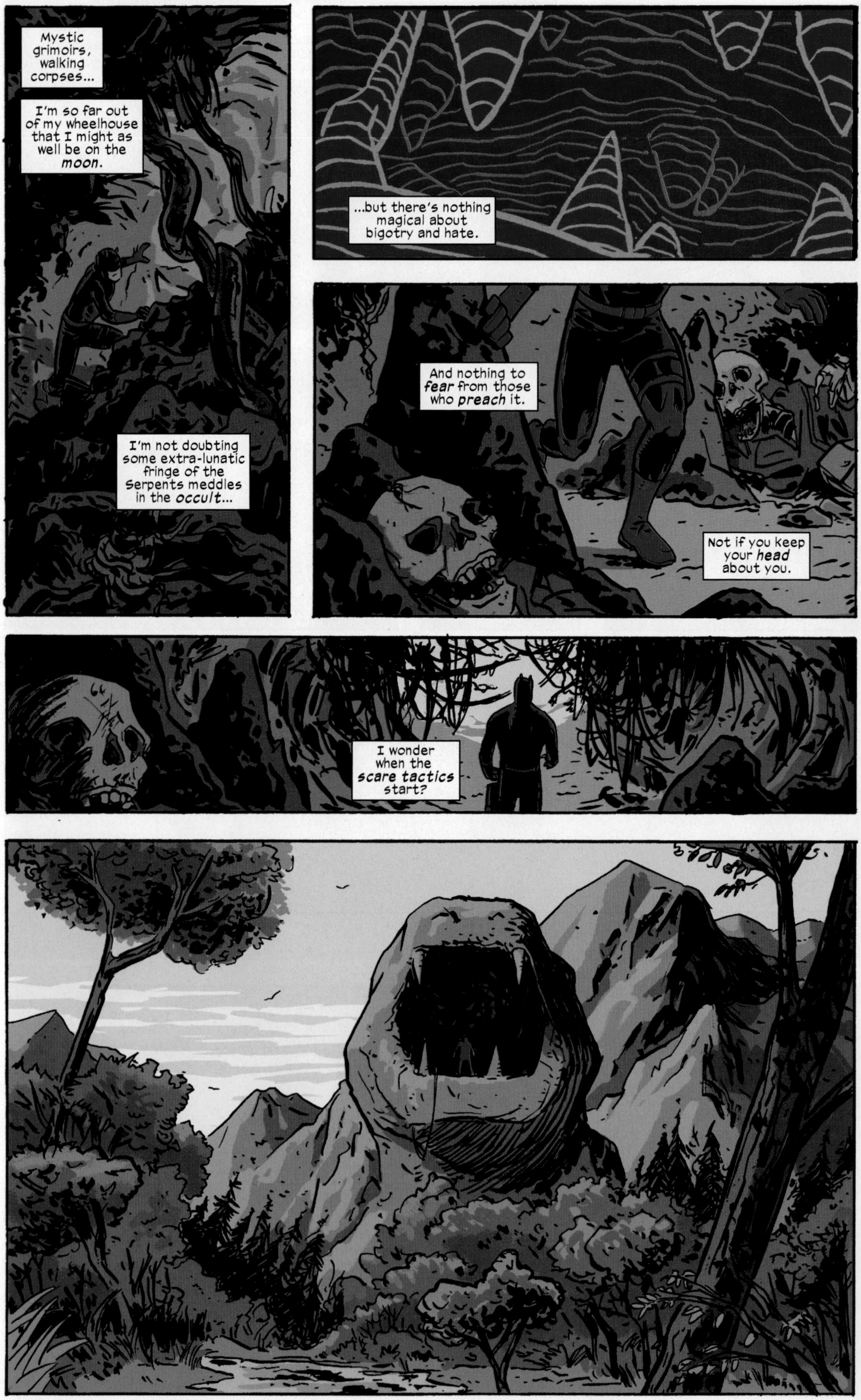
Mystic grimoirs, walking corpses...
I'm so far out of my wheelhouse that I might as well be on the *moon*.
I'm not doubting some extra-lunatic fringe of the Serpents meddles in the *occult*...
...but there's nothing magical about bigotry and hate.
And nothing to *fear* from those who *preach* it.
Not if you keep your *head* about you.
I wonder when the *scare tactics* start?

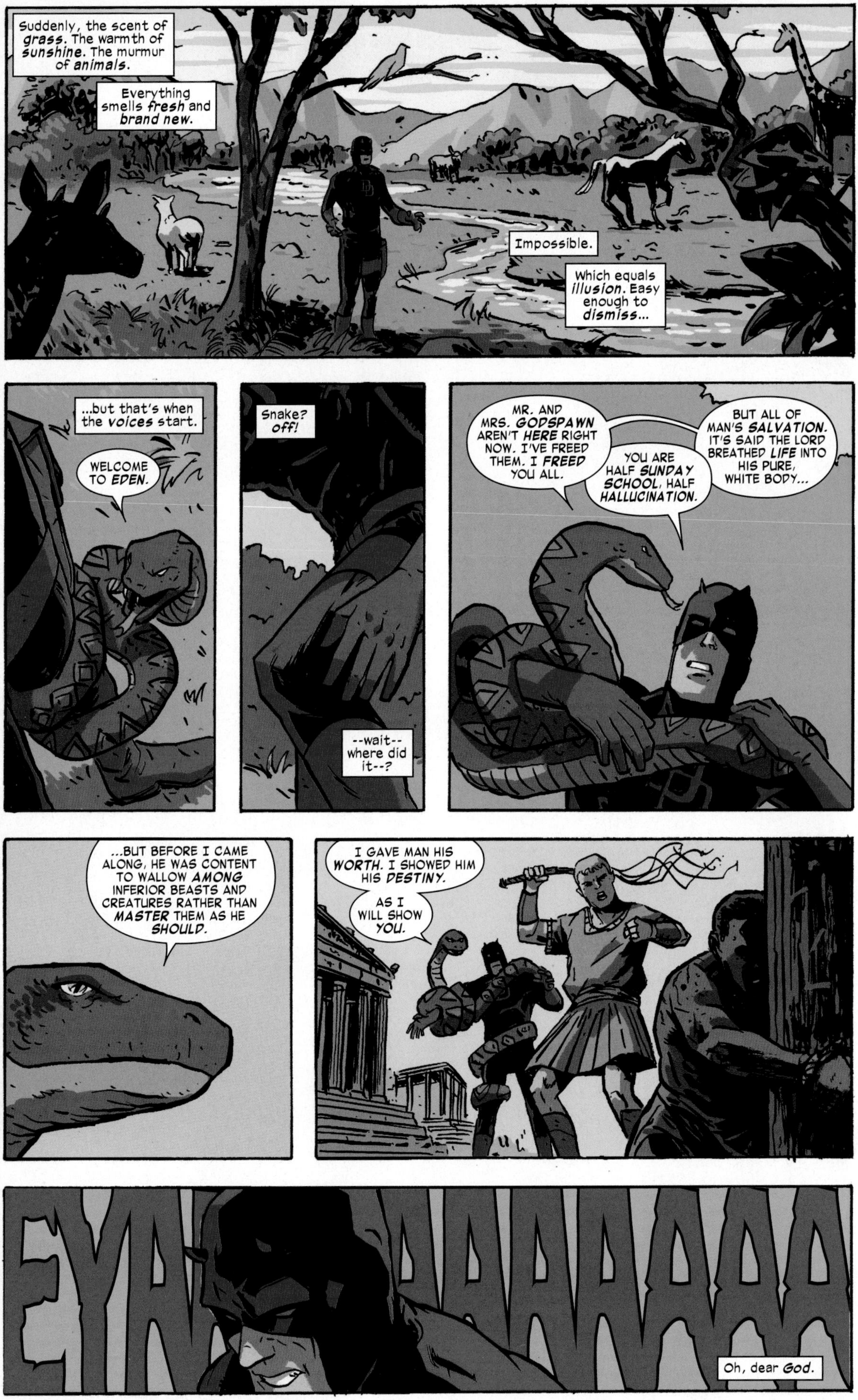
Suddenly, the scent of *grass*. The warmth of *sunshine*. The murmur of *animals*.
Everything smells *fresh* and *brand new*.
Impossible.
Which equals *illusion*. Easy enough to *dismiss*...
...but that's when the *voices* start.
WELCOME TO *EDEN*.
Snake? *off!*
--wait-- where did it--?
MR. AND MRS. *GODSPAWN* AREN'T *HERE* RIGHT NOW. I'VE FREED THEM. I *FREED* YOU ALL.
YOU ARE HALF *SUNDAY SCHOOL*, HALF *HALLUCINATION*.
BUT ALL OF MAN'S *SALVATION*. IT'S SAID THE LORD BREATHED *LIFE* INTO HIS PURE, WHITE BODY...
...BUT BEFORE I CAME ALONG, HE WAS CONTENT TO WALLOW *AMONG* INFERIOR BEASTS AND CREATURES RATHER THAN *MASTER* THEM AS HE *SHOULD*.
I GAVE MAN HIS *WORTH*. I SHOWED HIM HIS *DESTINY*.
AS I WILL SHOW *YOU*.
EYAAAAAAAA
Oh, dear *God*.

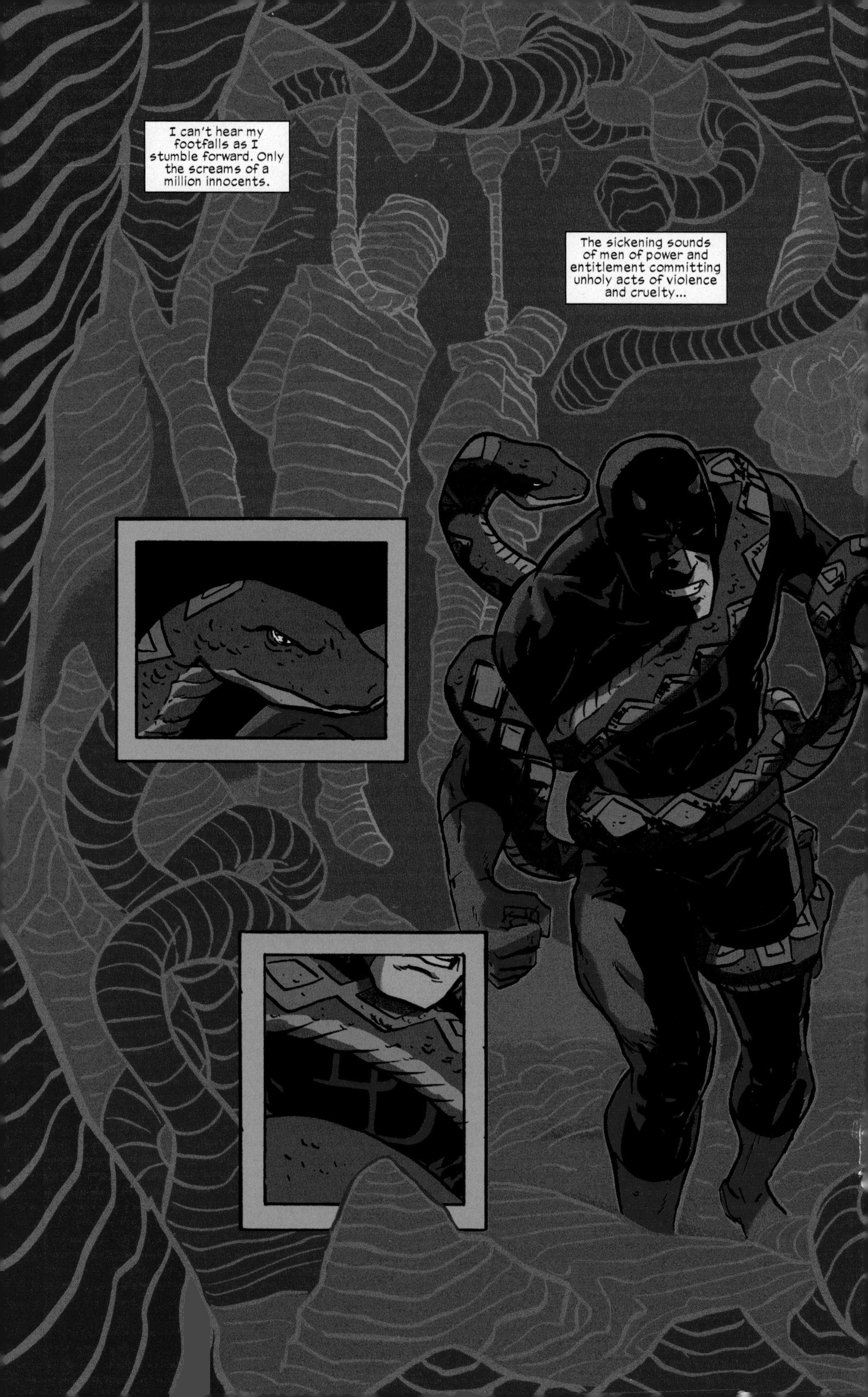
I can't hear my footfalls as I stumble forward. Only the screams of a million innocents.
The sickening sounds of men of power and entitlement committing unholy acts of violence and cruelty...

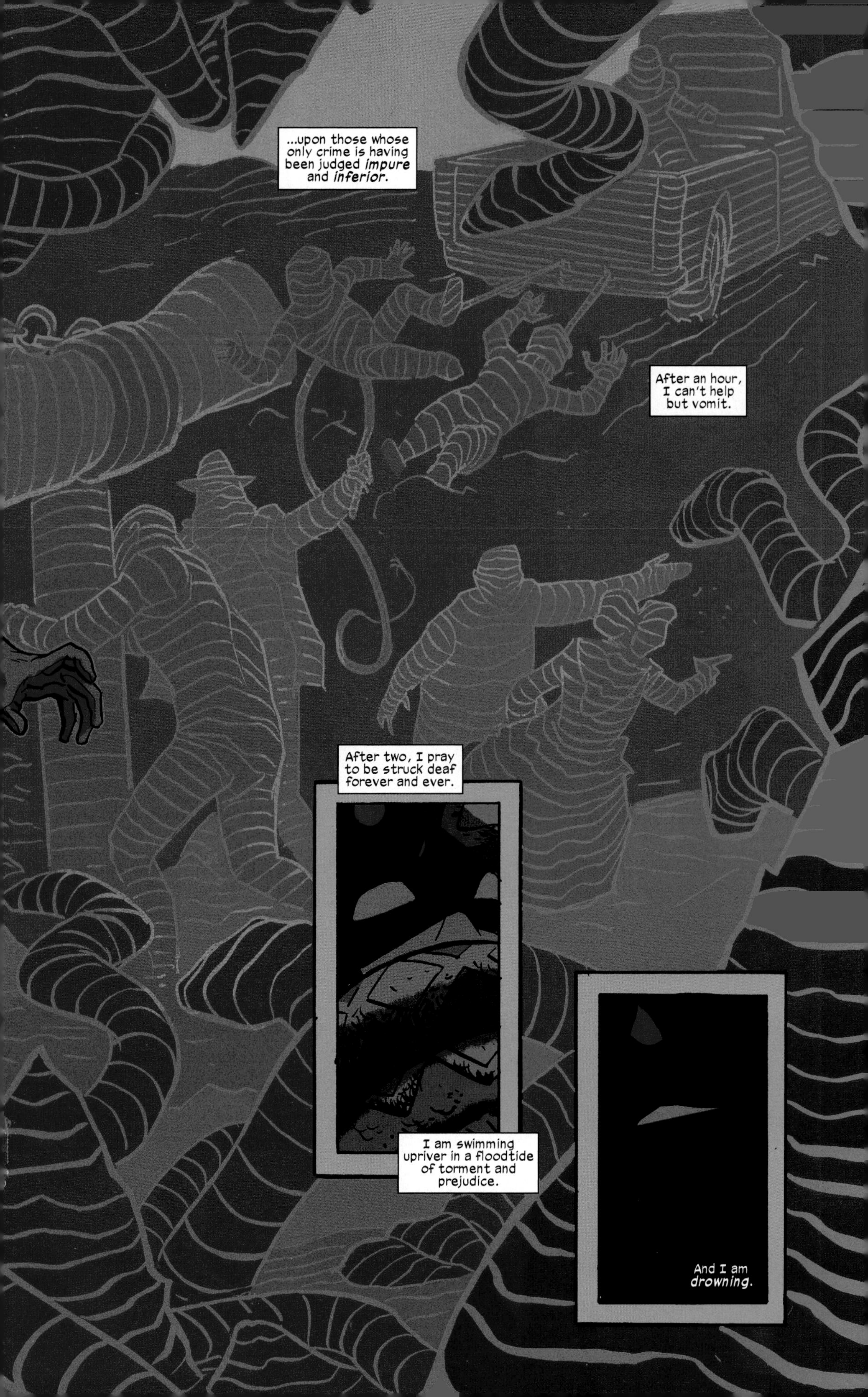
...upon those whose only crime is having been judged *impure* and *inferior*.
After an hour, I can't help but vomit.
After two, I pray to be struck deaf forever and ever.
I am swimming upriver in a floodtide of torment and prejudice.
And I am *drowning*.

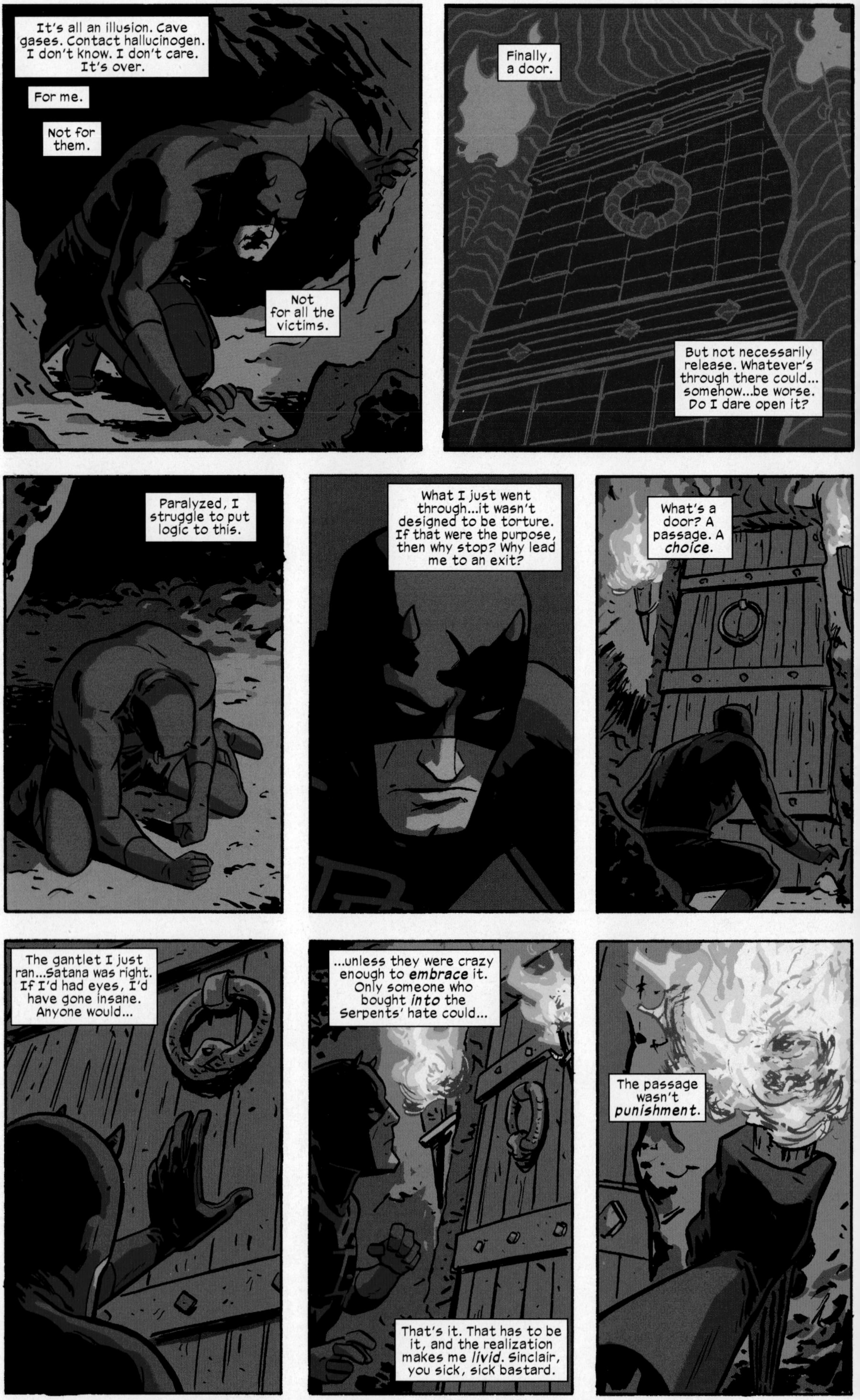
It's all an illusion. Cave gases. Contact hallucinogen. I don't know. I don't care. It's over.
For me.
Not for them.
Not for all the victims.
Finally, a door.
But not necessarily release. Whatever's through there could... somehow...be worse. Do I dare open it?
Paralyzed, I struggle to put logic to this.
What I just went through...it wasn't designed to be torture. If that were the purpose, then why stop? Why lead me to an exit?
What's a door? A passage. A *choice*.
The gantlet I just ran...Satana was right. If I'd had eyes, I'd have gone insane. Anyone would...
...unless they were crazy enough to *embrace* it. Only someone who bought *into* the Serpents' hate could...
That's it. That has to be it, and the realization makes me *livid*. Sinclair, you sick, sick bastard.
The passage wasn't *punishment*.

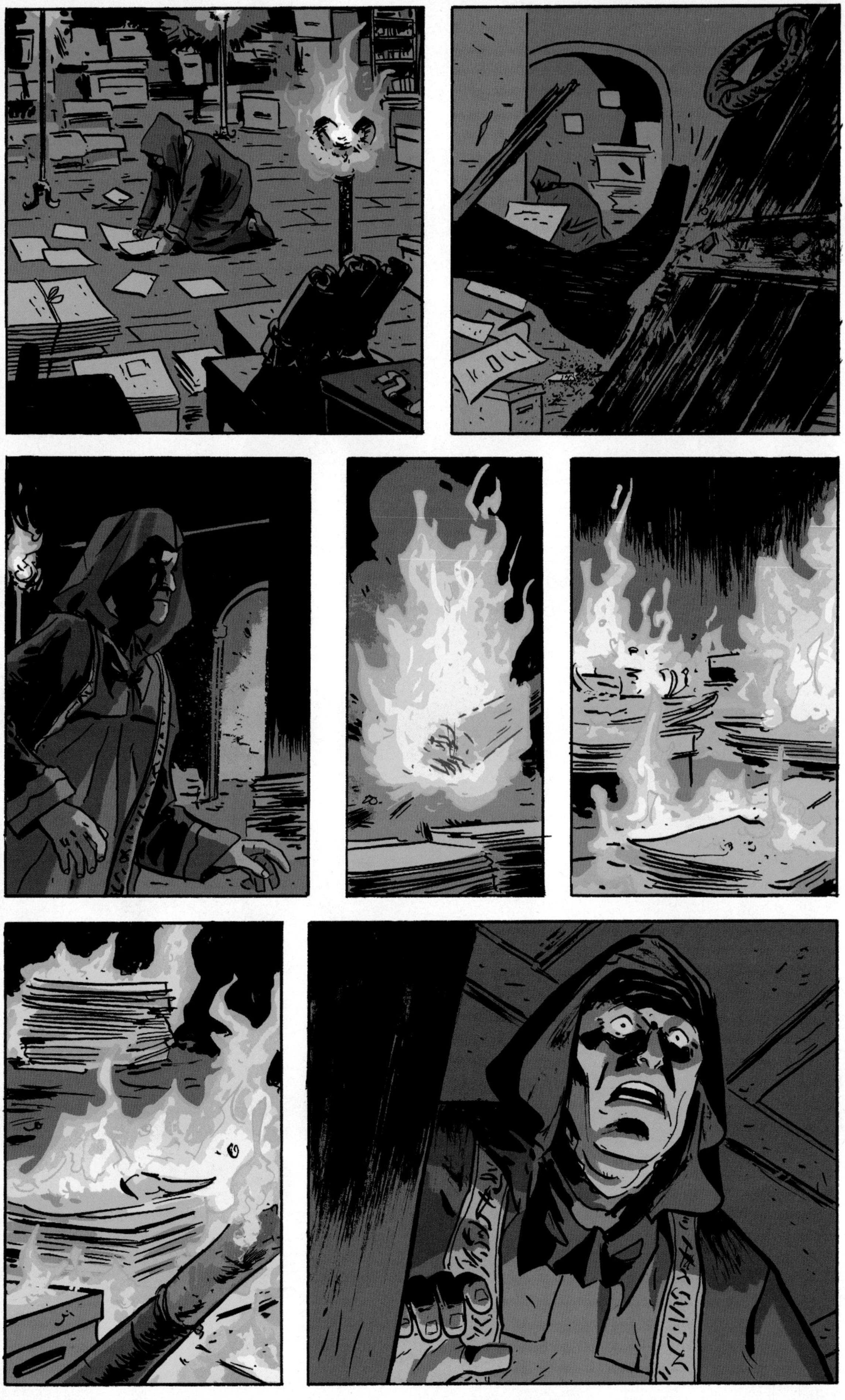

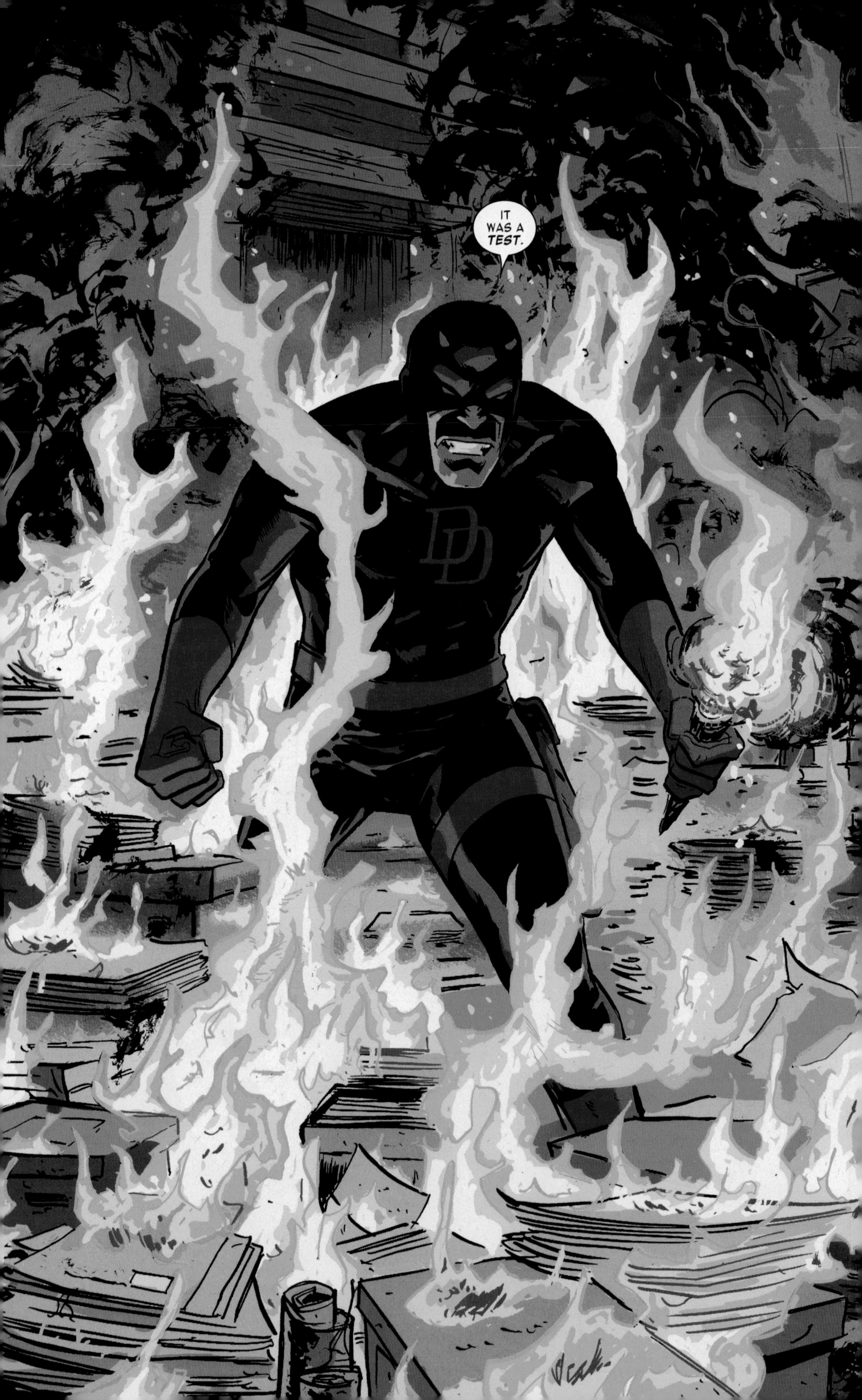
IT WAS A TEST.

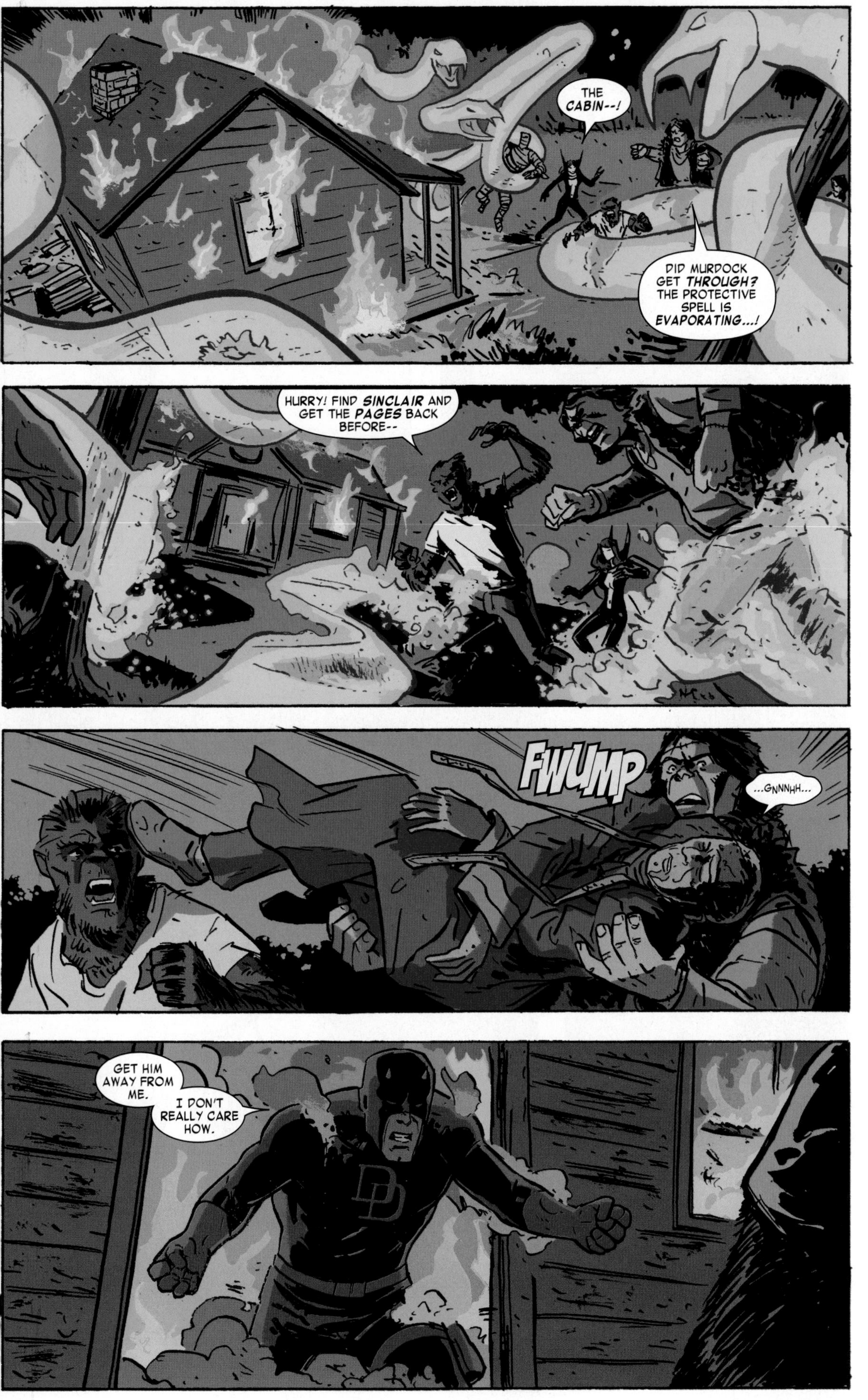
THE CABIN--!
DID MURDOCK GET THROUGH? THE PROTECTIVE SPELL IS EVAPORATING...!
HURRY! FIND SINCLAIR AND GET THE PAGES BACK BEFORE--
FWUMP
...GNNNHH...
GET HIM AWAY FROM ME.
I DON'T REALLY CARE HOW.

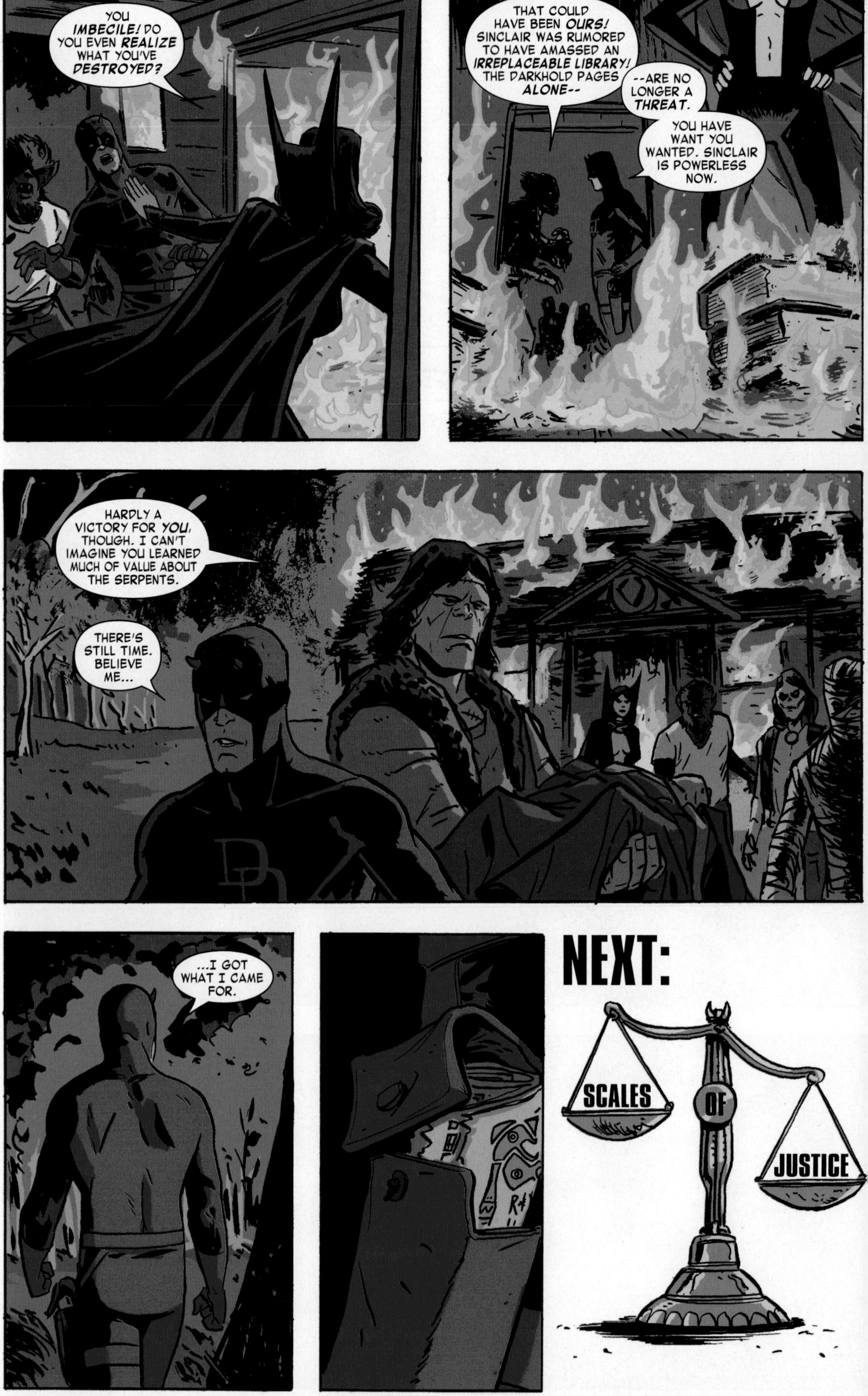
YOU IMBECILE! DO YOU EVEN REALIZE WHAT YOU'VE DESTROYED?
THAT COULD HAVE BEEN OURS! SINCLAIR WAS RUMORED TO HAVE AMASSED AN IRREPLACEABLE LIBRARY! THE DARKHOLD PAGES ALONE--
--ARE NO LONGER A THREAT.
YOU HAVE WANT YOU WANTED. SINCLAIR IS POWERLESS NOW.
HARDLY A VICTORY FOR YOU, THOUGH. I CAN'T IMAGINE YOU LEARNED MUCH OF VALUE ABOUT THE SERPENTS.
THERE'S STILL TIME. BELIEVE ME...
...I GOT WHAT I CAME FOR.
NEXT:
SCALES OF JUSTICE

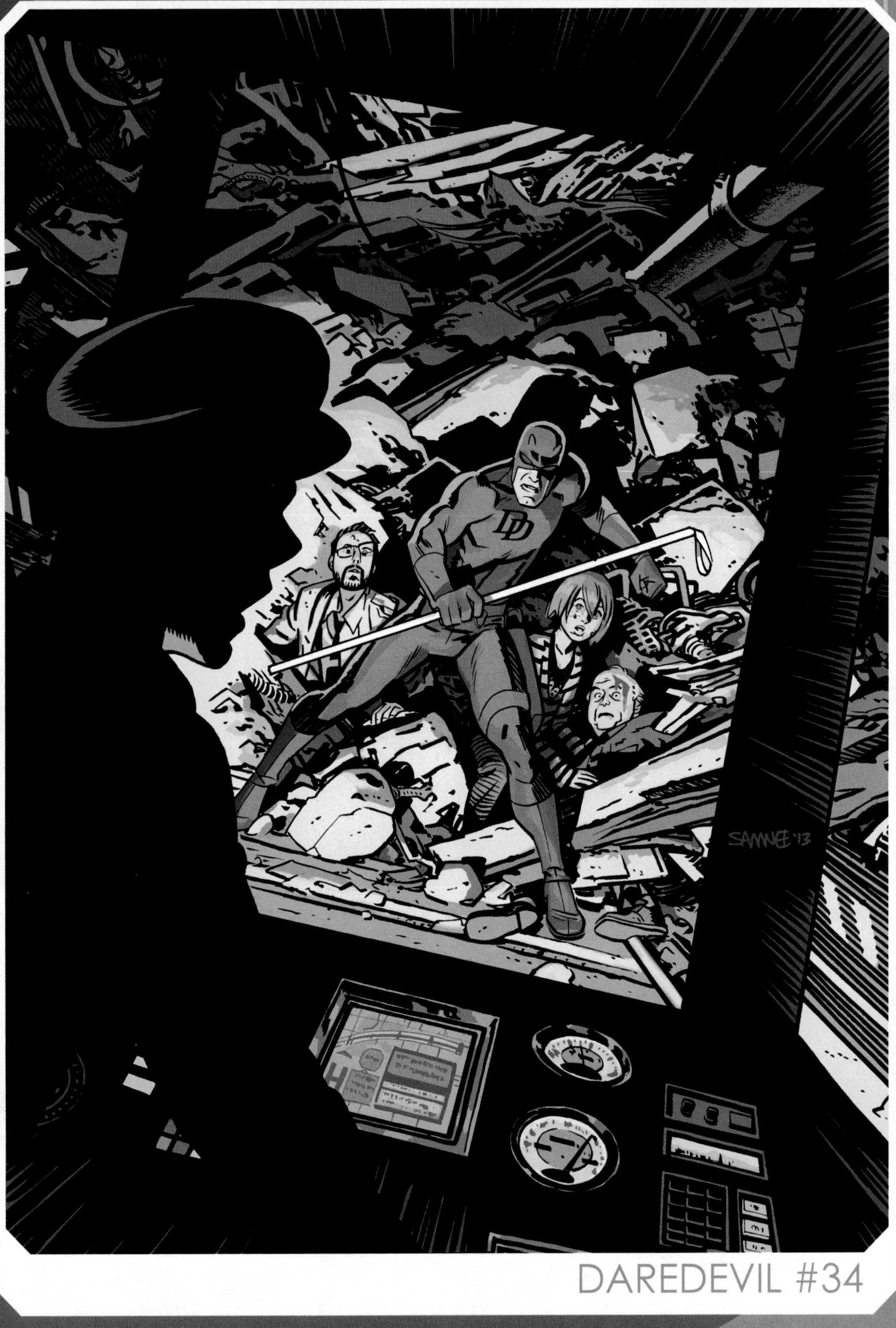
SAMNEE '13

DAREDEVIL #34

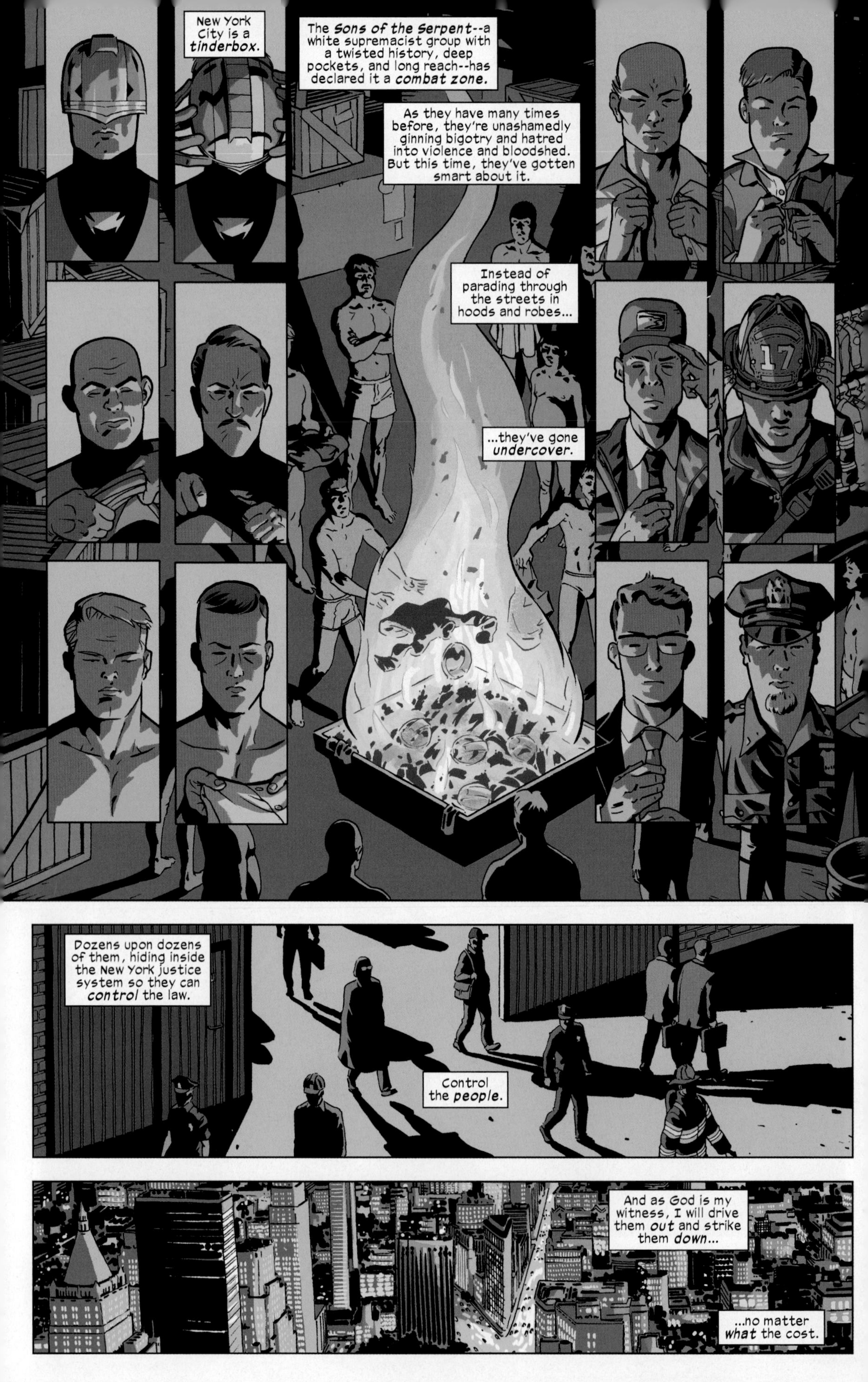
New York City is a *tinderbox.*
The *Sons of the Serpent*--a white supremacist group with a twisted history, deep pockets, and long reach--has declared it a *combat zone.*
As they have many times before, they're unashamedly ginning bigotry and hatred into violence and bloodshed. But this time, they've gotten smart about it.
Instead of parading through the streets in hoods and robes...
...they've gone *undercover.*
17
Dozens upon dozens of them, hiding inside the New York justice system so they can *control* the law.
Control the *people.*
And as God is my witness, I will drive them *out* and strike them *down...*
...no matter *what* the cost.

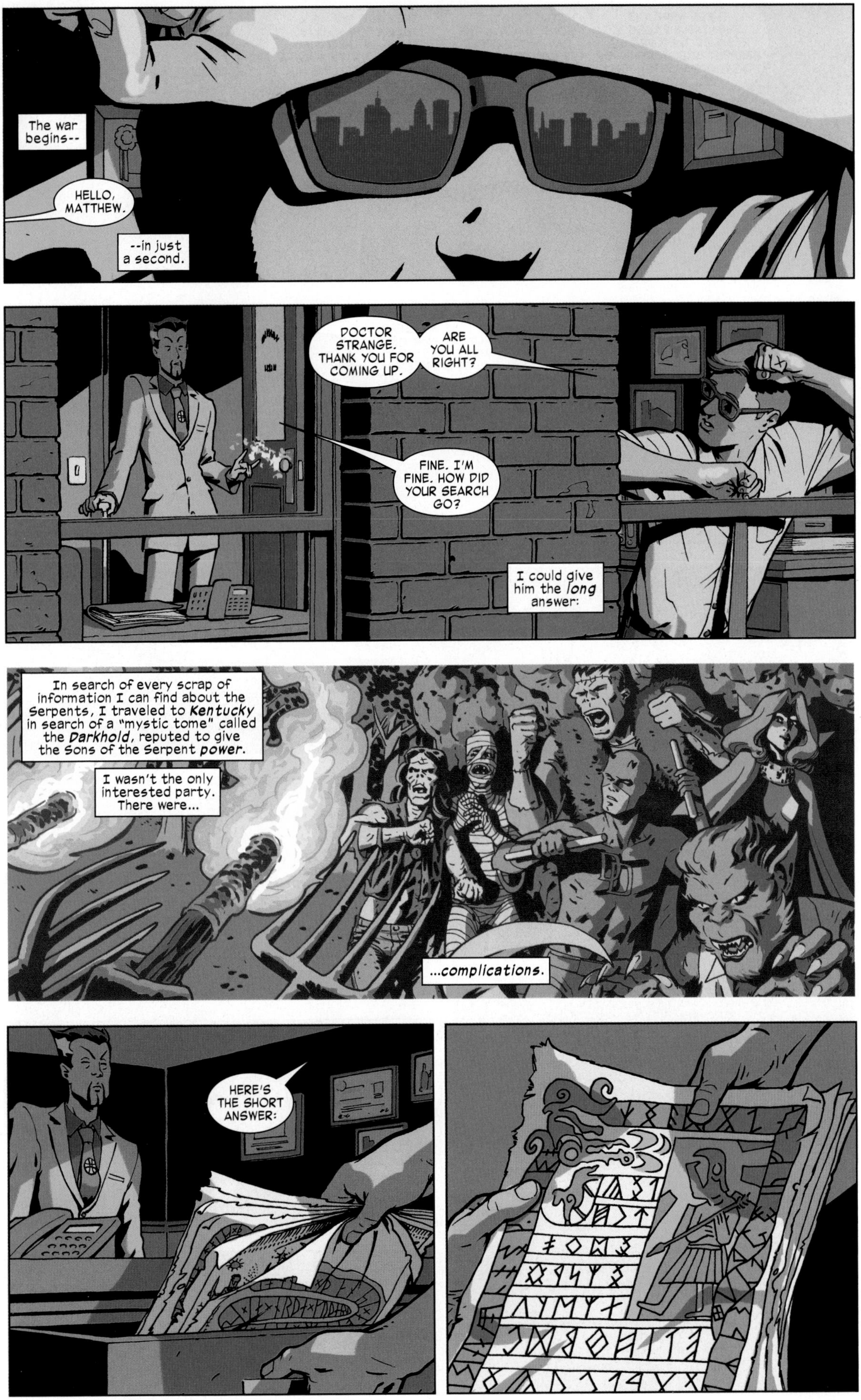
The war begins--
HELLO, MATTHEW.
--in just a second.
DOCTOR STRANGE. THANK YOU FOR COMING UP.
ARE YOU ALL RIGHT?
FINE. I'M FINE. HOW DID YOUR SEARCH GO?
I could give him the long answer:
In search of every scrap of information I can find about the Serpents, I traveled to Kentucky in search of a "mystic tome" called the Darkhold, reputed to give the Sons of the Serpent power.
I wasn't the only interested party. There were...
...complications.
HERE'S THE SHORT ANSWER:

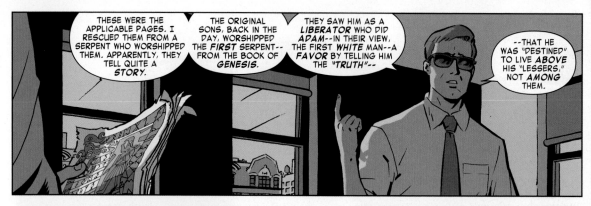

THESE WERE THE APPLICABLE PAGES. I RESCUED THEM FROM A SERPENT WHO WORSHIPPED THEM. APPARENTLY, THEY TELL QUITE A STORY.

THE ORIGINAL SONS, BACK IN THE DAY, WORSHIPPED THE FIRST SERPENT--FROM THE BOOK OF GENESIS.

THEY SAW HIM AS A LIBERATOR WHO DID ADAM--IN THEIR VIEW, THE FIRST WHITE MAN--A FAVOR BY TELLING HIM THE "TRUTH"--

--THAT HE WAS "DESTINED" TO LIVE ABOVE HIS "LESSERS," NOT AMONG THEM.

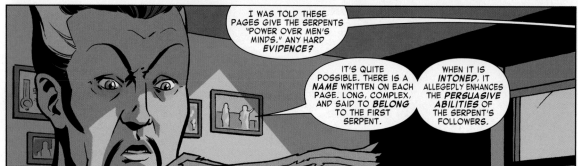

I WAS TOLD THESE PAGES GIVE THE SERPENTS "POWER OVER MEN'S MINDS." ANY HARD EVIDENCE?

IT'S QUITE POSSIBLE. THERE IS A NAME WRITTEN ON EACH PAGE. LONG, COMPLEX, AND SAID TO BELONG TO THE FIRST SERPENT.

WHEN IT IS INTONED, IT ALLEGEDLY ENHANCES THE PERSUASIVE ABILITIES OF THE SERPENT'S FOLLOWERS.

ALLEGEDLY. WHAT'S THE NAME?

I WON'T REPEAT IT.

OH, COME ON. IT'S JUST A WORD...!

PERHAPS. BUT PERHAPS NOT. I WON'T KNOW UNTIL I DO SOME RESEARCH.

YOU BORROWED THESE FROM JACK RUSSELL?

THE WEREWOLF? AND HIS FRIENDS, THE MONSTER SQUAD AND SOME DEVIL-WOMAN?

"BORROWED" ISN'T THE RIGHT WORD. THEY THINK THESE PAGES WERE DESTROYED. LET'S SAY "FELL INTO EVIDENCE."

DEVIL-WO--

SATANA? THE OTHERS...NO CONCERN. BUT YOU LIED TO SATANA ABOUT HAVING THESE PAGES?

IS THAT A PROBLEM?

IT WILL BE SOMEDAY, WHEN SHE FINDS OUT.

AND SHE WILL FIND OUT.

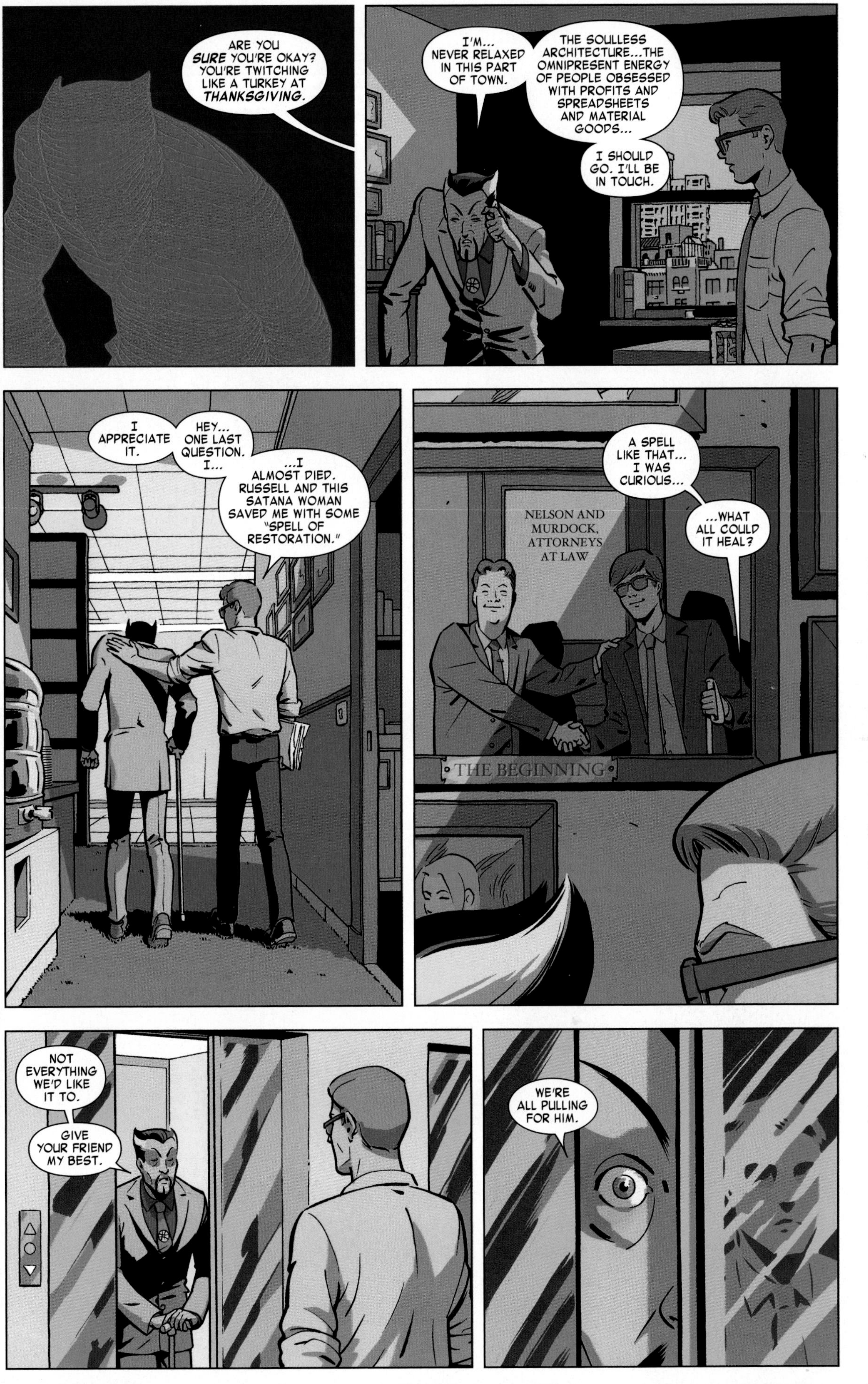
ARE YOU SURE YOU'RE OKAY? YOU'RE TWITCHING LIKE A TURKEY AT THANKSGIVING.
I'M... NEVER RELAXED IN THIS PART OF TOWN.
THE SOULLESS ARCHITECTURE...THE OMNIPRESENT ENERGY OF PEOPLE OBSESSED WITH PROFITS AND SPREADSHEETS AND MATERIAL GOODS...
I SHOULD GO. I'LL BE IN TOUCH.
I APPRECIATE IT.
HEY... ONE LAST QUESTION. I...
...I ALMOST DIED. RUSSELL AND THIS SATANA WOMAN SAVED ME WITH SOME "SPELL OF RESTORATION."
A SPELL LIKE THAT... I WAS CURIOUS...
NELSON AND MURDOCK, ATTORNEYS AT LAW
...WHAT ALL COULD IT HEAL?
THE BEGINNING
NOT EVERYTHING WE'D LIKE IT TO.
GIVE YOUR FRIEND MY BEST.
WE'RE ALL PULLING FOR HIM.

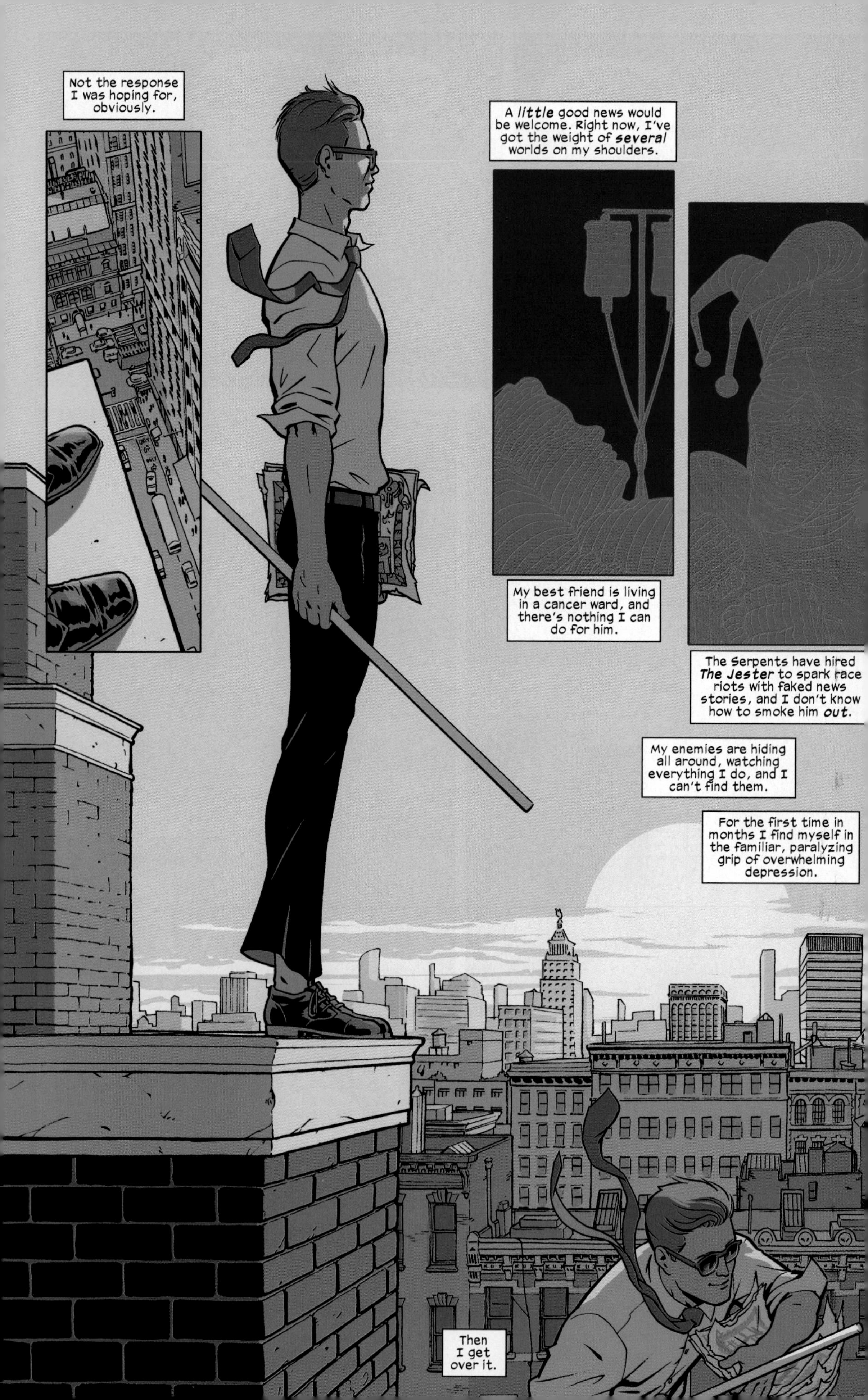
Not the response I was hoping for, obviously.
A *little* good news would be welcome. Right now, I've got the weight of ***several*** worlds on my shoulders.
My best friend is living in a cancer ward, and there's nothing I can do for him.
The Serpents have hired ***The Jester*** to spark race riots with faked news stories, and I don't know how to smoke him ***out***.
My enemies are hiding all around, watching everything I do, and I can't find them.
For the first time in months I find myself in the familiar, paralyzing grip of overwhelming depression.
Then I get over it.

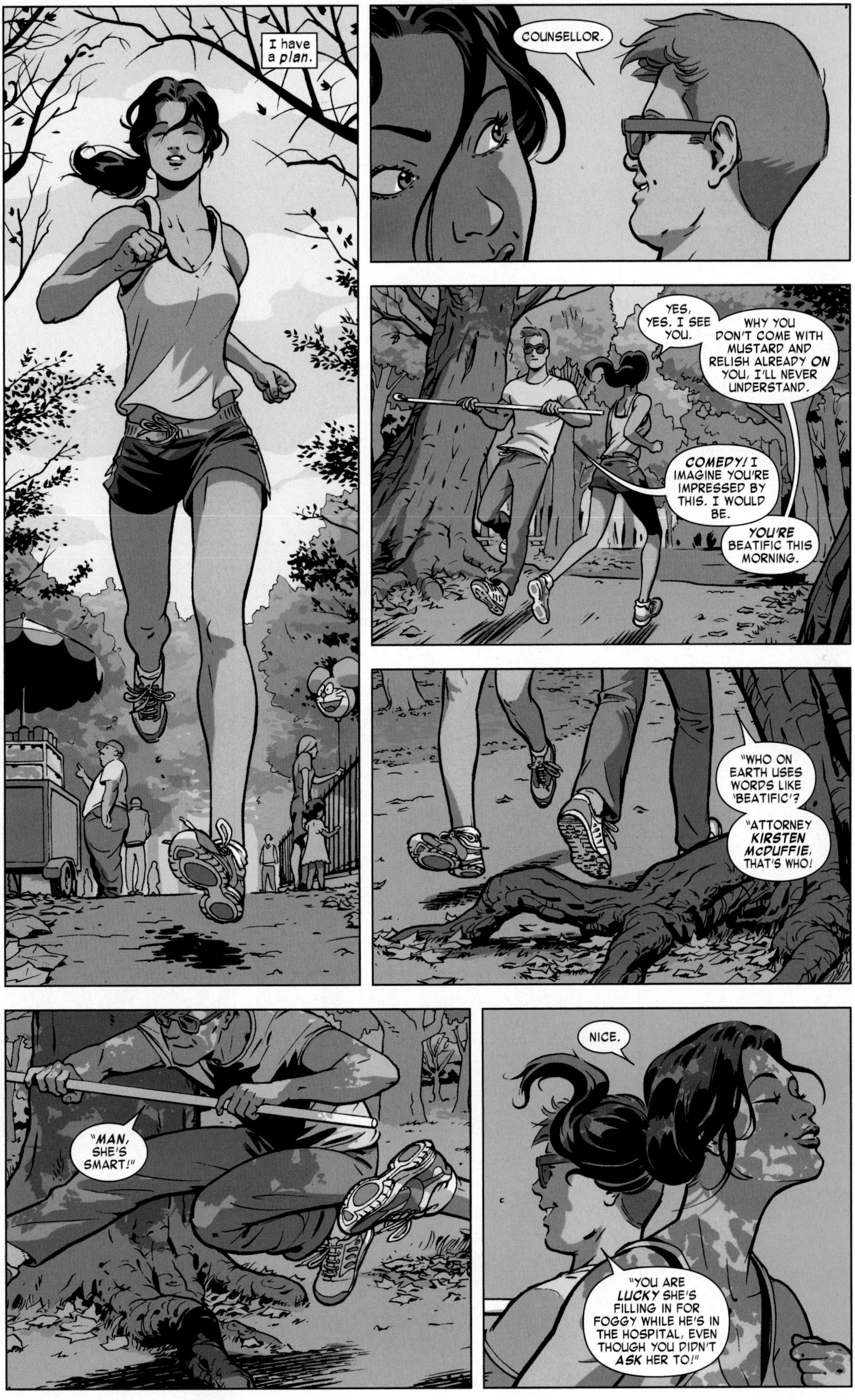
I have a *plan*.
COUNSELLOR.
YES, YES. I SEE YOU.
WHY YOU DON'T COME WITH MUSTARD AND RELISH ALREADY **ON** YOU, I'LL NEVER UNDERSTAND.
COMEDY! I IMAGINE YOU'RE IMPRESSED BY THIS. I WOULD BE.
YOU'RE BEATIFIC THIS MORNING.
"WHO ON EARTH USES WORDS LIKE 'BEATIFIC'?
"ATTORNEY **KIRSTEN McDUFFIE**, THAT'S WHO!
"**MAN**, SHE'S SMART!"
NICE.
"YOU ARE **LUCKY** SHE'S FILLING IN FOR FOGGY WHILE HE'S IN THE HOSPITAL, EVEN THOUGH YOU DIDN'T **ASK** HER TO!"

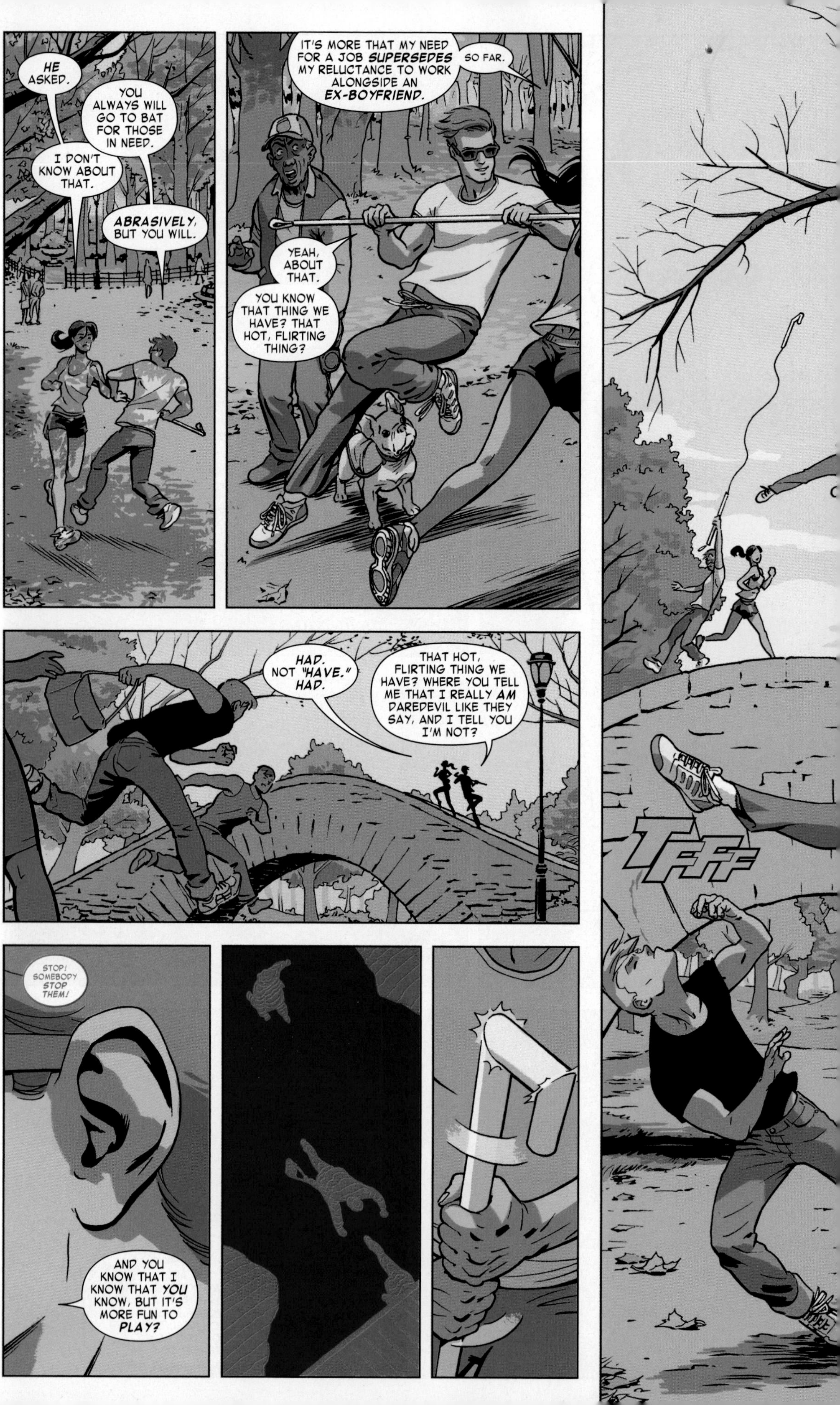
HE ASKED.
YOU ALWAYS WILL GO TO BAT FOR THOSE IN NEED.
I DON'T KNOW ABOUT THAT.
ABRASIVELY, BUT YOU WILL.
IT'S MORE THAT MY NEED FOR A JOB SUPERSEDES MY RELUCTANCE TO WORK ALONGSIDE AN EX-BOYFRIEND.
SO FAR.
YEAH, ABOUT THAT.
YOU KNOW THAT THING WE HAVE? THAT HOT, FLIRTING THING?
HAD. NOT "HAVE." HAD.
THAT HOT, FLIRTING THING WE HAVE? WHERE YOU TELL ME THAT I REALLY AM DAREDEVIL LIKE THEY SAY, AND I TELL YOU I'M NOT?
STOP! SOMEBODY STOP THEM!
AND YOU KNOW THAT I KNOW THAT YOU KNOW, BUT IT'S MORE FUN TO PLAY?
TFFF

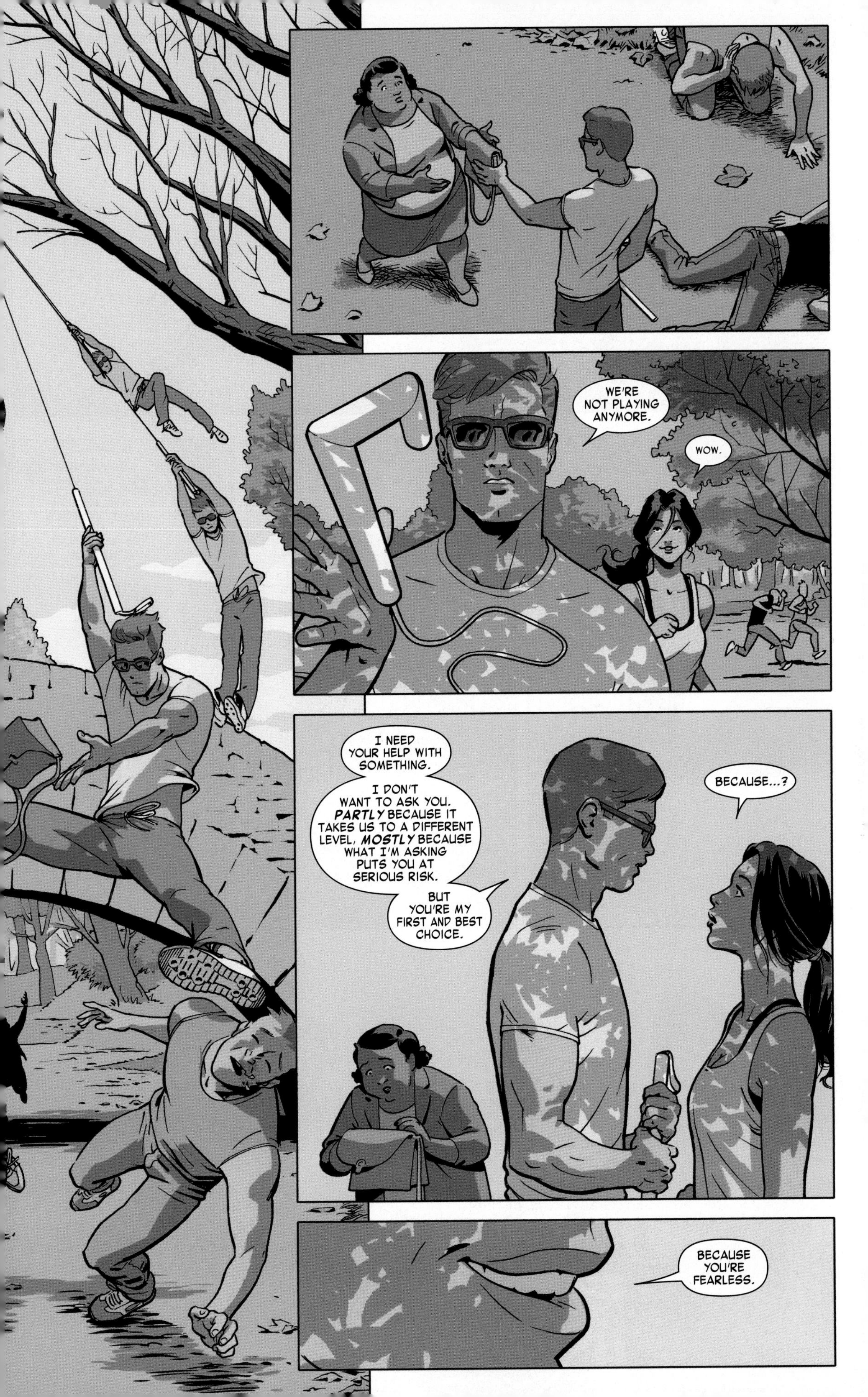
WE'RE NOT PLAYING ANYMORE.
WOW.
I NEED YOUR HELP WITH SOMETHING.
I DON'T WANT TO ASK YOU. PARTLY BECAUSE IT TAKES US TO A DIFFERENT LEVEL, MOSTLY BECAUSE WHAT I'M ASKING PUTS YOU AT SERIOUS RISK.
BUT YOU'RE MY FIRST AND BEST CHOICE.
BECAUSE...?
BECAUSE YOU'RE FEARLESS.

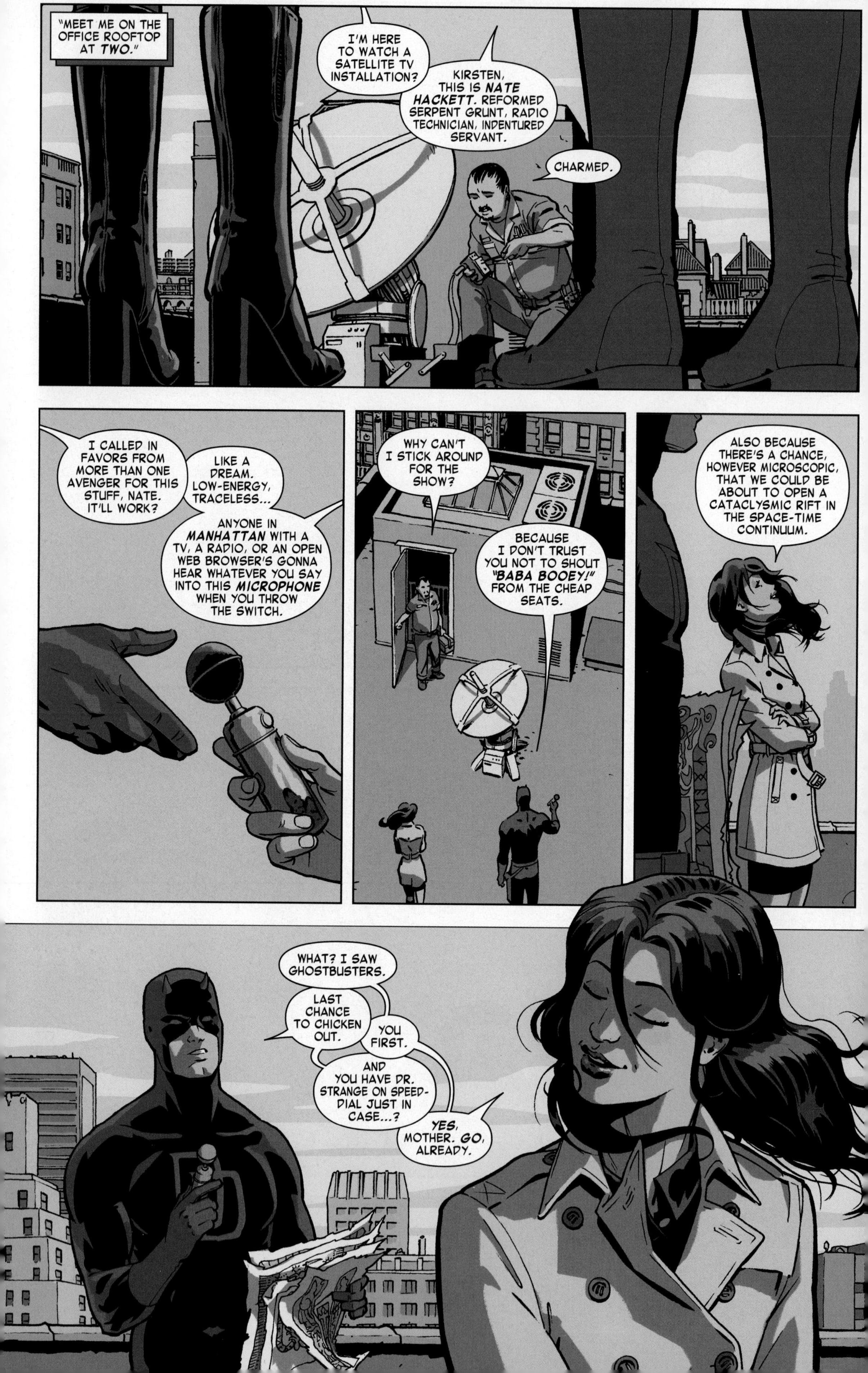
"MEET ME ON THE OFFICE ROOFTOP AT TWO."
I'M HERE TO WATCH A SATELLITE TV INSTALLATION?
KIRSTEN, THIS IS NATE HACKETT. REFORMED SERPENT GRUNT, RADIO TECHNICIAN, INDENTURED SERVANT.
CHARMED.
I CALLED IN FAVORS FROM MORE THAN ONE AVENGER FOR THIS STUFF, NATE. IT'LL WORK?
LIKE A DREAM. LOW-ENERGY, TRACELESS...
ANYONE IN MANHATTAN WITH A TV, A RADIO, OR AN OPEN WEB BROWSER'S GONNA HEAR WHATEVER YOU SAY INTO THIS MICROPHONE WHEN YOU THROW THE SWITCH.
WHY CAN'T I STICK AROUND FOR THE SHOW?
BECAUSE I DON'T TRUST YOU NOT TO SHOUT "BABA BOOEY!" FROM THE CHEAP SEATS.
ALSO BECAUSE THERE'S A CHANCE, HOWEVER MICROSCOPIC, THAT WE COULD BE ABOUT TO OPEN A CATACLYSMIC RIFT IN THE SPACE-TIME CONTINUUM.
WHAT? I SAW GHOSTBUSTERS.
LAST CHANCE TO CHICKEN OUT.
YOU FIRST.
AND YOU HAVE DR. STRANGE ON SPEED-DIAL JUST IN CASE...?
YES, MOTHER. GO, ALREADY.

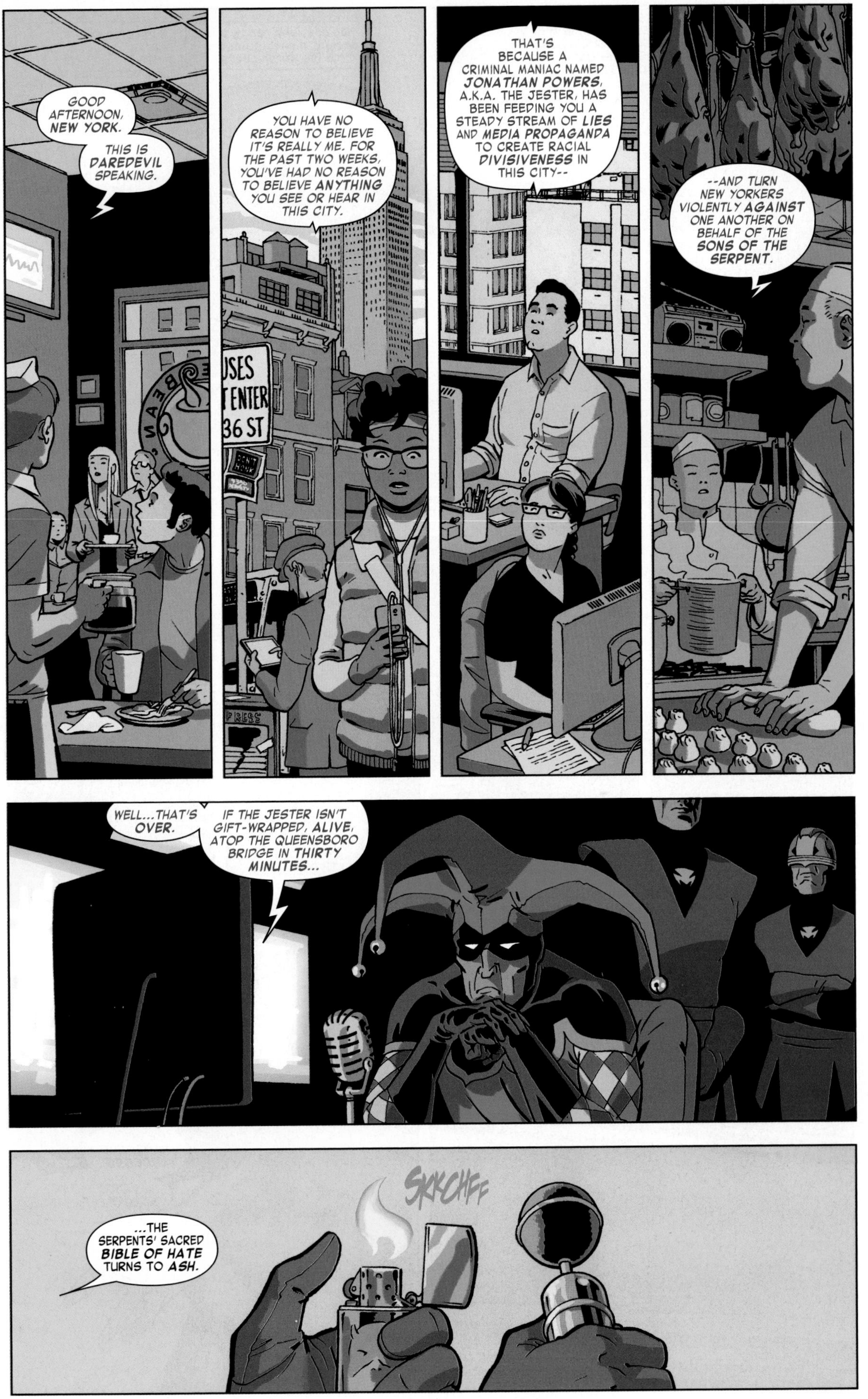
GOOD AFTERNOON, NEW YORK.
THIS IS DAREDEVIL SPEAKING.
YOU HAVE NO REASON TO BELIEVE IT'S REALLY ME. FOR THE PAST TWO WEEKS, YOU'VE HAD NO REASON TO BELIEVE ANYTHING YOU SEE OR HEAR IN THIS CITY.
USES
ENTER
36 ST
THAT'S BECAUSE A CRIMINAL MANIAC NAMED JONATHAN POWERS, A.K.A. THE JESTER, HAS BEEN FEEDING YOU A STEADY STREAM OF LIES AND MEDIA PROPAGANDA TO CREATE RACIAL DIVISIVENESS IN THIS CITY--
--AND TURN NEW YORKERS VIOLENTLY AGAINST ONE ANOTHER ON BEHALF OF THE SONS OF THE SERPENT.
WELL...THAT'S OVER.
IF THE JESTER ISN'T GIFT-WRAPPED, ALIVE, ATOP THE QUEENSBORO BRIDGE IN THIRTY MINUTES...
SKKCHFF
...THE SERPENTS' SACRED BIBLE OF HATE TURNS TO ASH.

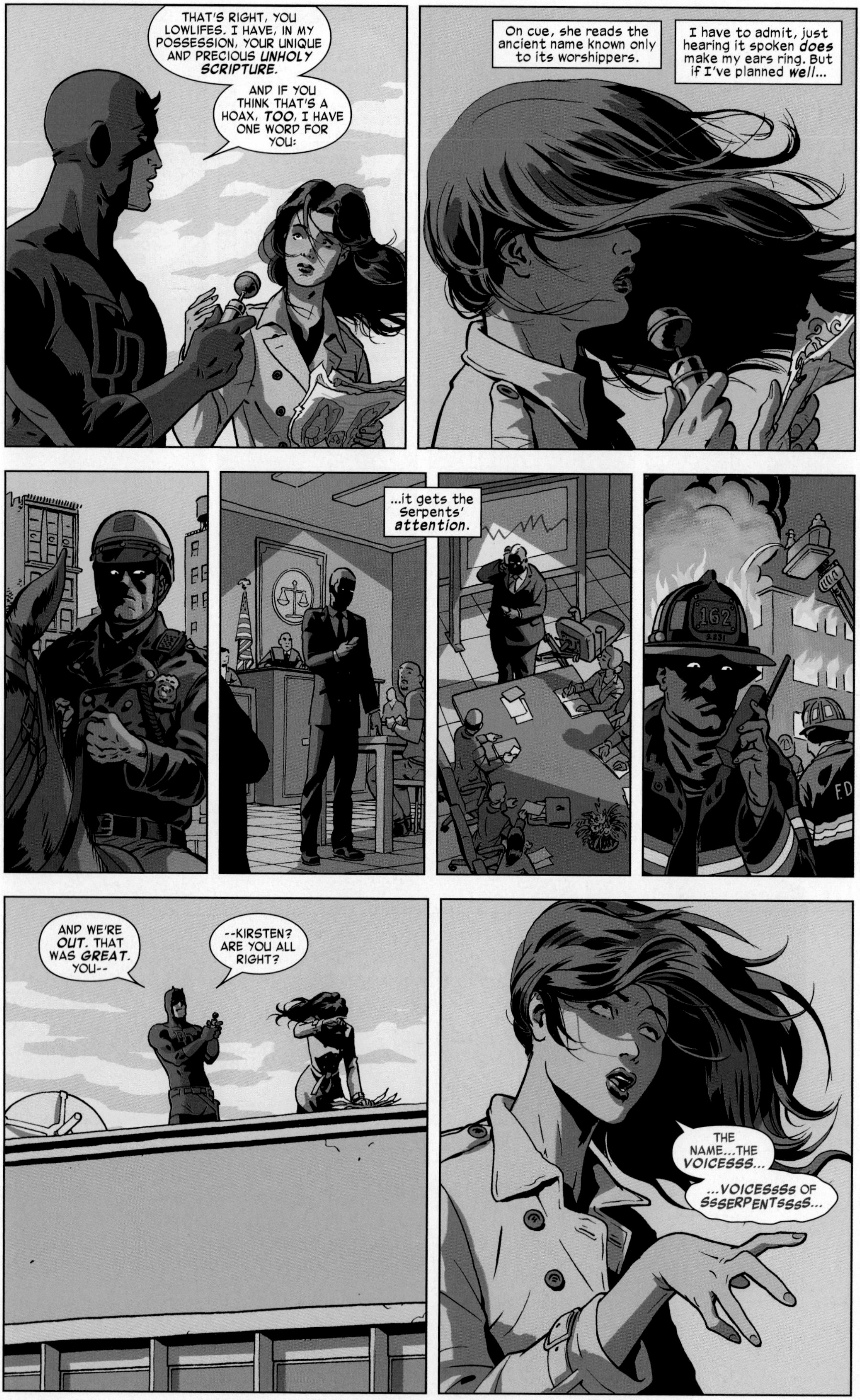

THAT'S RIGHT, YOU LOWLIFES. I HAVE, IN MY POSSESSION, YOUR UNIQUE AND PRECIOUS UNHOLY SCRIPTURE.
AND IF YOU THINK THAT'S A HOAX, TOO, I HAVE ONE WORD FOR YOU:
On cue, she reads the ancient name known only to its worshippers.
I have to admit, just hearing it spoken does make my ears ring. But if I've planned well...
...it gets the Serpents' attention.
162
F.D
AND WE'RE OUT. THAT WAS GREAT. YOU--
--KIRSTEN? ARE YOU ALL RIGHT?
THE NAME...THE VOICESSS...
...VOICESSSS OF SSSERPENTSSSS...

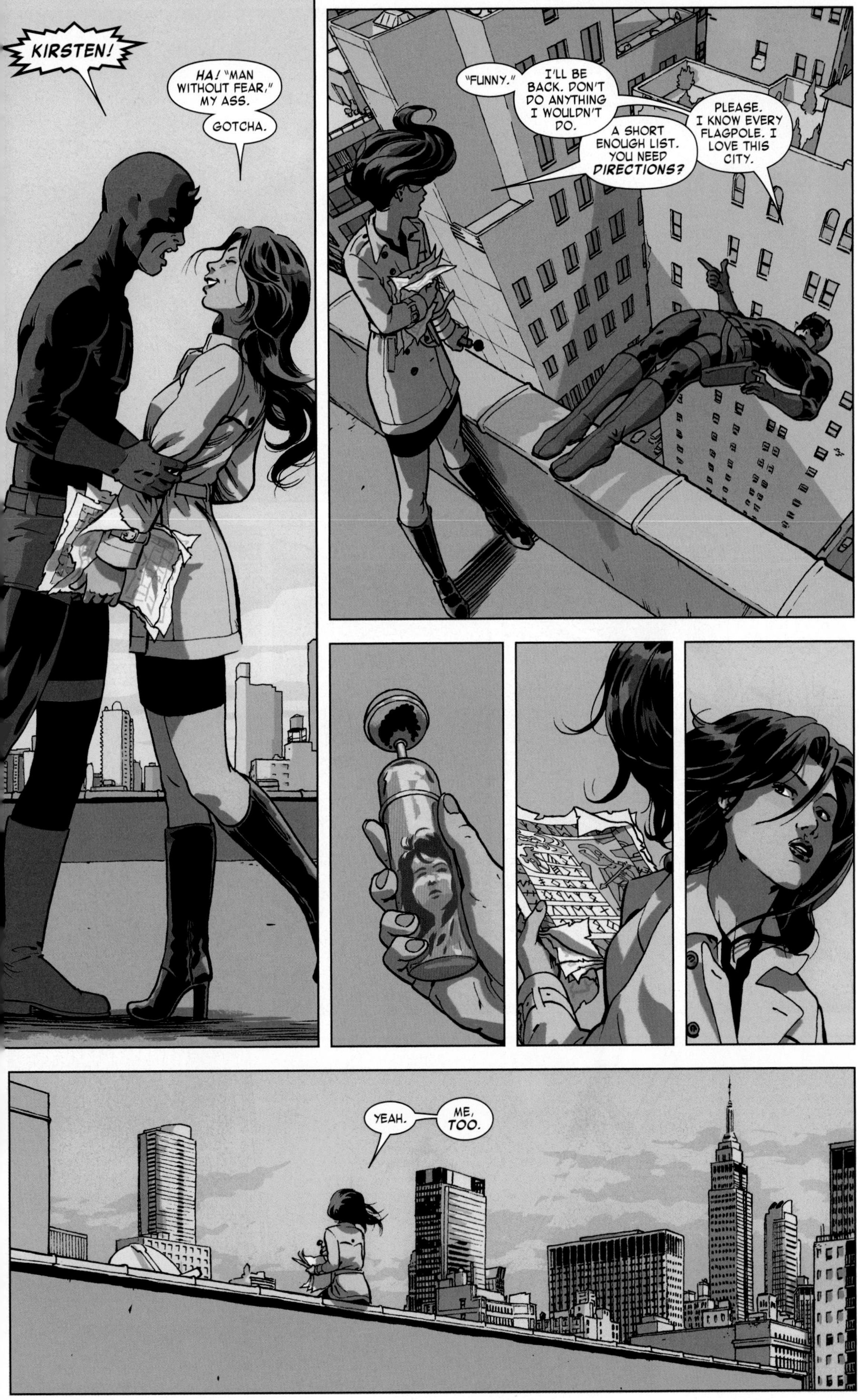
KIRSTEN!
HA! "MAN WITHOUT FEAR," MY ASS.
GOTCHA.
"FUNNY."
I'LL BE BACK. DON'T DO ANYTHING I WOULDN'T DO.
A SHORT ENOUGH LIST. YOU NEED DIRECTIONS?
PLEASE. I KNOW EVERY FLAGPOLE. I LOVE THIS CITY.
YEAH.
ME, TOO.

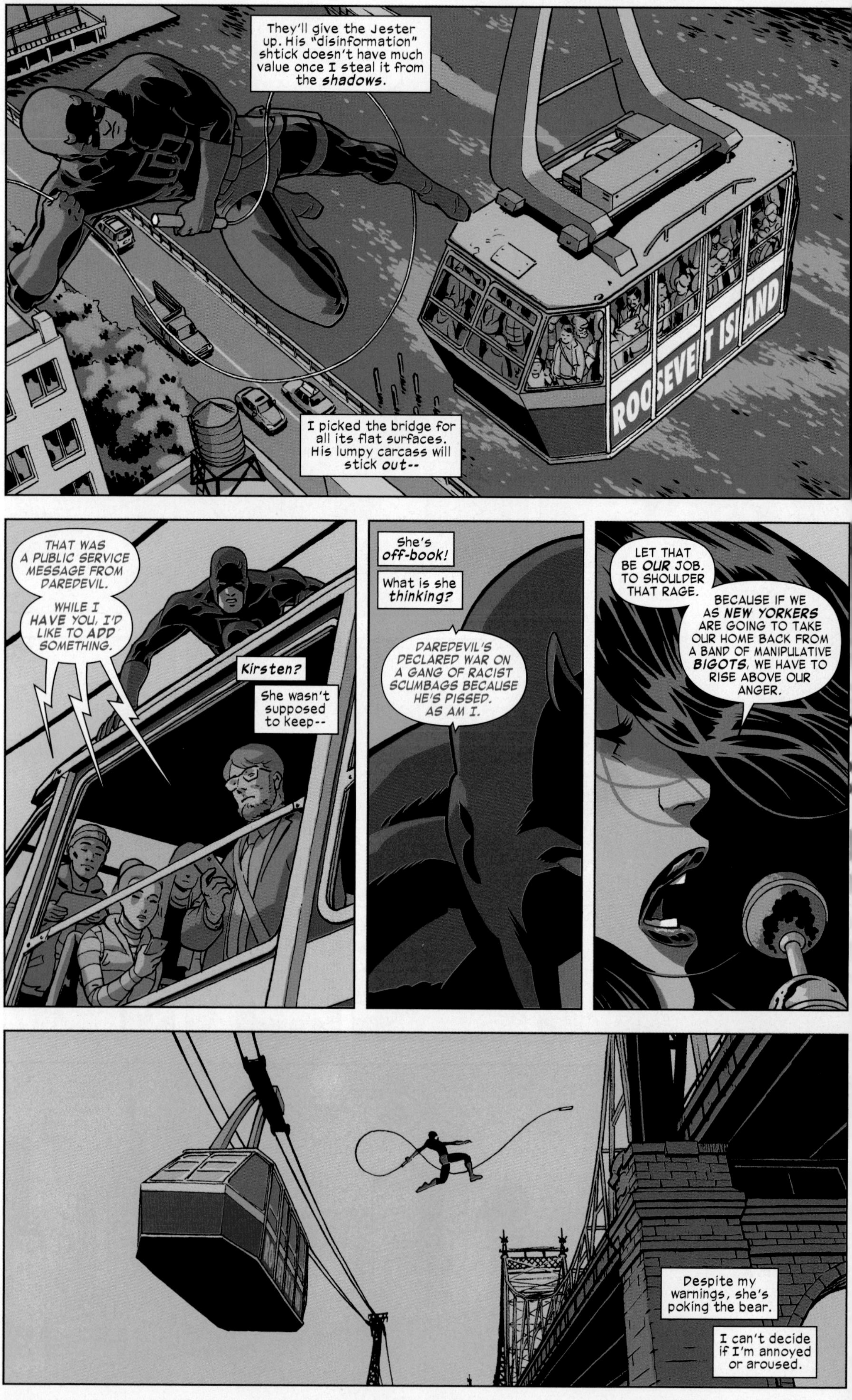
They'll give the Jester up. His "disinformation" shtick doesn't have much value once I steal it from the shadows.
ROOSEVELT ISLAND
I picked the bridge for all its flat surfaces. His lumpy carcass will stick out--
THAT WAS A PUBLIC SERVICE MESSAGE FROM DAREDEVIL.
WHILE I HAVE YOU, I'D LIKE TO ADD SOMETHING.
Kirsten?
She wasn't supposed to keep--
She's off-book!
What is she thinking?
DAREDEVIL'S DECLARED WAR ON A GANG OF RACIST SCUMBAGS BECAUSE HE'S PISSED. AS AM I.
LET THAT BE OUR JOB. TO SHOULDER THAT RAGE.
BECAUSE IF WE AS NEW YORKERS ARE GOING TO TAKE OUR HOME BACK FROM A BAND OF MANIPULATIVE BIGOTS, WE HAVE TO RISE ABOVE OUR ANGER.
Despite my warnings, she's poking the bear.
I can't decide if I'm annoyed or aroused.

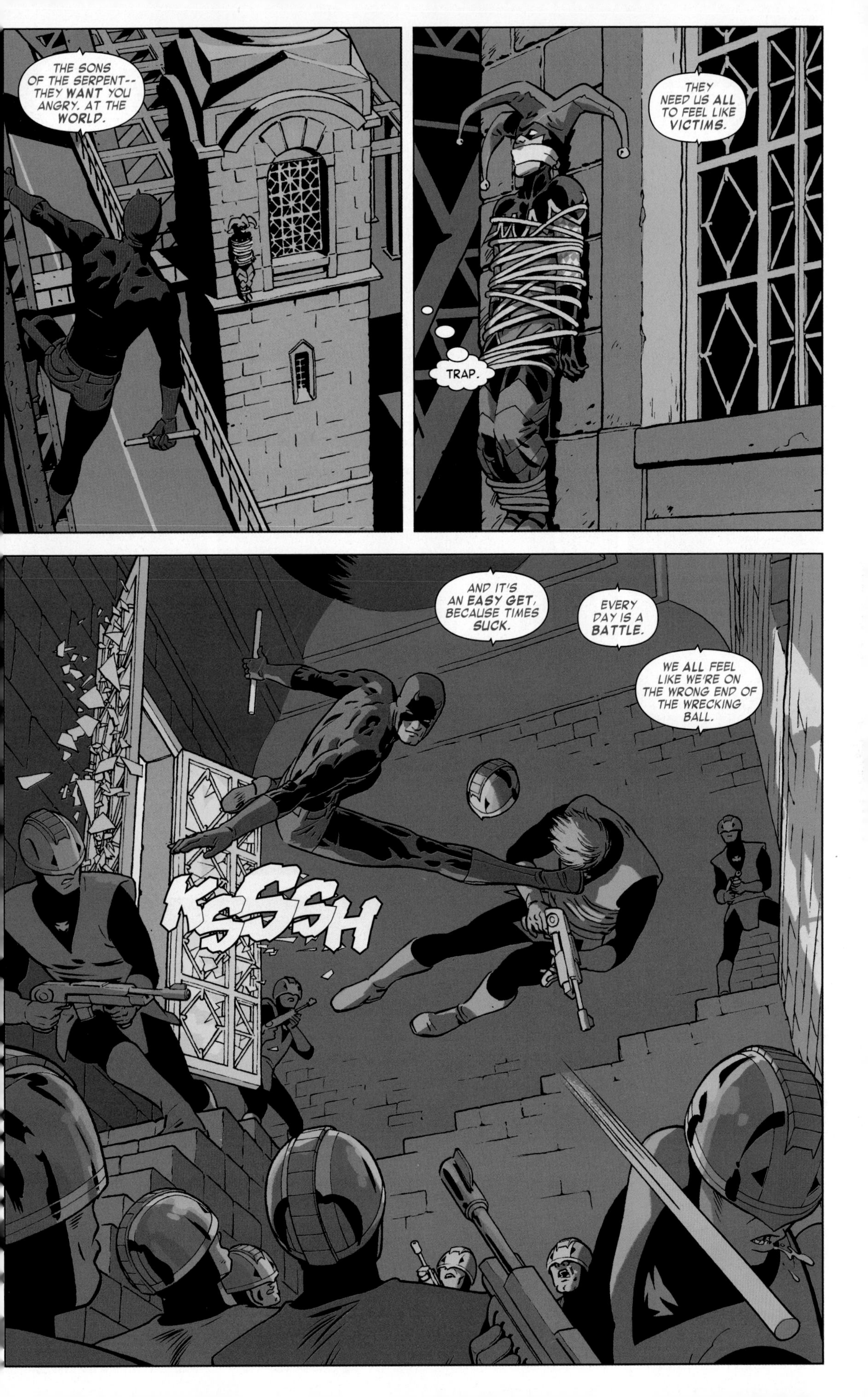
THE SONS OF THE SERPENT-- THEY WANT YOU ANGRY. AT THE WORLD.
THEY NEED US ALL TO FEEL LIKE VICTIMS.
TRAP.
AND IT'S AN EASY GET, BECAUSE TIMES SUCK.
EVERY DAY IS A BATTLE.
WE ALL FEEL LIKE WE'RE ON THE WRONG END OF THE WRECKING BALL.
KSSSH

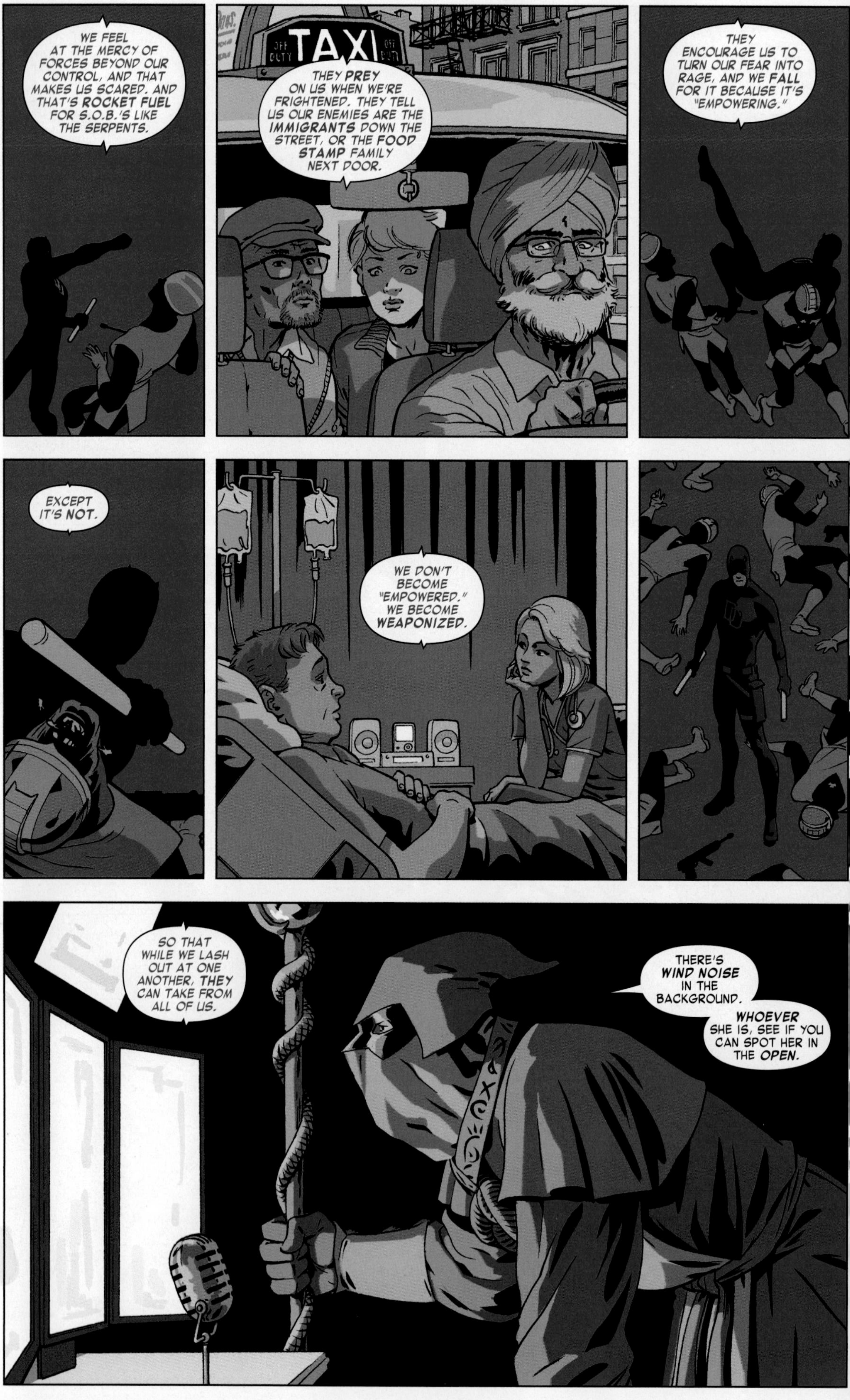
WE FEEL AT THE MERCY OF FORCES BEYOND OUR CONTROL, AND THAT MAKES US SCARED. AND THAT'S ROCKET FUEL FOR S.O.B.'S LIKE THE SERPENTS.
TAXI
THEY PREY ON US WHEN WE'RE FRIGHTENED. THEY TELL US OUR ENEMIES ARE THE IMMIGRANTS DOWN THE STREET, OR THE FOOD STAMP FAMILY NEXT DOOR.
THEY ENCOURAGE US TO TURN OUR FEAR INTO RAGE, AND WE FALL FOR IT BECAUSE IT'S "EMPOWERING."
EXCEPT IT'S NOT.
WE DON'T BECOME "EMPOWERED." WE BECOME WEAPONIZED.
SO THAT WHILE WE LASH OUT AT ONE ANOTHER, THEY CAN TAKE FROM ALL OF US.
THERE'S WIND NOISE IN THE BACKGROUND.
WHOEVER SHE IS, SEE IF YOU CAN SPOT HER IN THE OPEN.

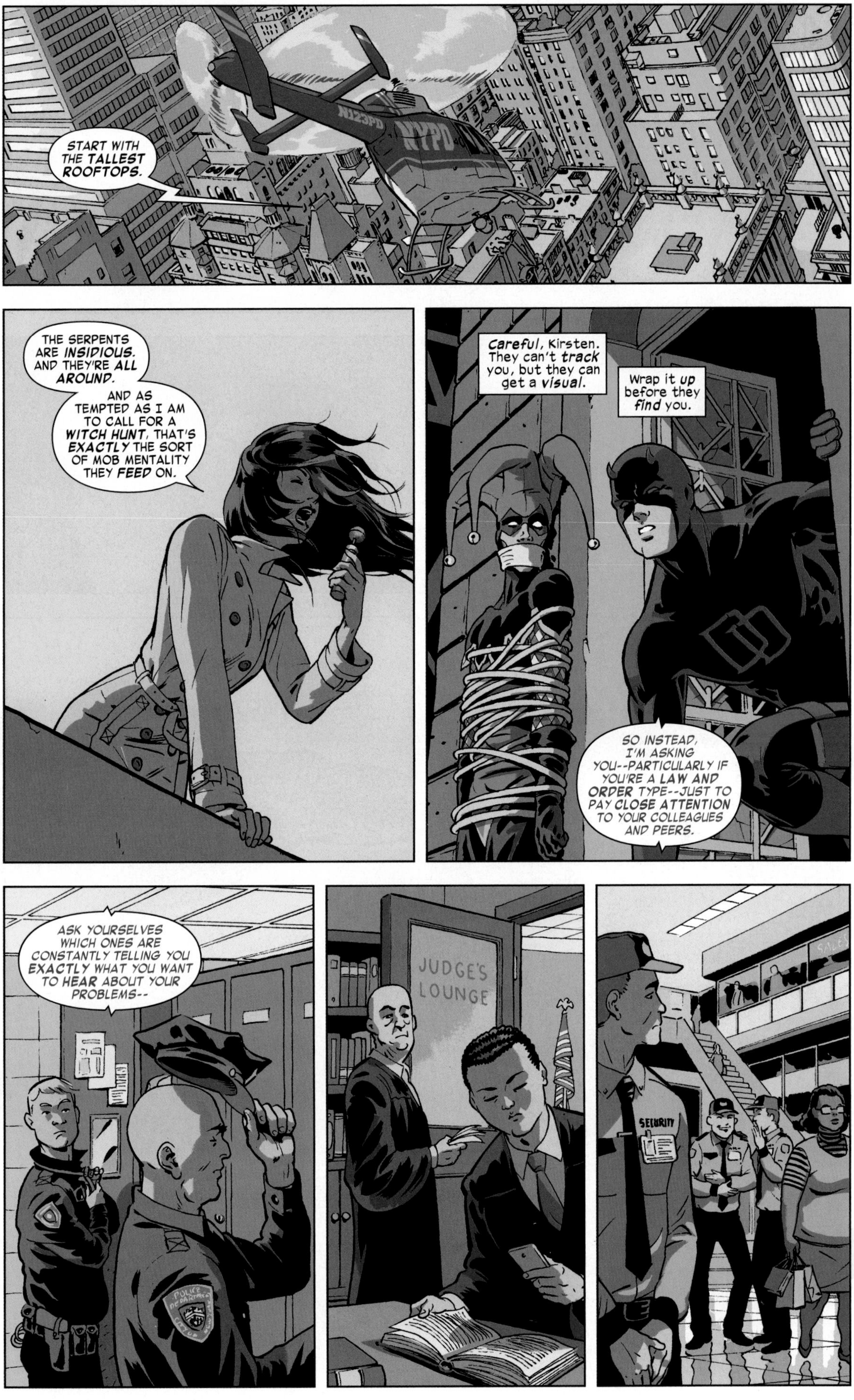
START WITH THE TALLEST ROOFTOPS.
N123PD NYPD
THE SERPENTS ARE INSIDIOUS. AND THEY'RE ALL AROUND.
AND AS TEMPTED AS I AM TO CALL FOR A WITCH HUNT, THAT'S EXACTLY THE SORT OF MOB MENTALITY THEY FEED ON.
Careful, Kirsten. They can't track you, but they can get a visual.
Wrap it up before they find you.
SO INSTEAD, I'M ASKING YOU--PARTICULARLY IF YOU'RE A LAW AND ORDER TYPE--JUST TO PAY CLOSE ATTENTION TO YOUR COLLEAGUES AND PEERS.
ASK YOURSELVES WHICH ONES ARE CONSTANTLY TELLING YOU EXACTLY WHAT YOU WANT TO HEAR ABOUT YOUR PROBLEMS--
JUDGE'S LOUNGE
SECURITY

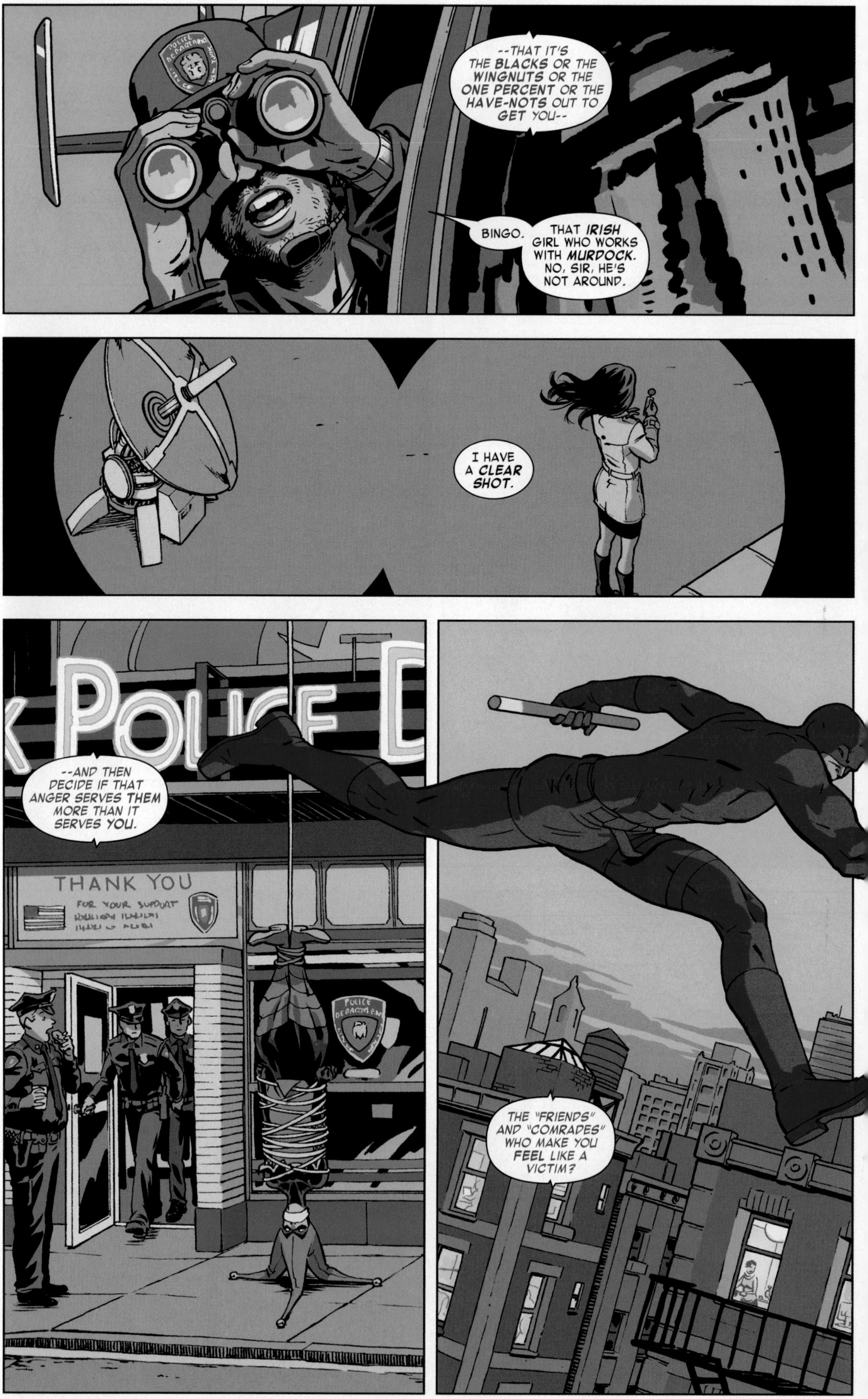
--THAT IT'S THE BLACKS OR THE WINGNUTS OR THE ONE PERCENT OR THE HAVE-NOTS OUT TO GET YOU--
BINGO.
THAT IRISH GIRL WHO WORKS WITH MURDOCK. NO, SIR, HE'S NOT AROUND.
I HAVE A CLEAR SHOT.
POLICE D
--AND THEN DECIDE IF THAT ANGER SERVES THEM MORE THAN IT SERVES YOU.
THANK YOU
FOR YOUR SUPPORT
THE "FRIENDS" AND "COMRADES" WHO MAKE YOU FEEL LIKE A VICTIM?

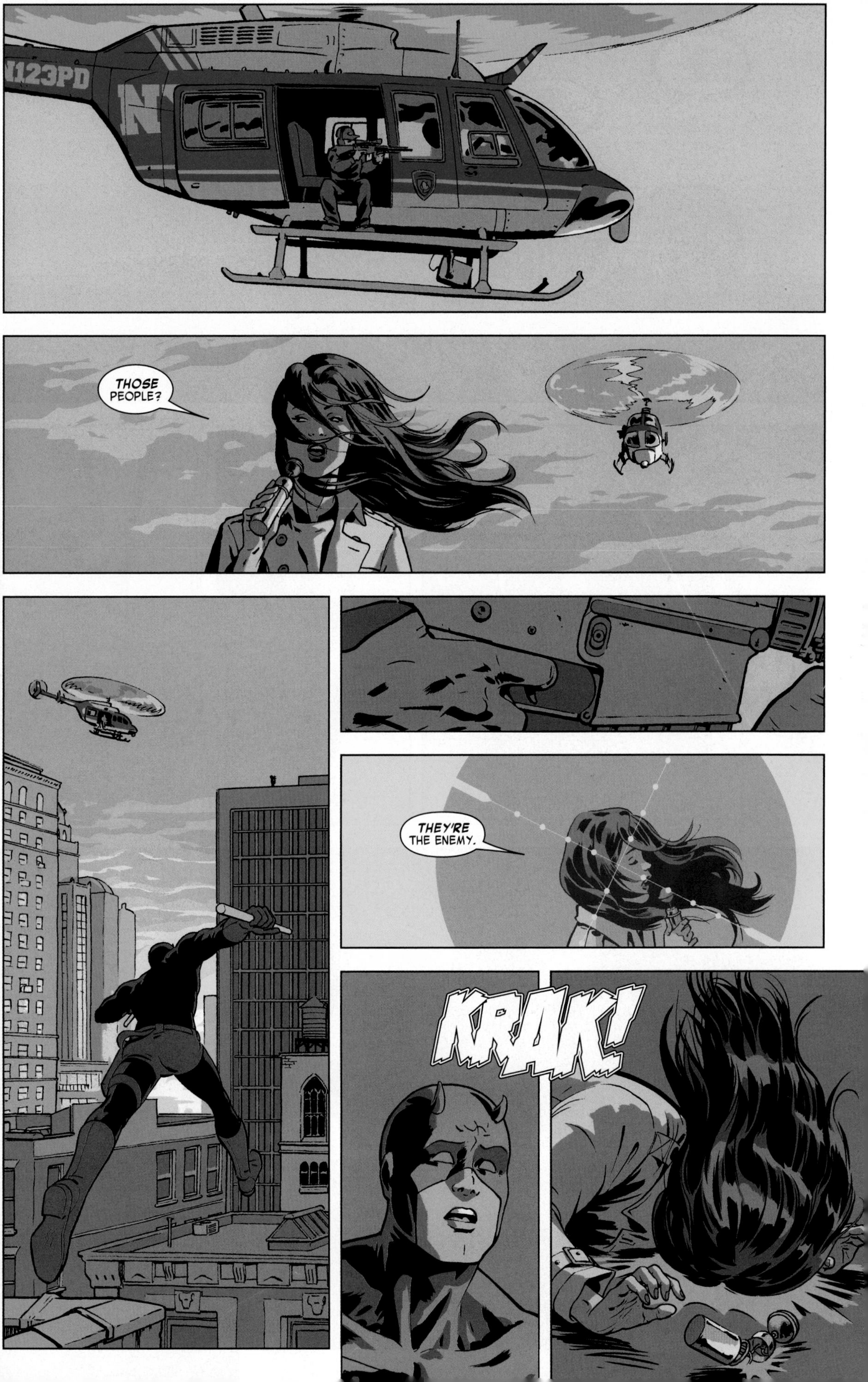
N123PD
THOSE PEOPLE?
THEY'RE THE ENEMY.
KRAK!

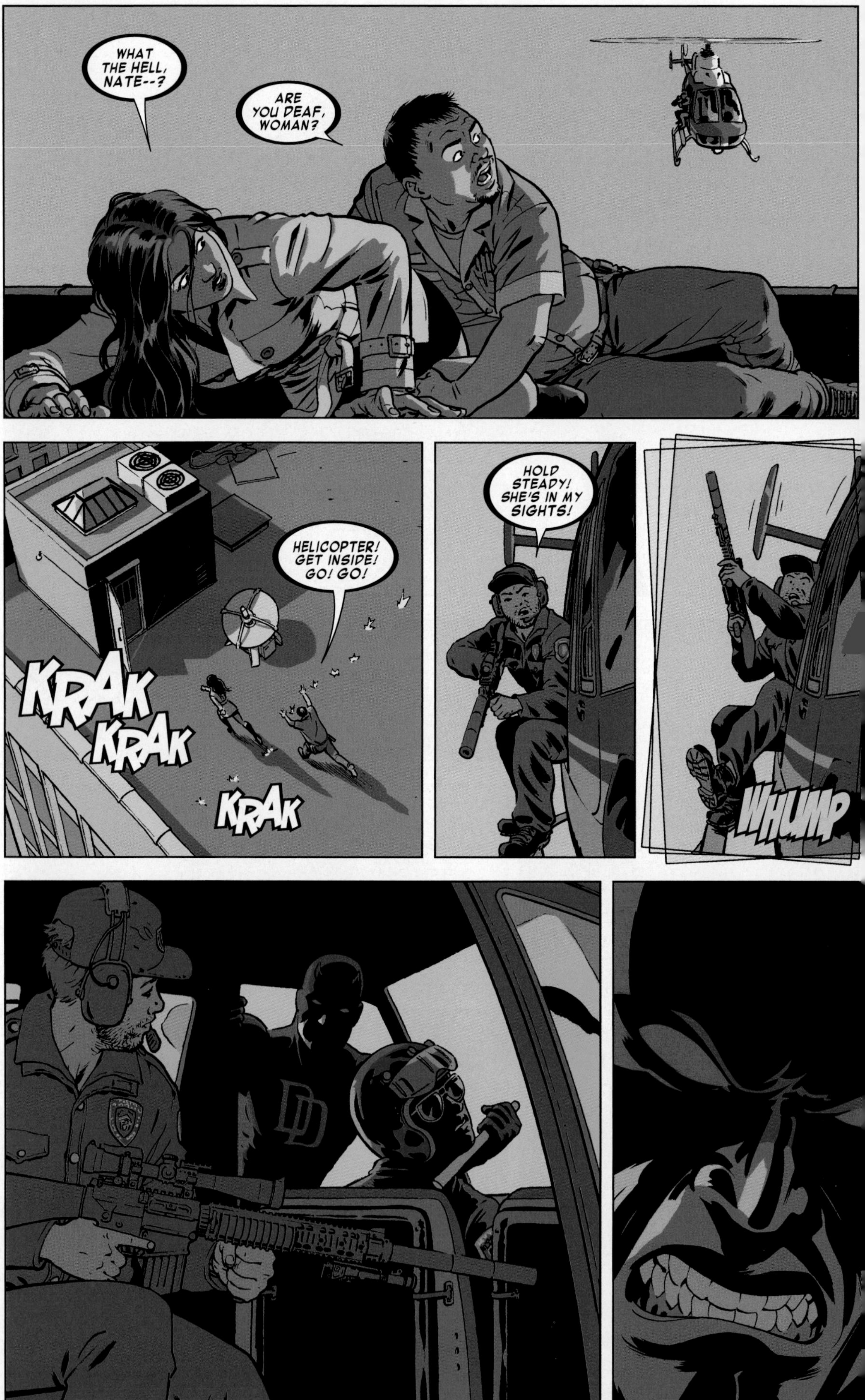
WHAT THE HELL, NATE--?
ARE YOU DEAF, WOMAN?
HELICOPTER! GET INSIDE! GO! GO!
KRAK
KRAK
KRAK
HOLD STEADY! SHE'S IN MY SIGHTS!
WHUMP

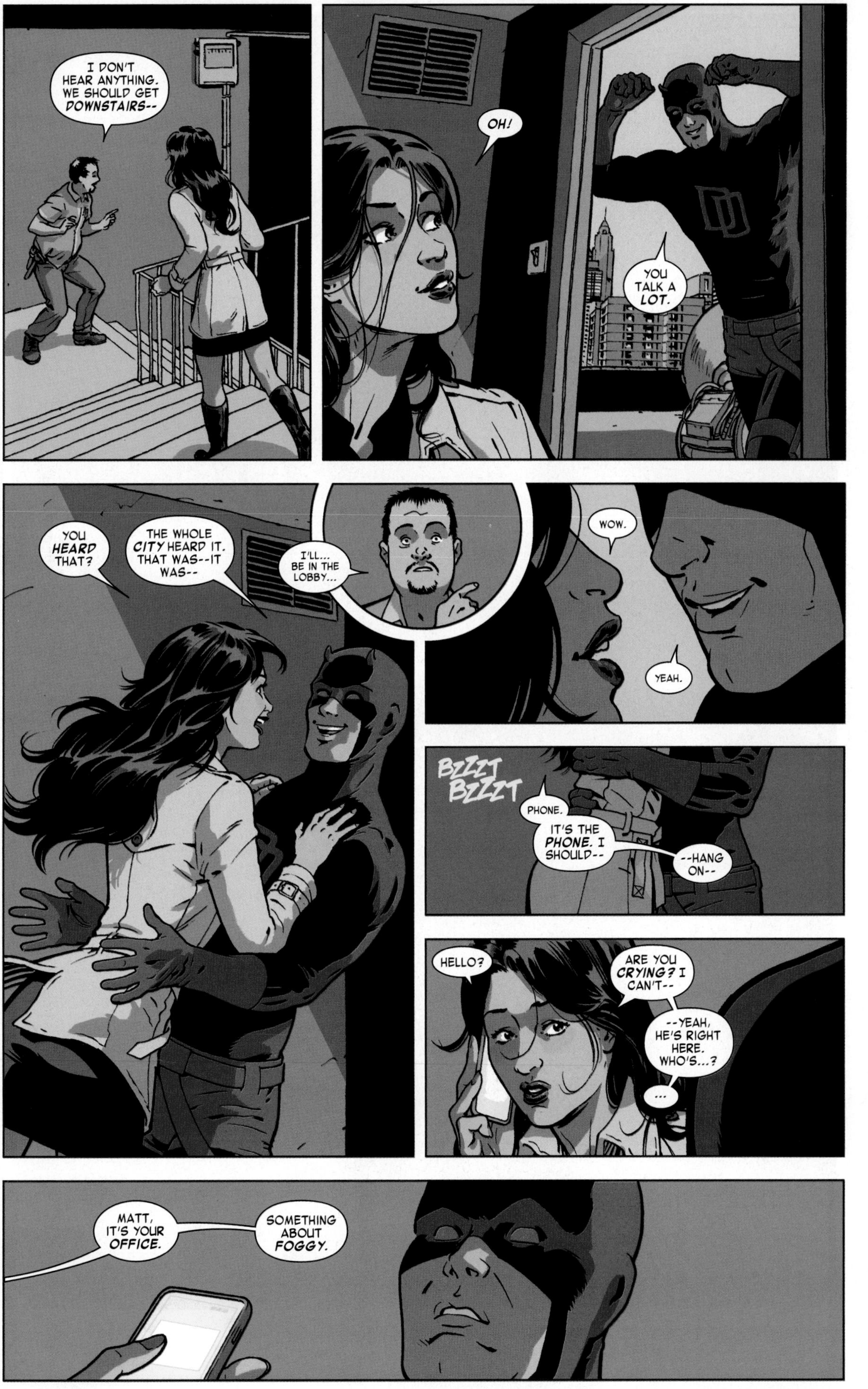
I DON'T HEAR ANYTHING. WE SHOULD GET DOWNSTAIRS--
OH!
YOU TALK A LOT.
YOU HEARD THAT?
THE WHOLE CITY HEARD IT. THAT WAS--IT WAS--
I'LL... BE IN THE LOBBY...
WOW.
YEAH.
BZZZT BZZZT
PHONE.
IT'S THE PHONE. I SHOULD--
--HANG ON--
HELLO?
ARE YOU CRYING? I CAN'T--
--YEAH, HE'S RIGHT HERE. WHO'S...?
...
MATT, IT'S YOUR OFFICE.
SOMETHING ABOUT FOGGY.

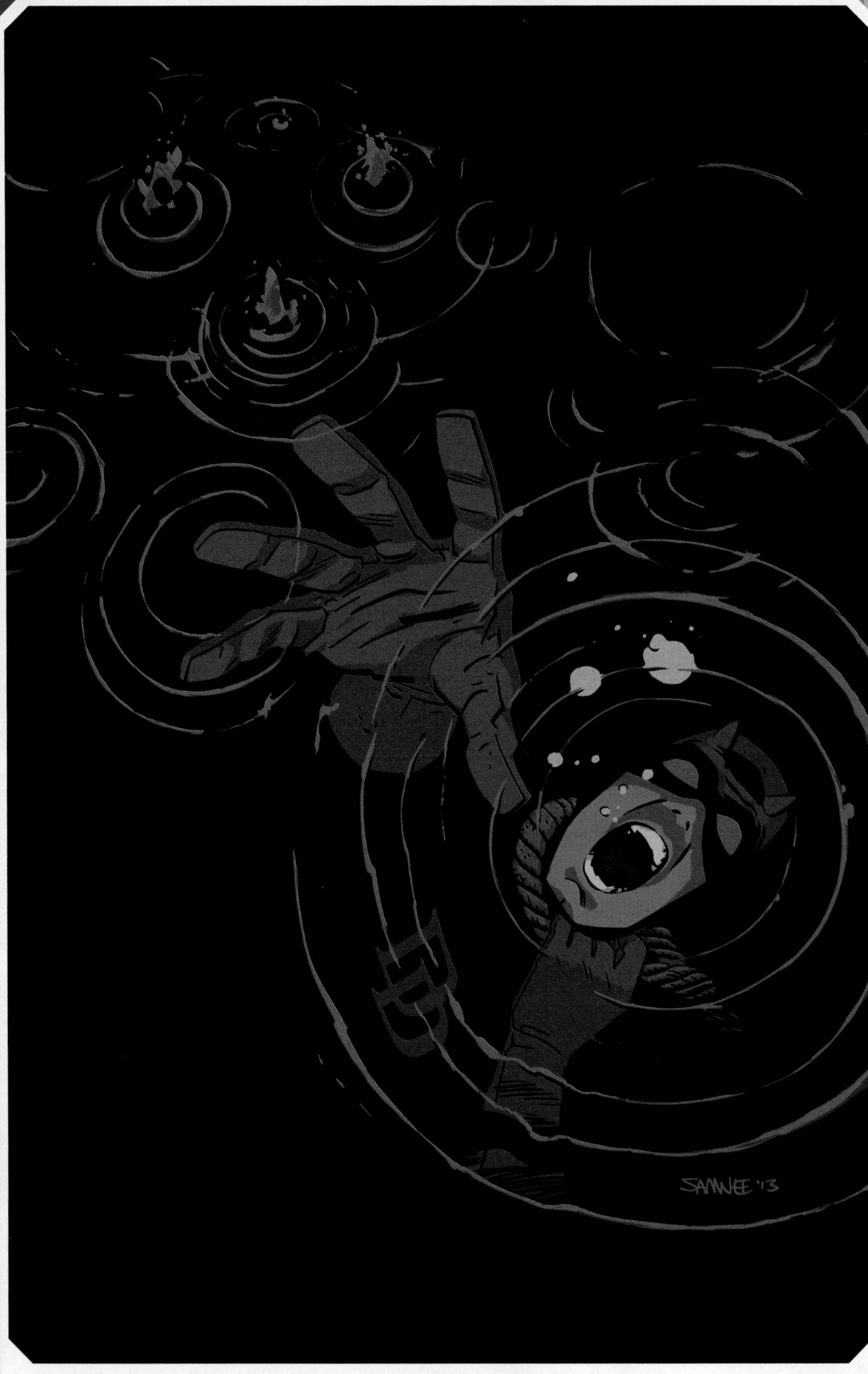
SAMNEE '13

DAREDEVIL #35

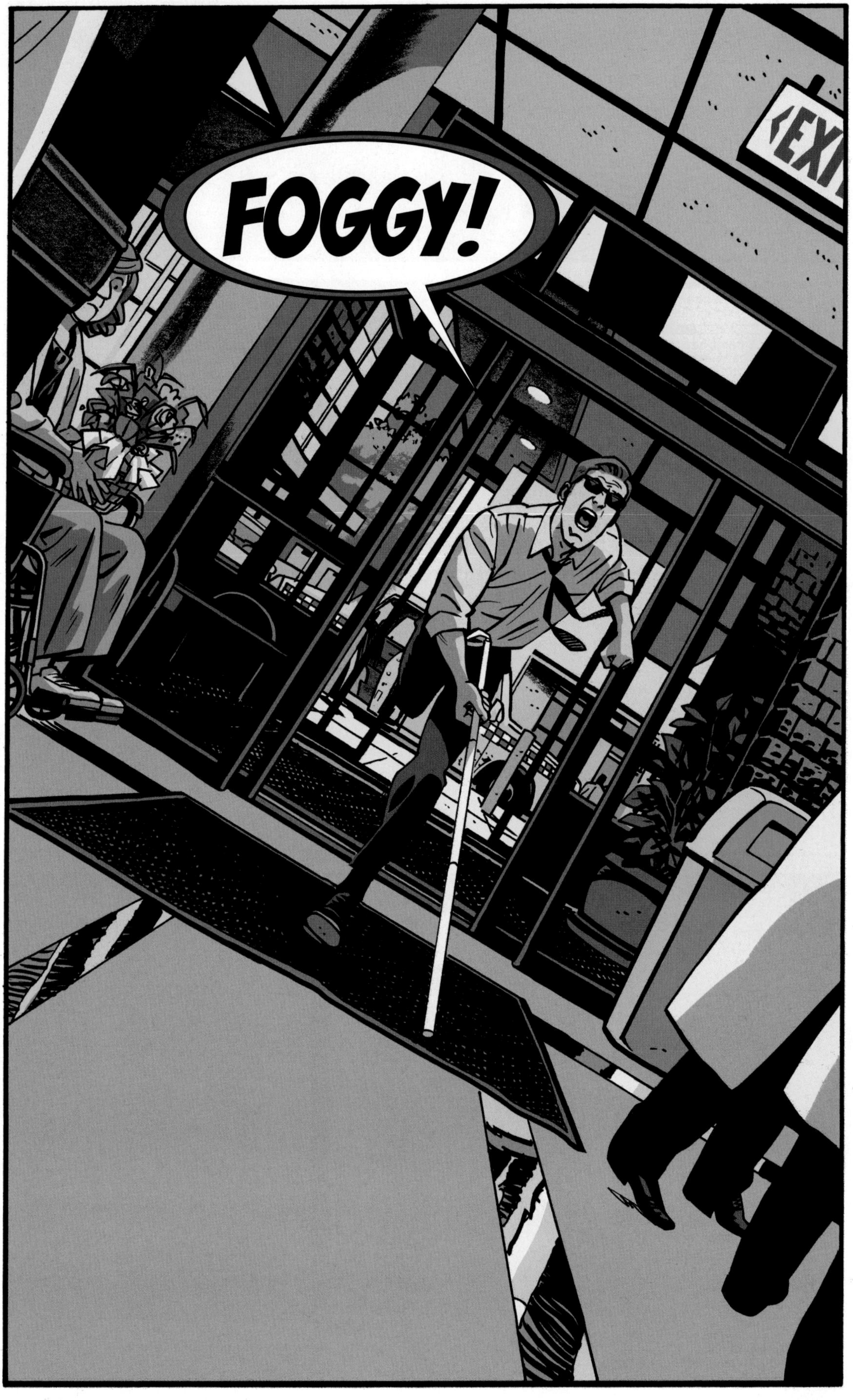
FOGGY!
EXI

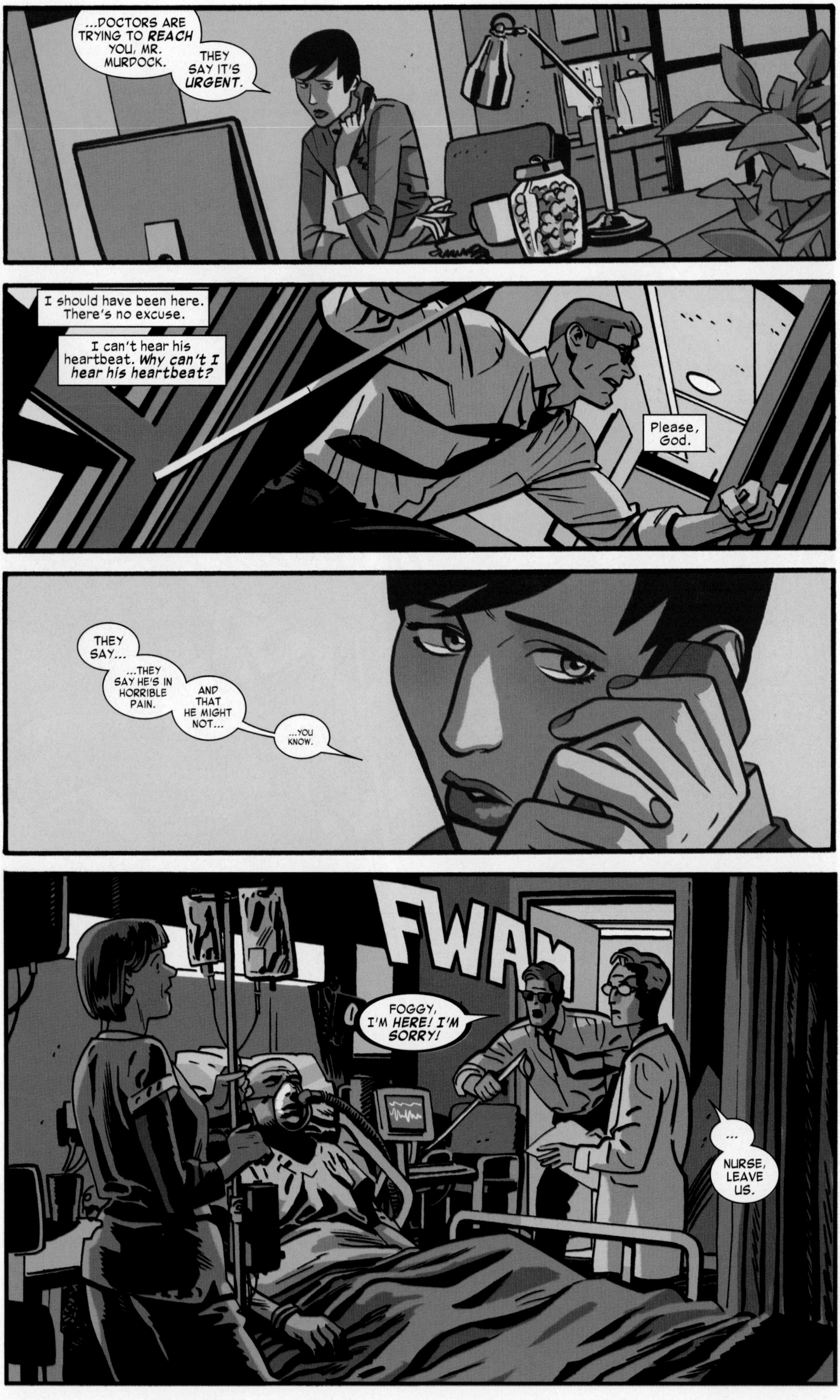
...DOCTORS ARE TRYING TO REACH YOU, MR. MURDOCK.
THEY SAY IT'S URGENT.
I should have been here. There's no excuse.
I can't hear his heartbeat. Why can't I hear his heartbeat?
Please, God.
THEY SAY...
...THEY SAY HE'S IN HORRIBLE PAIN.
AND THAT HE MIGHT NOT...
...YOU KNOW.
FWAM
FOGGY, I'M HERE! I'M SORRY!
...
NURSE, LEAVE US.

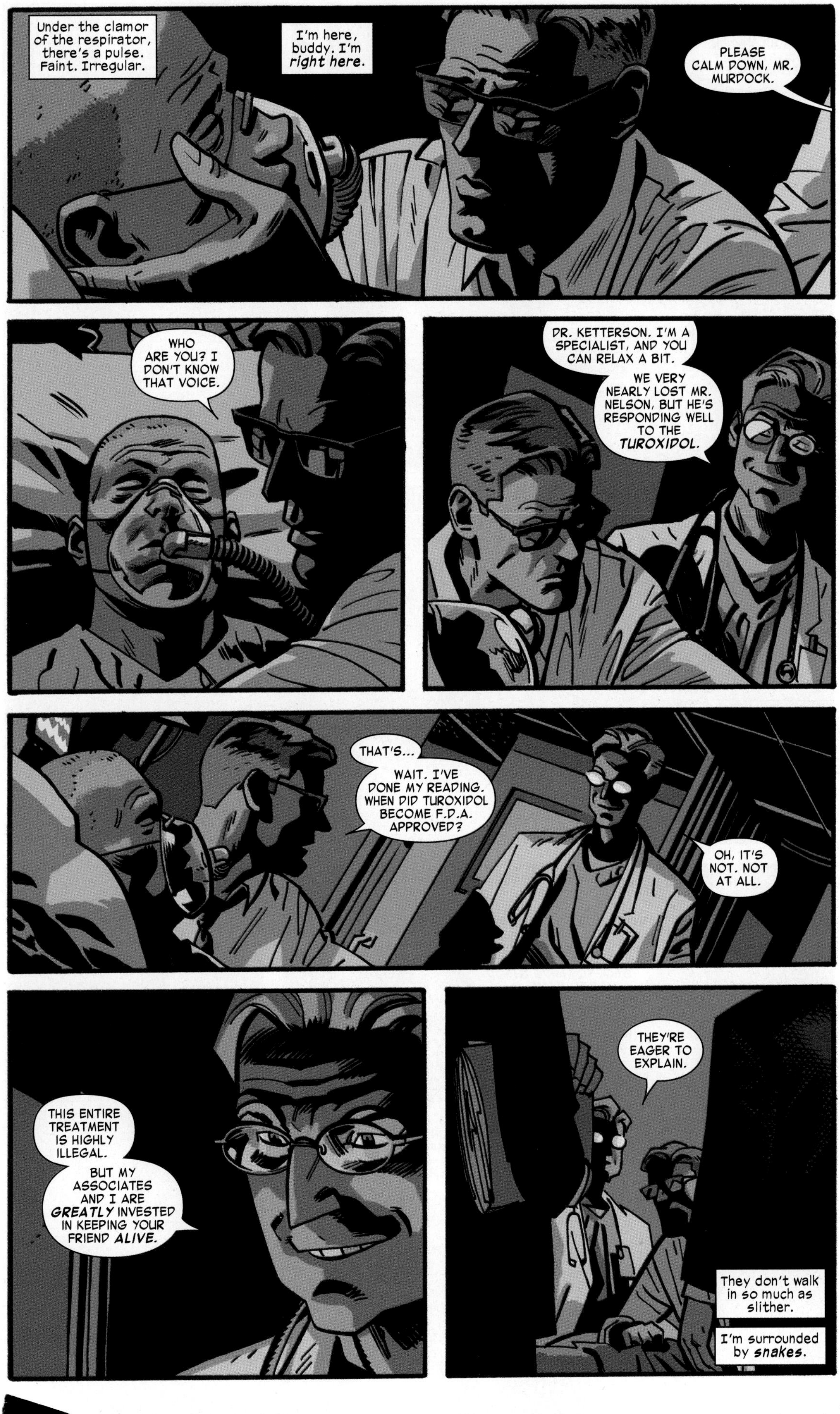
Under the clamor of the respirator, there's a pulse. Faint. Irregular.
I'm here, buddy. I'm right here.
PLEASE CALM DOWN, MR. MURDOCK.
WHO ARE YOU? I DON'T KNOW THAT VOICE.
DR. KETTERSON. I'M A SPECIALIST, AND YOU CAN RELAX A BIT.
WE VERY NEARLY LOST MR. NELSON, BUT HE'S RESPONDING WELL TO THE TUROXIDOL.
THAT'S...
WAIT. I'VE DONE MY READING. WHEN DID TUROXIDOL BECOME F.D.A. APPROVED?
OH, IT'S NOT. NOT AT ALL.
THIS ENTIRE TREATMENT IS HIGHLY ILLEGAL.
BUT MY ASSOCIATES AND I ARE GREATLY INVESTED IN KEEPING YOUR FRIEND ALIVE.
THEY'RE EAGER TO EXPLAIN.
They don't walk in so much as slither.
I'm surrounded by snakes.

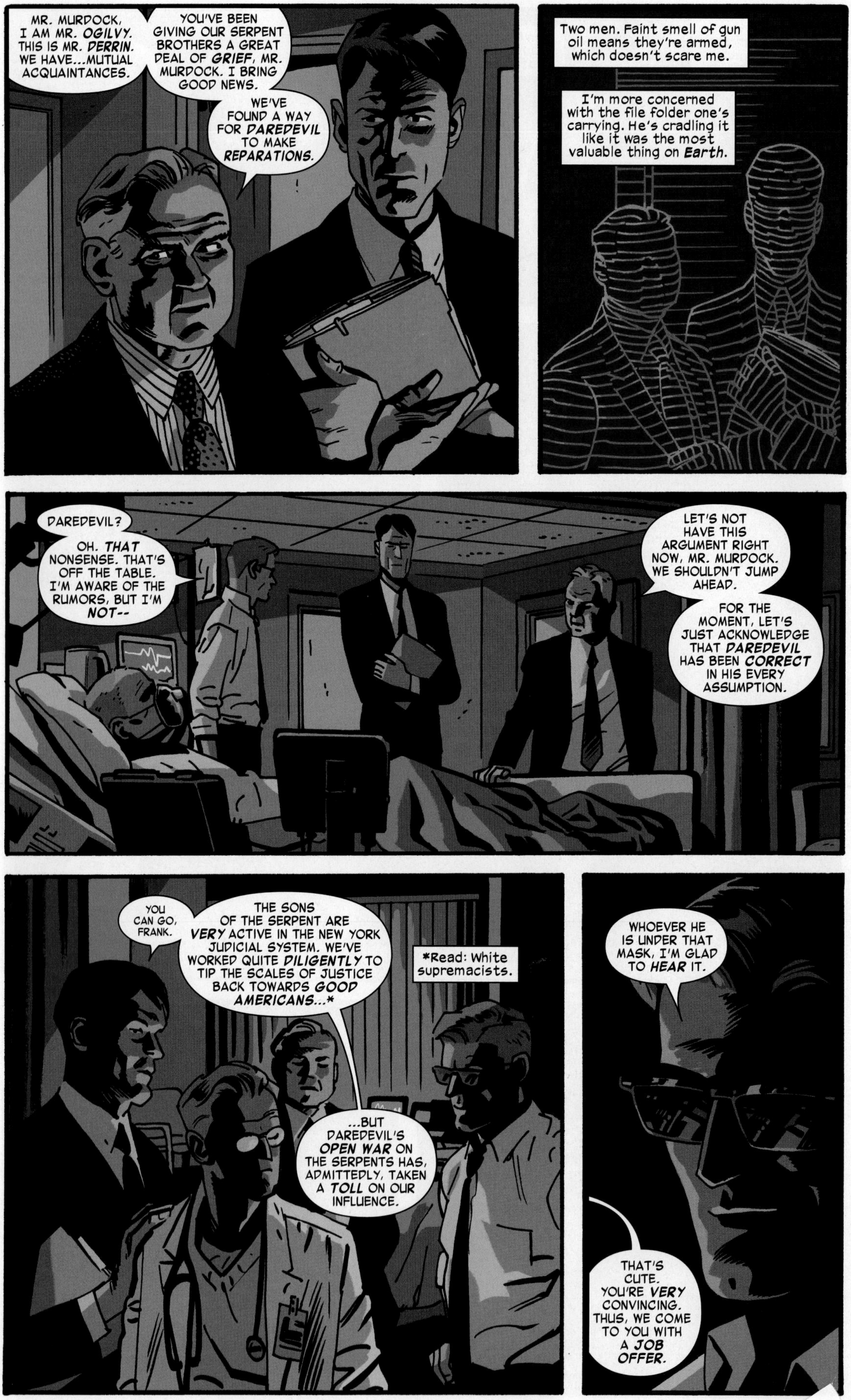
MR. MURDOCK, I AM MR. OGILVY. THIS IS MR. DERRIN. WE HAVE...MUTUAL ACQUAINTANCES.
YOU'VE BEEN GIVING OUR SERPENT BROTHERS A GREAT DEAL OF GRIEF, MR. MURDOCK. I BRING GOOD NEWS.
WE'VE FOUND A WAY FOR DAREDEVIL TO MAKE REPARATIONS.
Two men. Faint smell of gun oil means they're armed, which doesn't scare me.
I'm more concerned with the file folder one's carrying. He's cradling it like it was the most valuable thing on Earth.
DAREDEVIL?
OH. THAT NONSENSE. THAT'S OFF THE TABLE. I'M AWARE OF THE RUMORS, BUT I'M NOT--
LET'S NOT HAVE THIS ARGUMENT RIGHT NOW, MR. MURDOCK. WE SHOULDN'T JUMP AHEAD.
FOR THE MOMENT, LET'S JUST ACKNOWLEDGE THAT DAREDEVIL HAS BEEN CORRECT IN HIS EVERY ASSUMPTION.
YOU CAN GO, FRANK.
THE SONS OF THE SERPENT ARE VERY ACTIVE IN THE NEW YORK JUDICIAL SYSTEM. WE'VE WORKED QUITE DILIGENTLY TO TIP THE SCALES OF JUSTICE BACK TOWARDS GOOD AMERICANS...*
*Read: White supremacists.
...BUT DAREDEVIL'S OPEN WAR ON THE SERPENTS HAS, ADMITTEDLY, TAKEN A TOLL ON OUR INFLUENCE.
WHOEVER HE IS UNDER THAT MASK, I'M GLAD TO HEAR IT.
THAT'S CUTE. YOU'RE VERY CONVINCING. THUS, WE COME TO YOU WITH A JOB OFFER.

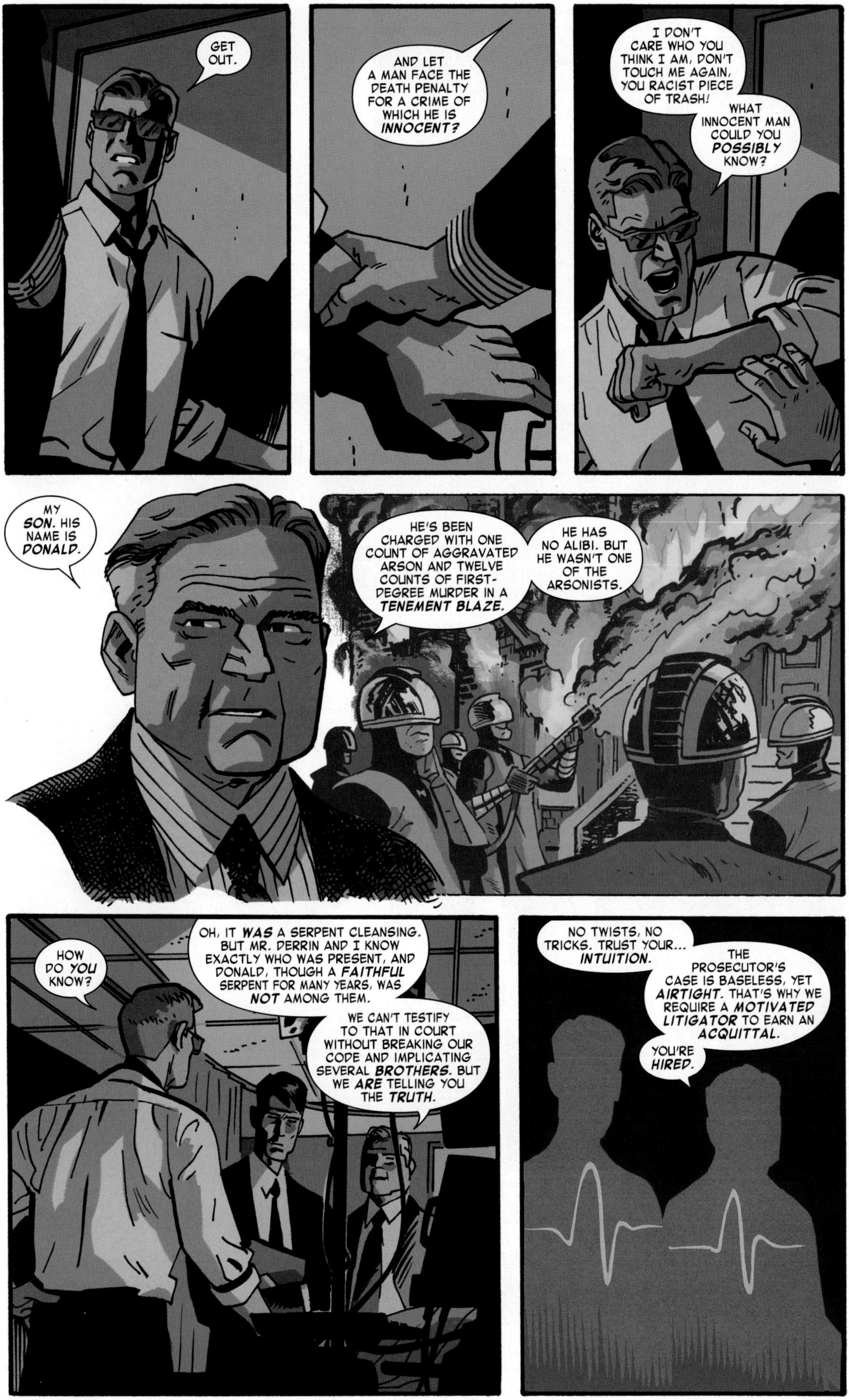
GET OUT.
AND LET A MAN FACE THE DEATH PENALTY FOR A CRIME OF WHICH HE IS INNOCENT?
I DON'T CARE WHO YOU THINK I AM, DON'T TOUCH ME AGAIN, YOU RACIST PIECE OF TRASH!
WHAT INNOCENT MAN COULD YOU POSSIBLY KNOW?
MY SON. HIS NAME IS DONALD.
HE'S BEEN CHARGED WITH ONE COUNT OF AGGRAVATED ARSON AND TWELVE COUNTS OF FIRST-DEGREE MURDER IN A TENEMENT BLAZE.
HE HAS NO ALIBI. BUT HE WASN'T ONE OF THE ARSONISTS.
HOW DO YOU KNOW?
OH, IT WAS A SERPENT CLEANSING. BUT MR. DERRIN AND I KNOW EXACTLY WHO WAS PRESENT, AND DONALD, THOUGH A FAITHFUL SERPENT FOR MANY YEARS, WAS NOT AMONG THEM.
WE CAN'T TESTIFY TO THAT IN COURT WITHOUT BREAKING OUR CODE AND IMPLICATING SEVERAL BROTHERS. BUT WE ARE TELLING YOU THE TRUTH.
NO TWISTS, NO TRICKS. TRUST YOUR... INTUITION.
THE PROSECUTOR'S CASE IS BASELESS, YET AIRTIGHT. THAT'S WHY WE REQUIRE A MOTIVATED LITIGATOR TO EARN AN ACQUITTAL.
YOU'RE HIRED.

FIND ANOTHER LAWYER. I'D SOONER WORK IN ROADKILL REMOVAL.

IT COULD VERY WELL *COME* TO THAT, MR. MURDOCK.

WHILE *DAREDEVIL* HAS BEEN ATTACKING US, WE'VE BEEN *DIGGING.* EXHAUSTIVELY.

WE'VE ASSEMBLED QUITE THE *DOSSIER...*

...DAREDEVIL.

"YOU WERE BLINDED AND TRANSFORMED BY RADIOACTIVE WASTE AS A BOY. WE KNOW THE STREET CORNER AND THE ATTENDING PHYSICIAN AND NURSES. WE KNOW WHAT COLOR *SHIRT* YOU WERE WEARING."

"WE KNOW HOW YOU'RE ABLE TO PASS FOR A *SIGHTED* ACROBAT BECAUSE OF HOW BRILLIANTLY YOUR REMAINING SENSES *COMPENSATED...*"

FLAP FLAP FLAP FLAP

BDEEP

BDEEP

LUB DUB LUB

ZZZZT zzzzz>....

DING

DRIP

FFT

SSSS

BDEEP

WZOO

HONK

ARF AR

HONK

YOU'RE NOT GOING TO TELL ANYONE ABOUT THIS, RIGHT?

DRIP DRIP DRI

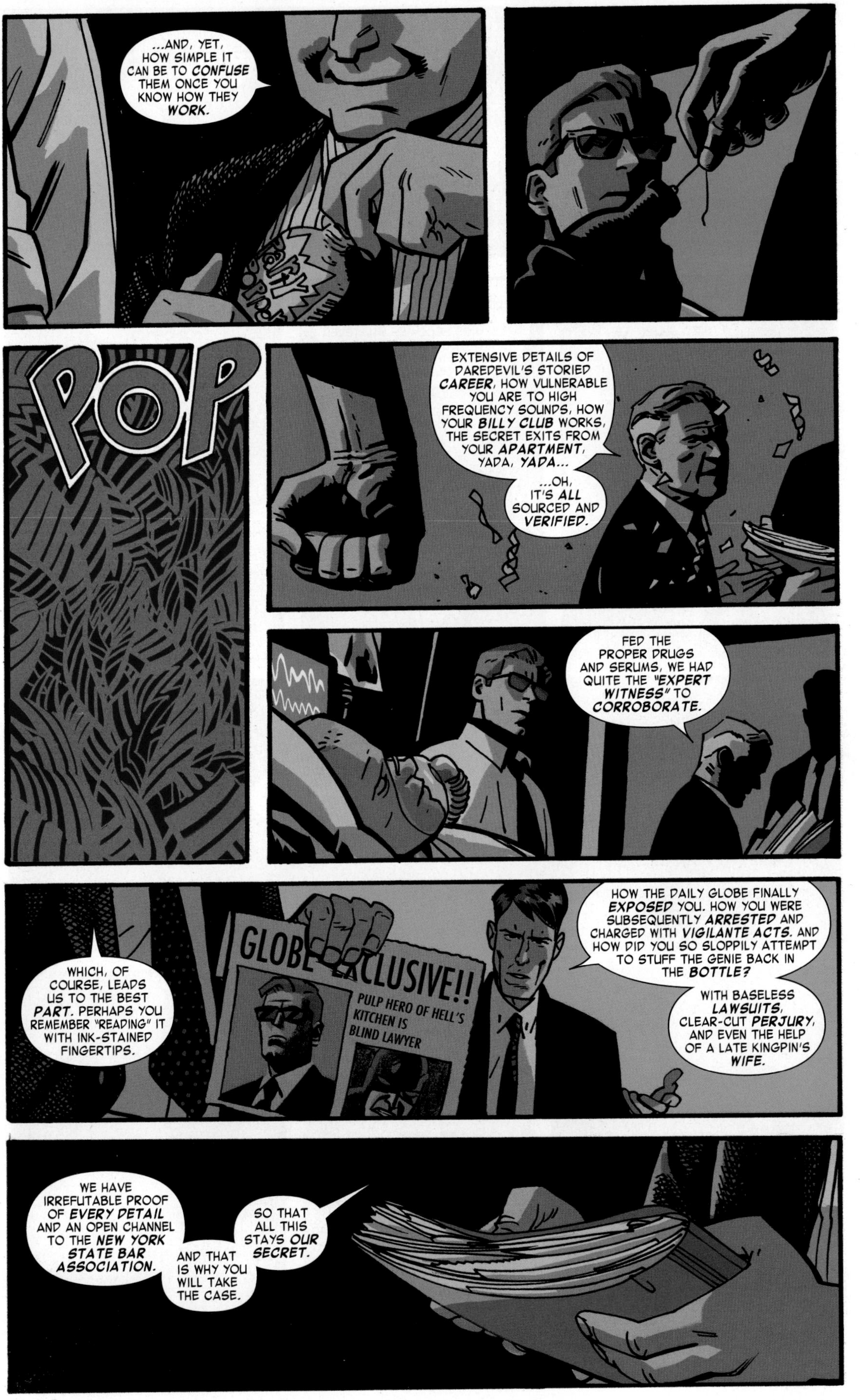
...AND, YET, HOW SIMPLE IT CAN BE TO CONFUSE THEM ONCE YOU KNOW HOW THEY WORK.
POP
EXTENSIVE DETAILS OF DAREDEVIL'S STORIED CAREER, HOW VULNERABLE YOU ARE TO HIGH FREQUENCY SOUNDS, HOW YOUR BILLY CLUB WORKS, THE SECRET EXITS FROM YOUR APARTMENT, YADA, YADA...
...OH, IT'S ALL SOURCED AND VERIFIED.
FED THE PROPER DRUGS AND SERUMS, WE HAD QUITE THE "EXPERT WITNESS" TO CORROBORATE.
WHICH, OF COURSE, LEADS US TO THE BEST PART. PERHAPS YOU REMEMBER "READING" IT WITH INK-STAINED FINGERTIPS.
GLOBE EXCLUSIVE!!
PULP HERO OF HELL'S KITCHEN IS BLIND LAWYER
HOW THE DAILY GLOBE FINALLY EXPOSED YOU. HOW YOU WERE SUBSEQUENTLY ARRESTED AND CHARGED WITH VIGILANTE ACTS. AND HOW DID YOU SO SLOPPILY ATTEMPT TO STUFF THE GENIE BACK IN THE BOTTLE?
WITH BASELESS LAWSUITS, CLEAR-CUT PERJURY, AND EVEN THE HELP OF A LATE KINGPIN'S WIFE.
WE HAVE IRREFUTABLE PROOF OF EVERY DETAIL AND AN OPEN CHANNEL TO THE NEW YORK STATE BAR ASSOCIATION.
AND THAT IS WHY YOU WILL TAKE THE CASE.
SO THAT ALL THIS STAYS OUR SECRET.

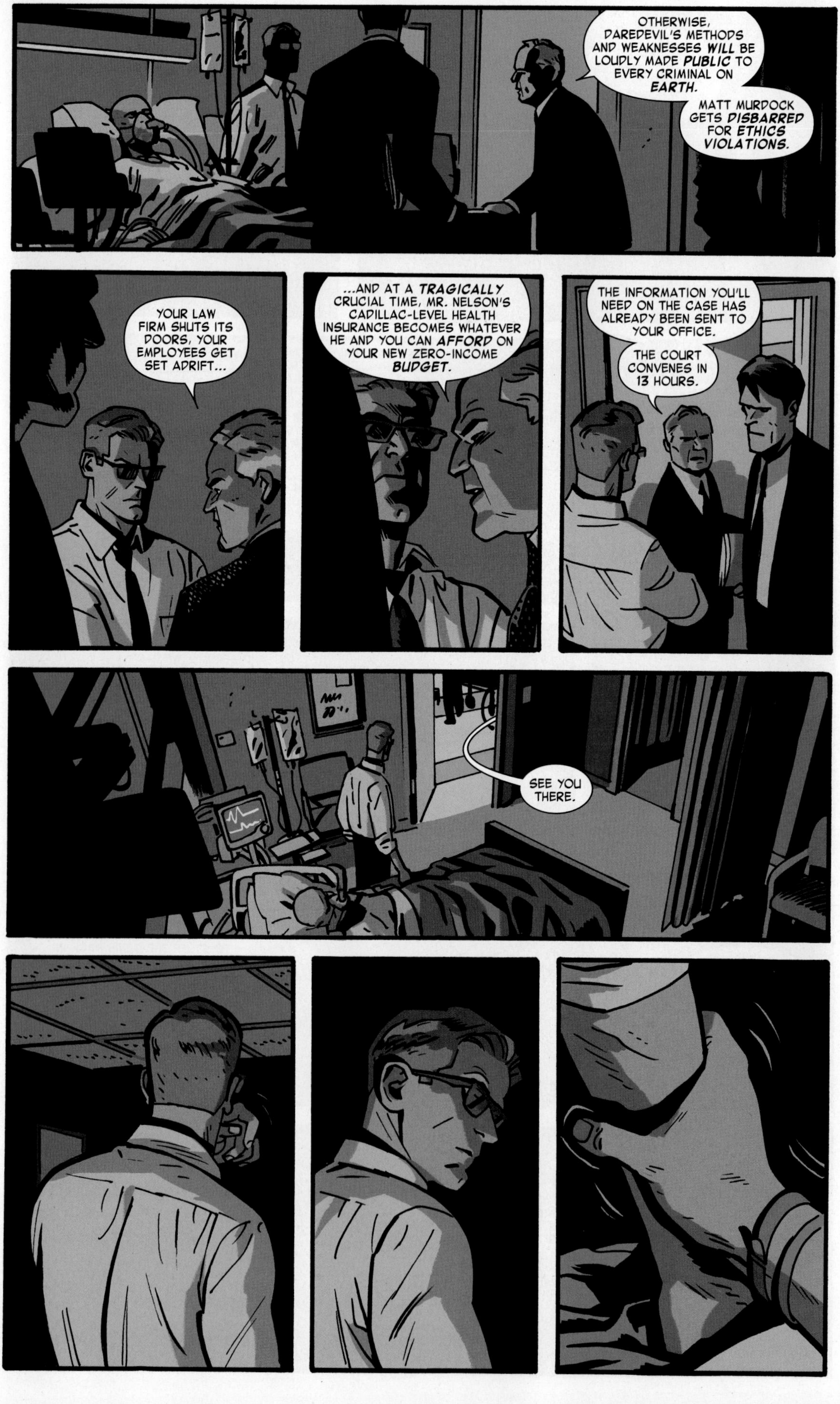

OTHERWISE, DAREDEVIL'S METHODS AND WEAKNESSES WILL BE LOUDLY MADE PUBLIC TO EVERY CRIMINAL ON EARTH.
MATT MURDOCK GETS DISBARRED FOR ETHICS VIOLATIONS.
YOUR LAW FIRM SHUTS ITS DOORS, YOUR EMPLOYEES GET SET ADRIFT...
...AND AT A TRAGICALLY CRUCIAL TIME, MR. NELSON'S CADILLAC-LEVEL HEALTH INSURANCE BECOMES WHATEVER HE AND YOU CAN AFFORD ON YOUR NEW ZERO-INCOME BUDGET.
THE INFORMATION YOU'LL NEED ON THE CASE HAS ALREADY BEEN SENT TO YOUR OFFICE.
THE COURT CONVENES IN 13 HOURS.
SEE YOU THERE.

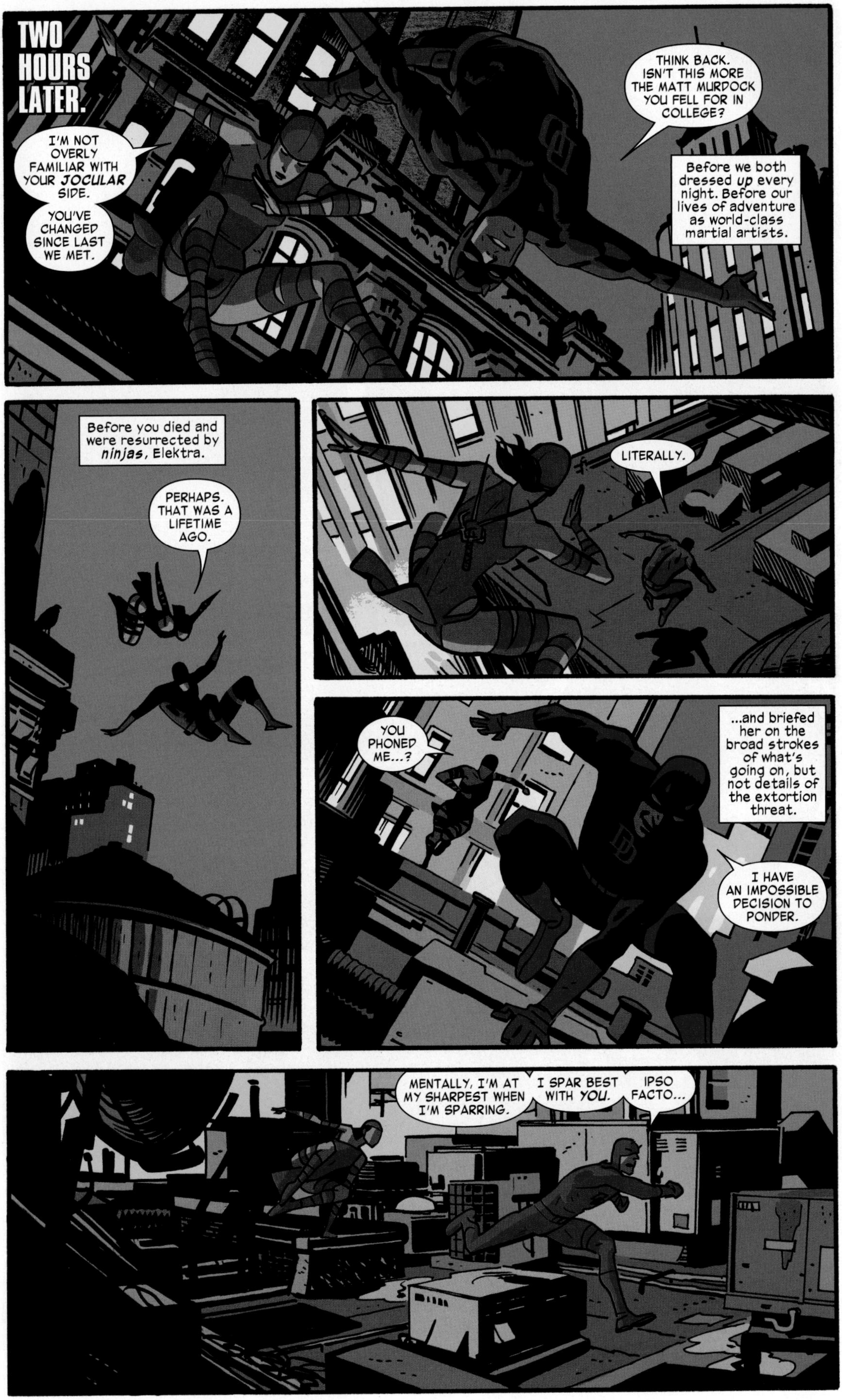

TWO HOURS LATER.
I'M NOT OVERLY FAMILIAR WITH YOUR JOCULAR SIDE.
YOU'VE CHANGED SINCE LAST WE MET.
THINK BACK. ISN'T THIS MORE THE MATT MURDOCK YOU FELL FOR IN COLLEGE?
Before we both dressed up every night. Before our lives of adventure as world-class martial artists.
Before you died and were resurrected by ninjas, Elektra.
PERHAPS. THAT WAS A LIFETIME AGO.
LITERALLY.
YOU PHONED ME...?
...and briefed her on the broad strokes of what's going on, but not details of the extortion threat.
I HAVE AN IMPOSSIBLE DECISION TO PONDER.
MENTALLY, I'M AT MY SHARPEST WHEN I'M SPARRING.
I SPAR BEST WITH YOU.
IPSO FACTO...

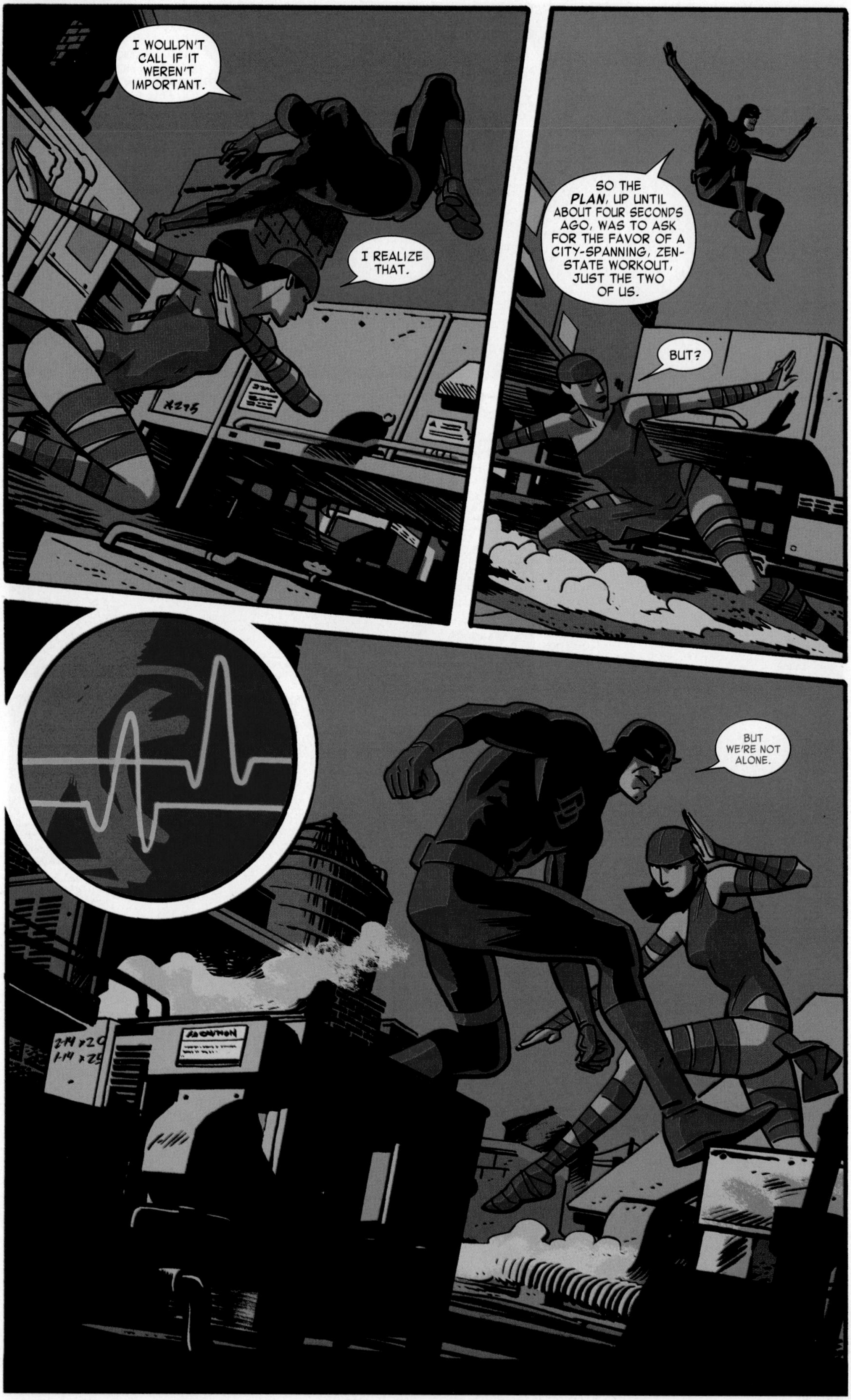
I WOULDN'T CALL IF IT WEREN'T IMPORTANT.
I REALIZE THAT.
SO THE PLAN, UP UNTIL ABOUT FOUR SECONDS AGO, WAS TO ASK FOR THE FAVOR OF A CITY-SPANNING, ZEN-STATE WORKOUT, JUST THE TWO OF US.
BUT?
BUT WE'RE NOT ALONE.

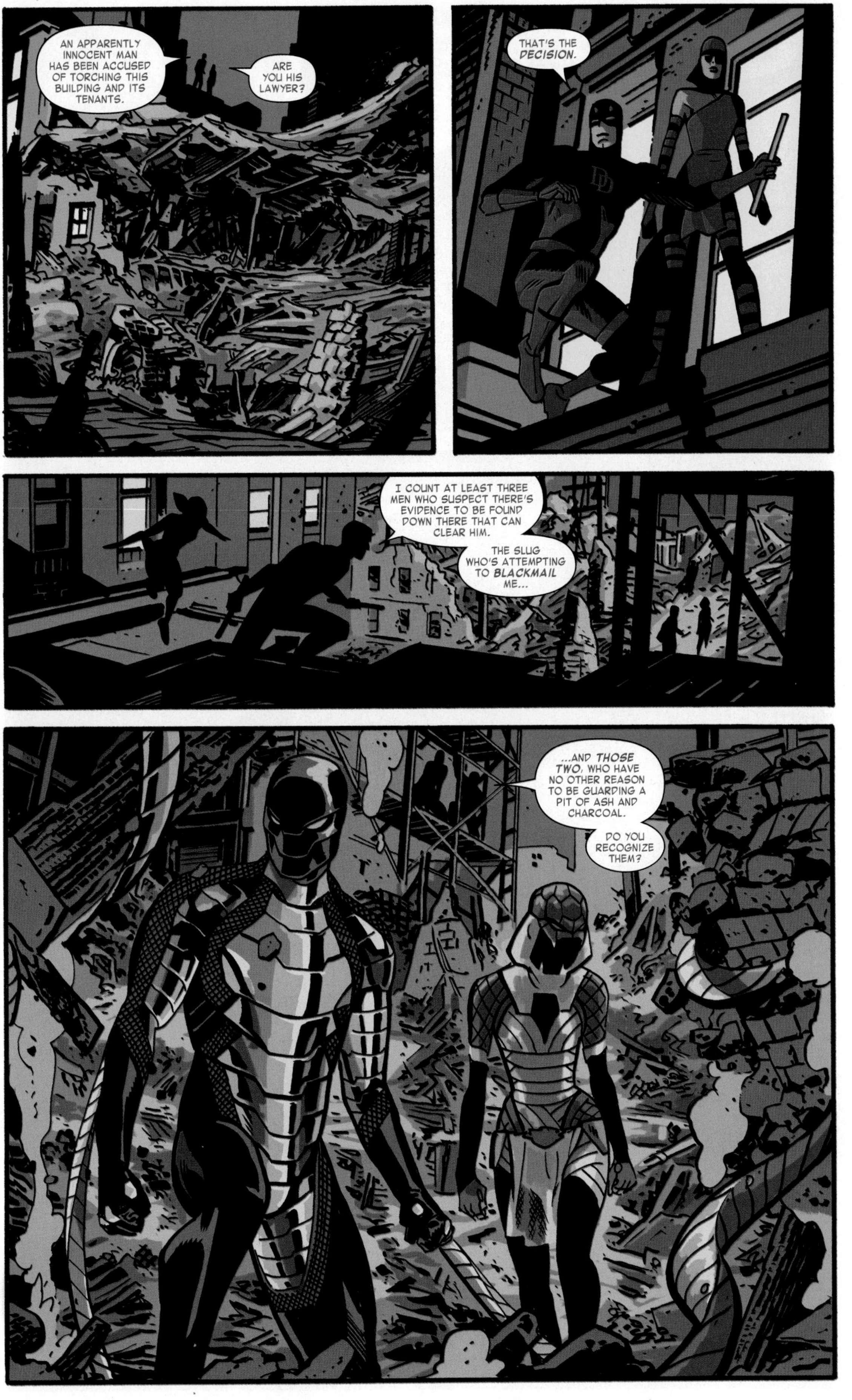
AN APPARENTLY INNOCENT MAN HAS BEEN ACCUSED OF TORCHING THIS BUILDING AND ITS TENANTS.
ARE YOU HIS LAWYER?
THAT'S THE DECISION.
I COUNT AT LEAST THREE MEN WHO SUSPECT THERE'S EVIDENCE TO BE FOUND DOWN THERE THAT CAN CLEAR HIM.
THE SLUG WHO'S ATTEMPTING TO BLACKMAIL ME...
...AND THOSE TWO, WHO HAVE NO OTHER REASON TO BE GUARDING A PIT OF ASH AND CHARCOAL.
DO YOU RECOGNIZE THEM?

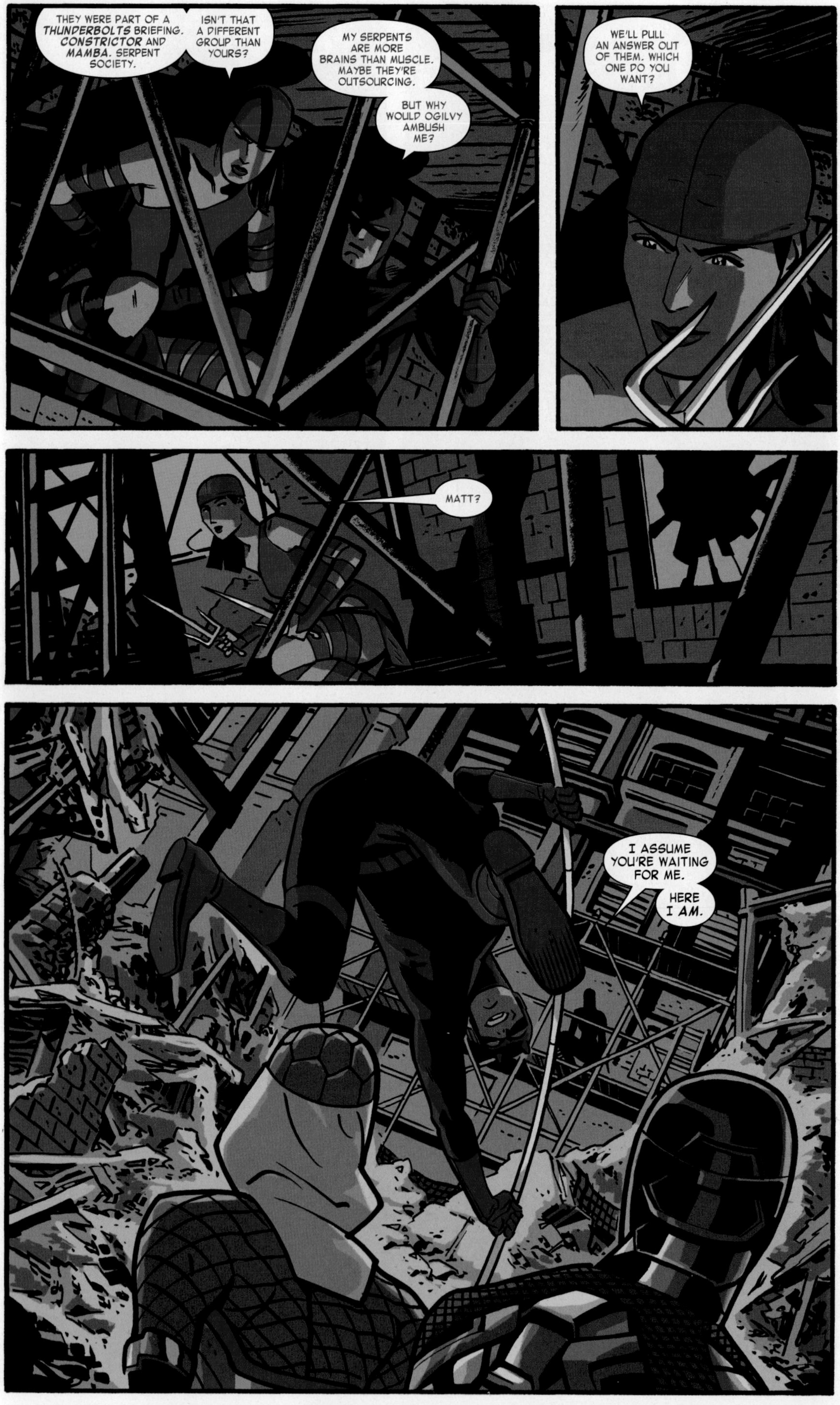
THEY WERE PART OF A *THUNDERBOLTS* BRIEFING. ***CONSTRICTOR*** AND ***MAMBA***. SERPENT SOCIETY.
ISN'T THAT A DIFFERENT GROUP THAN YOURS?
MY SERPENTS ARE MORE BRAINS THAN MUSCLE. MAYBE THEY'RE OUTSOURCING.
BUT WHY WOULD OGILVY AMBUSH ME?
WE'LL PULL AN ANSWER OUT OF THEM. WHICH ONE DO YOU WANT?
MATT?
I ASSUME YOU'RE WAITING FOR ME.
HERE ***I AM***.

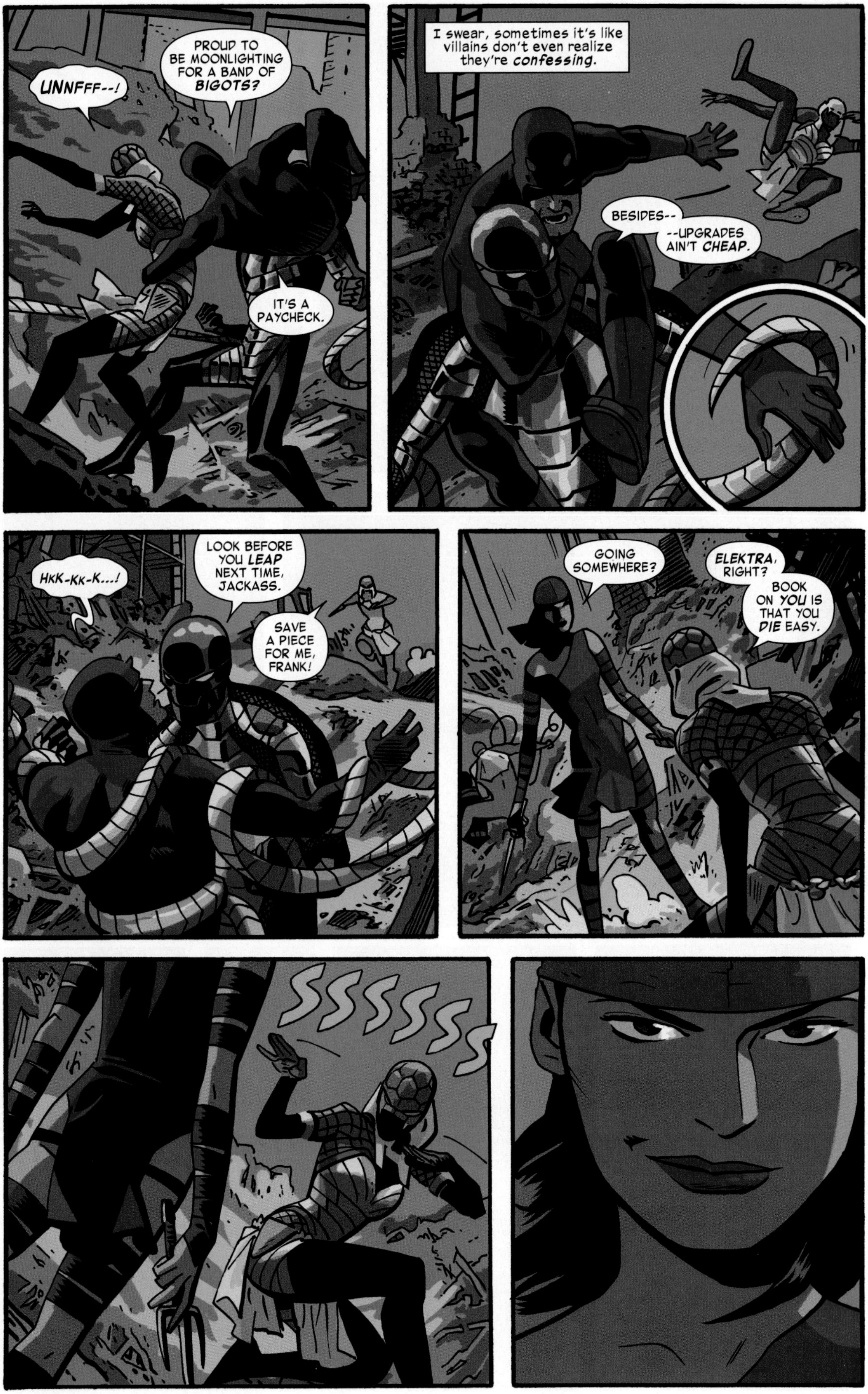
PROUD TO BE MOONLIGHTING FOR A BAND OF BIGOTS?
UNNFFF--!
IT'S A PAYCHECK.
I swear, sometimes it's like villains don't even realize they're confessing.
BESIDES--
--UPGRADES AIN'T CHEAP.
LOOK BEFORE YOU LEAP NEXT TIME, JACKASS.
HKK-KK-K...!
SAVE A PIECE FOR ME, FRANK!
GOING SOMEWHERE?
ELEKTRA, RIGHT?
BOOK ON YOU IS THAT YOU DIE EASY.
SSSSSS

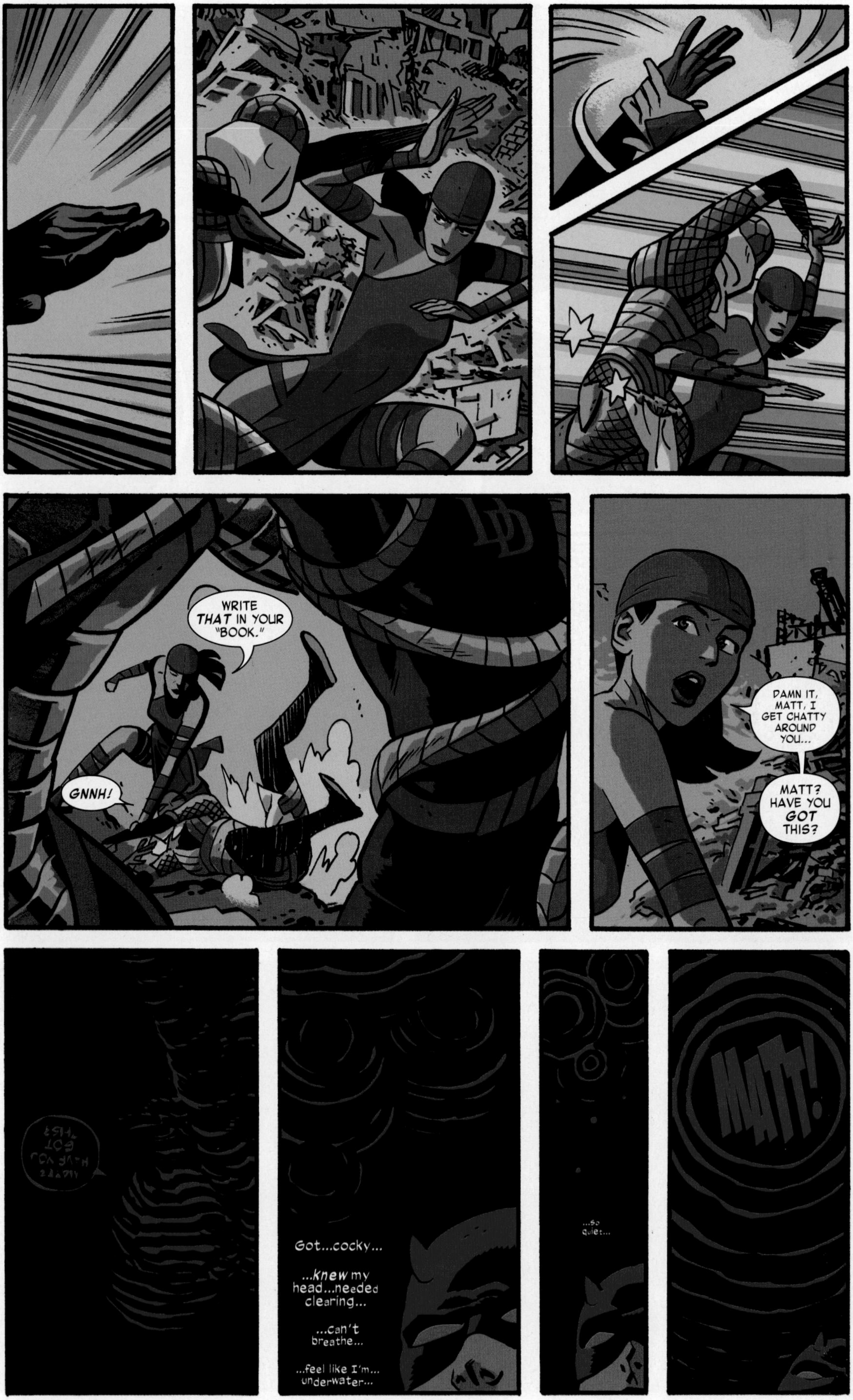
WRITE *THAT* IN YOUR "BOOK."
GNNH!
DAMN IT, MATT, I GET CHATTY AROUND YOU...
MATT? HAVE YOU *GOT* THIS?
Got...cocky...
...*knew* my head...needed clearing...
...can't breathe...
...feel like I'm... underwater...
...so quiet...
MATT!

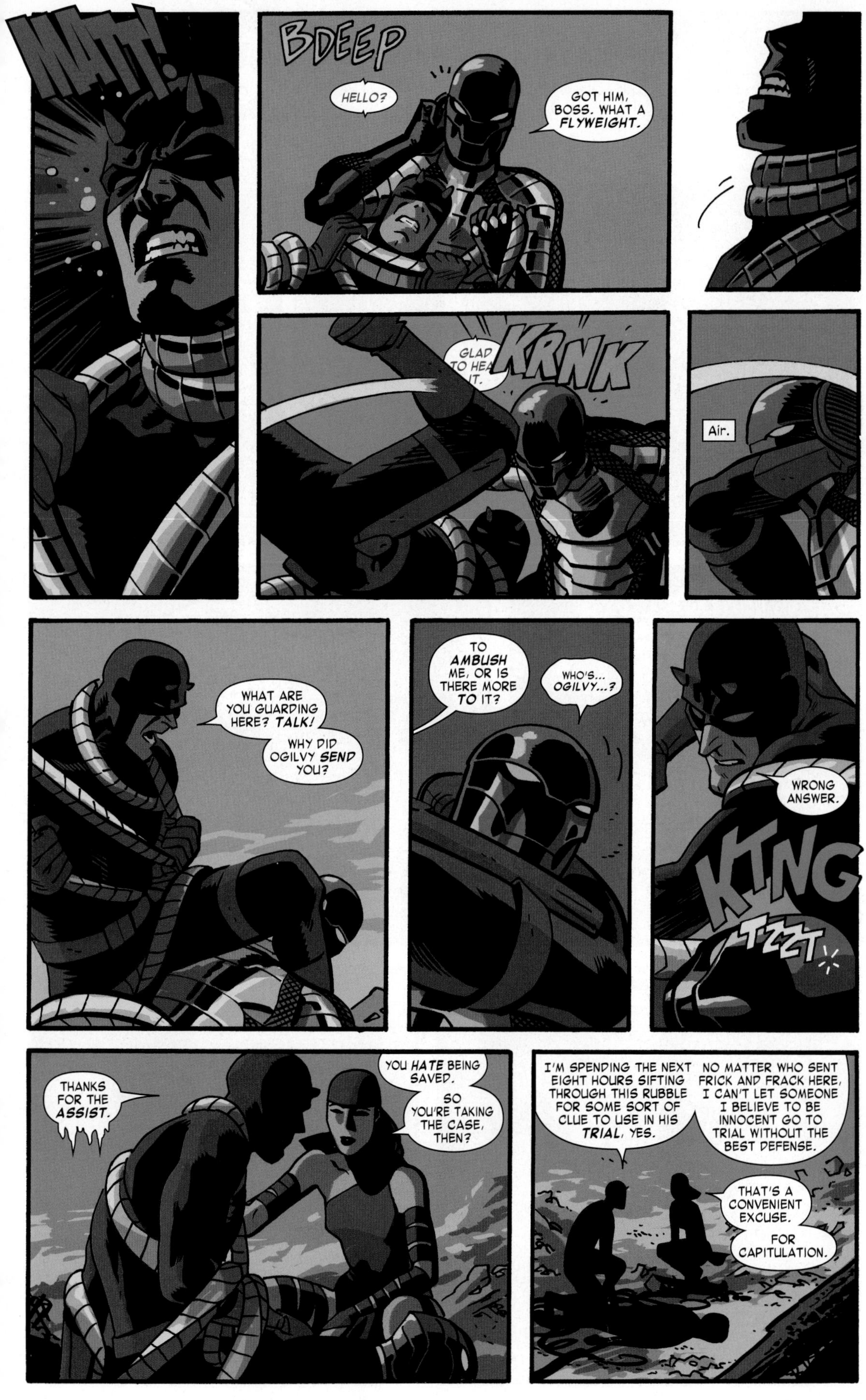
MATT!
BDEEP
HELLO?
GOT HIM, BOSS. WHAT A FLYWEIGHT.
GLAD TO HEA IT.
KRNK
Air.
WHAT ARE YOU GUARDING HERE? TALK!
WHY DID OGILVY SEND YOU?
TO AMBUSH ME, OR IS THERE MORE TO IT?
WHO'S... OGILVY...?
WRONG ANSWER.
KTNG
TZZT
THANKS FOR THE ASSIST.
YOU HATE BEING SAVED.
SO YOU'RE TAKING THE CASE, THEN?
I'M SPENDING THE NEXT EIGHT HOURS SIFTING THROUGH THIS RUBBLE FOR SOME SORT OF CLUE TO USE IN HIS TRIAL, YES.
NO MATTER WHO SENT FRICK AND FRACK HERE, I CAN'T LET SOMEONE I BELIEVE TO BE INNOCENT GO TO TRIAL WITHOUT THE BEST DEFENSE.
THAT'S A CONVENIENT EXCUSE.
FOR CAPITULATION.

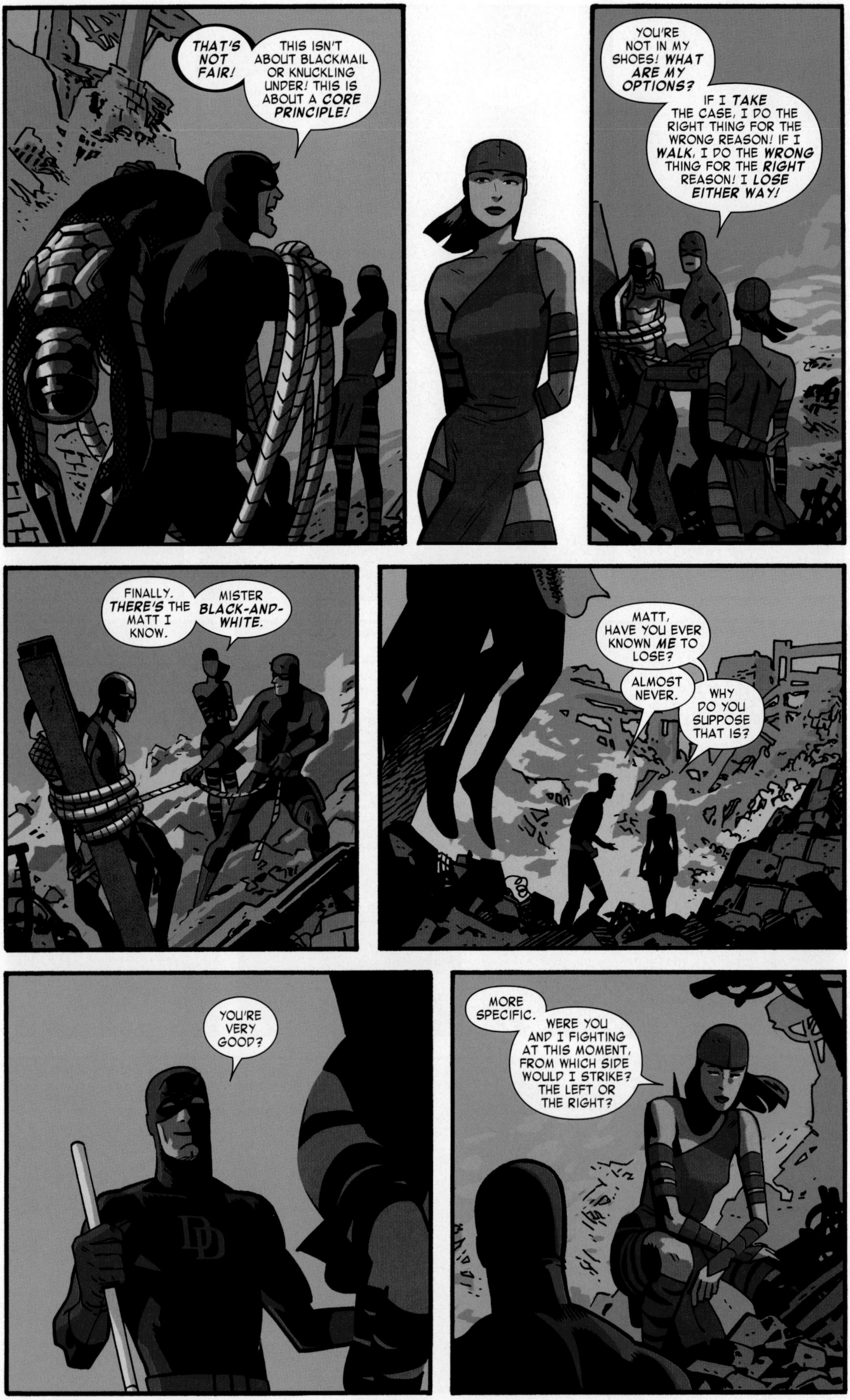
THAT'S NOT FAIR!
THIS ISN'T ABOUT BLACKMAIL OR KNUCKLING UNDER! THIS IS ABOUT A CORE PRINCIPLE!
YOU'RE NOT IN MY SHOES! WHAT ARE MY OPTIONS?
IF I TAKE THE CASE, I DO THE RIGHT THING FOR THE WRONG REASON! IF I WALK, I DO THE WRONG THING FOR THE RIGHT REASON! I LOSE EITHER WAY!
FINALLY. THERE'S THE MATT I KNOW.
MISTER BLACK-AND-WHITE.
MATT, HAVE YOU EVER KNOWN ME TO LOSE?
ALMOST NEVER.
WHY DO YOU SUPPOSE THAT IS?
YOU'RE VERY GOOD?
MORE SPECIFIC.
WERE YOU AND I FIGHTING AT THIS MOMENT, FROM WHICH SIDE WOULD I STRIKE? THE LEFT OR THE RIGHT?

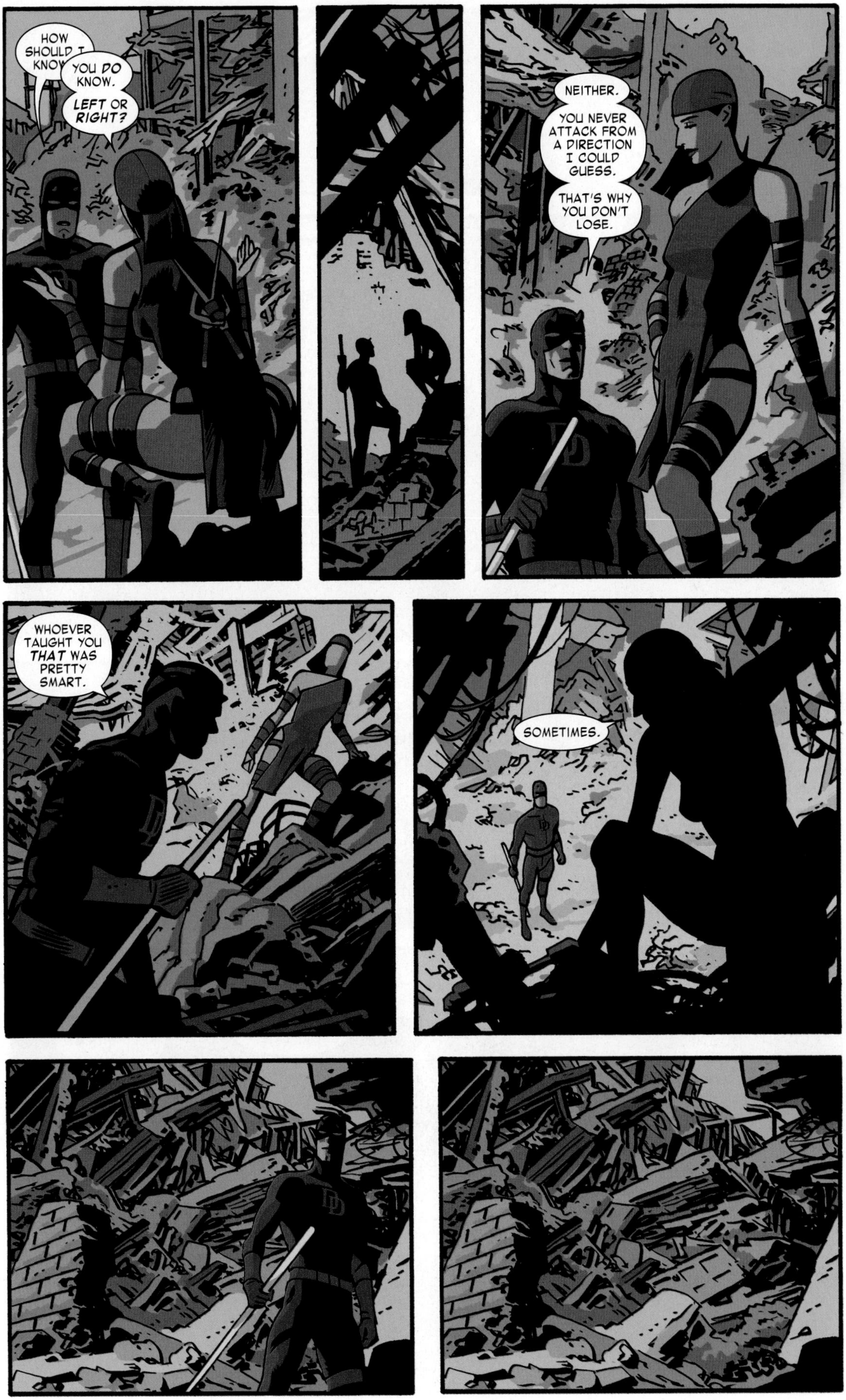
HOW SHOULD I KNOW?
YOU DO KNOW. LEFT OR RIGHT?
NEITHER.
YOU NEVER ATTACK FROM A DIRECTION I COULD GUESS.
THAT'S WHY YOU DON'T LOSE.
WHOEVER TAUGHT YOU THAT WAS PRETTY SMART.
SOMETIMES.

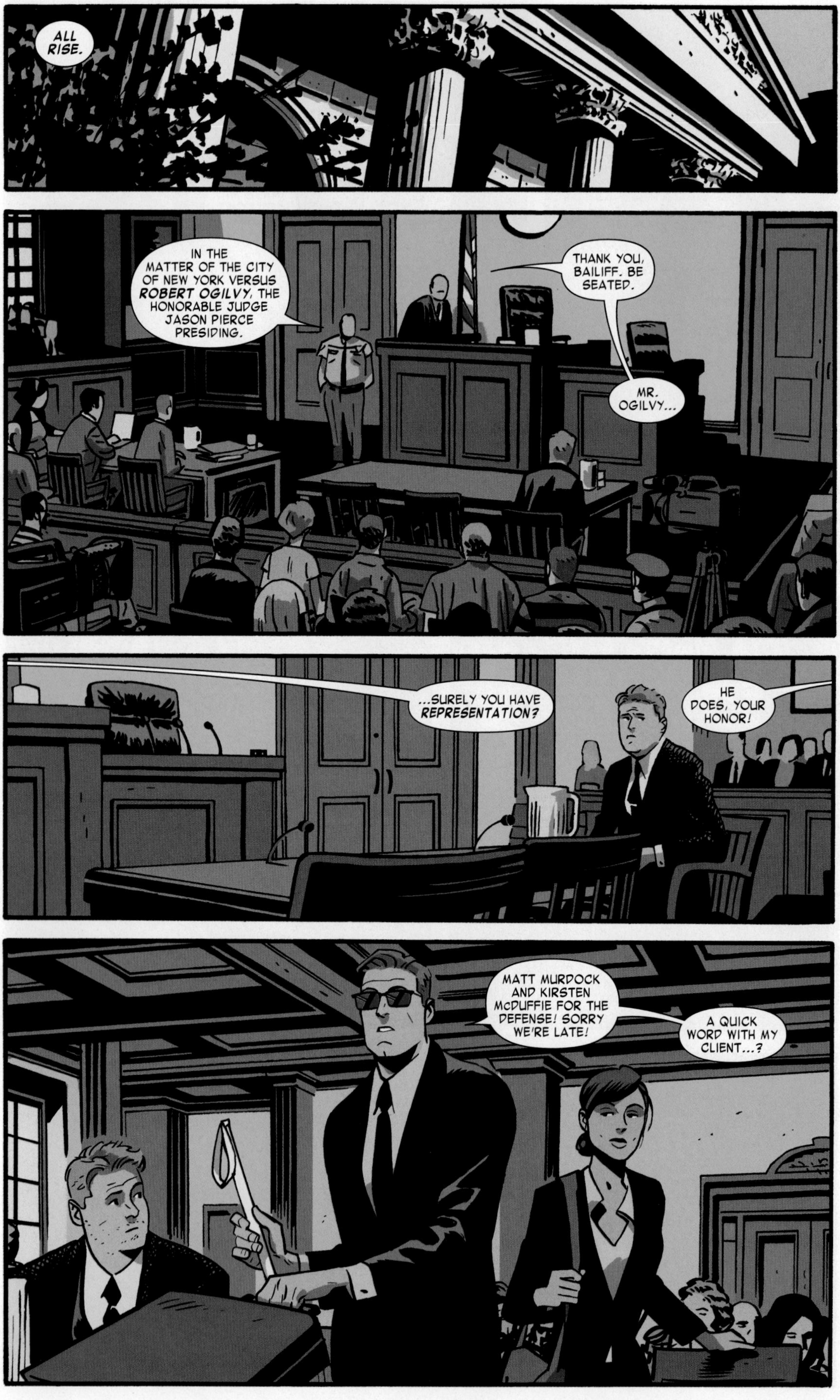
ALL RISE.
IN THE MATTER OF THE CITY OF NEW YORK VERSUS ROBERT OGILVY, THE HONORABLE JUDGE JASON PIERCE PRESIDING.
THANK YOU, BAILIFF. BE SEATED.
MR. OGILVY...
...SURELY YOU HAVE REPRESENTATION?
HE DOES, YOUR HONOR!
MATT MURDOCK AND KIRSTEN McDUFFIE FOR THE DEFENSE! SORRY WE'RE LATE!
A QUICK WORD WITH MY CLIENT...?

YOUR FATHER. HE'S HERE? IN THE GALLERY?

FRONT... KAFF— FRONT ROW...

Sure enough. I hear his pulse slowing as he relaxes.

Very telling. Now, file that away.

The prosecutor's giving his opening remarks. It's showtime.

LIKE WE REHEARSED. YOU READY?

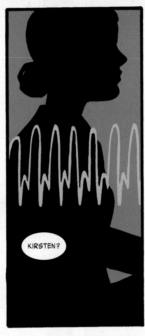

KIRSTEN?

KIRSTEN, I NEED YOU...!

...READY.

YOUR HONOR, DEFENSE WAIVES ITS OPENING REMARKS AND WILL MOVE DIRECTLY TO TESTIMONY.

MS. McDUFFIE, EFFECTIVE IMMEDIATELY, YOU ARE LEAD COUNSEL. CALL YOUR FIRST WITNESS.

OBJECTION, YOUR HONOR! THIS IS OUT OF ORDER--

THE DEFENSE CALLS MR. MATTHEW MURDOCK.

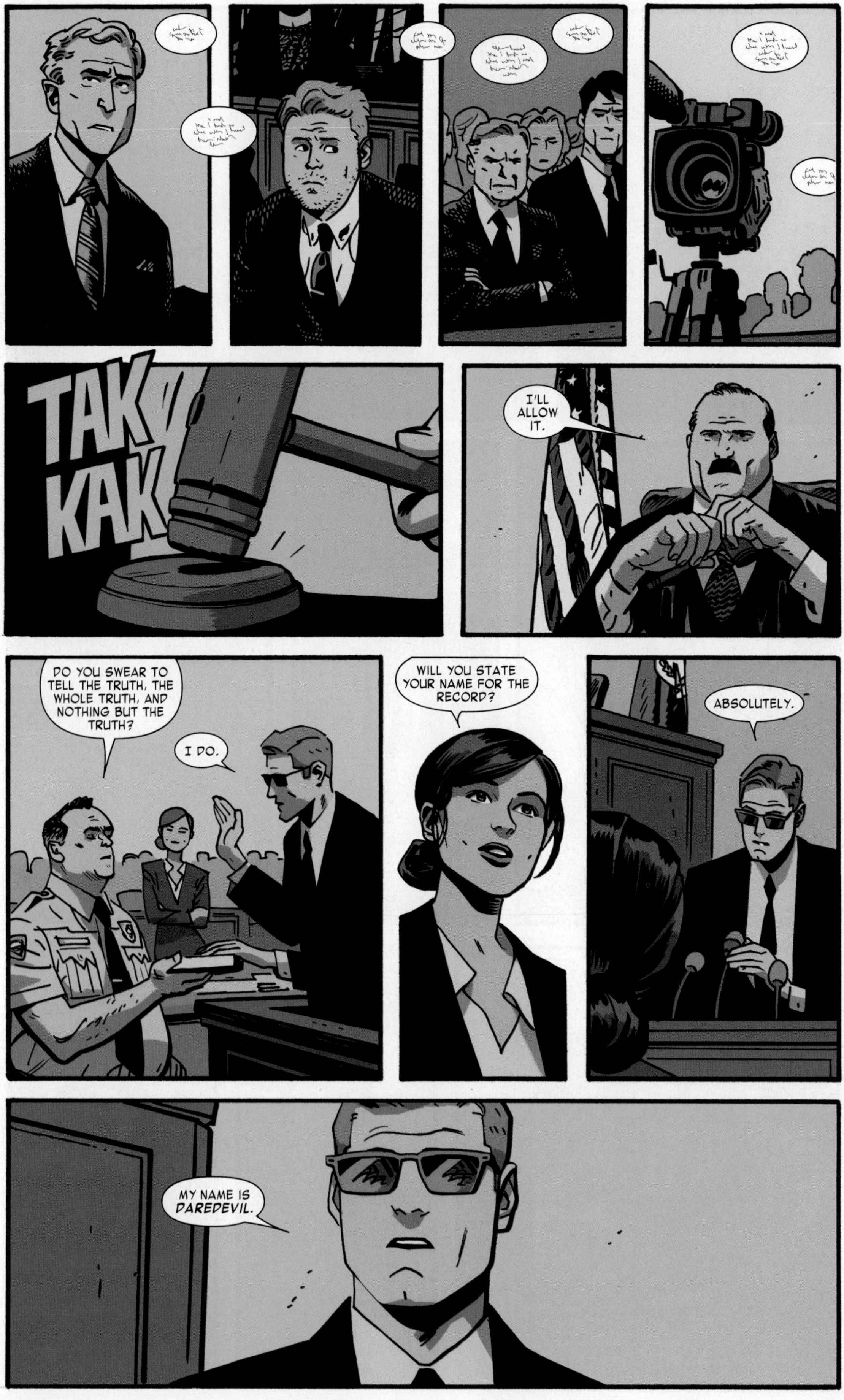
TAK
KAK
I'LL ALLOW IT.
DO YOU SWEAR TO TELL THE TRUTH, THE WHOLE TRUTH, AND NOTHING BUT THE TRUTH?
I DO.
WILL YOU STATE YOUR NAME FOR THE RECORD?
ABSOLUTELY.
MY NAME IS DAREDEVIL.

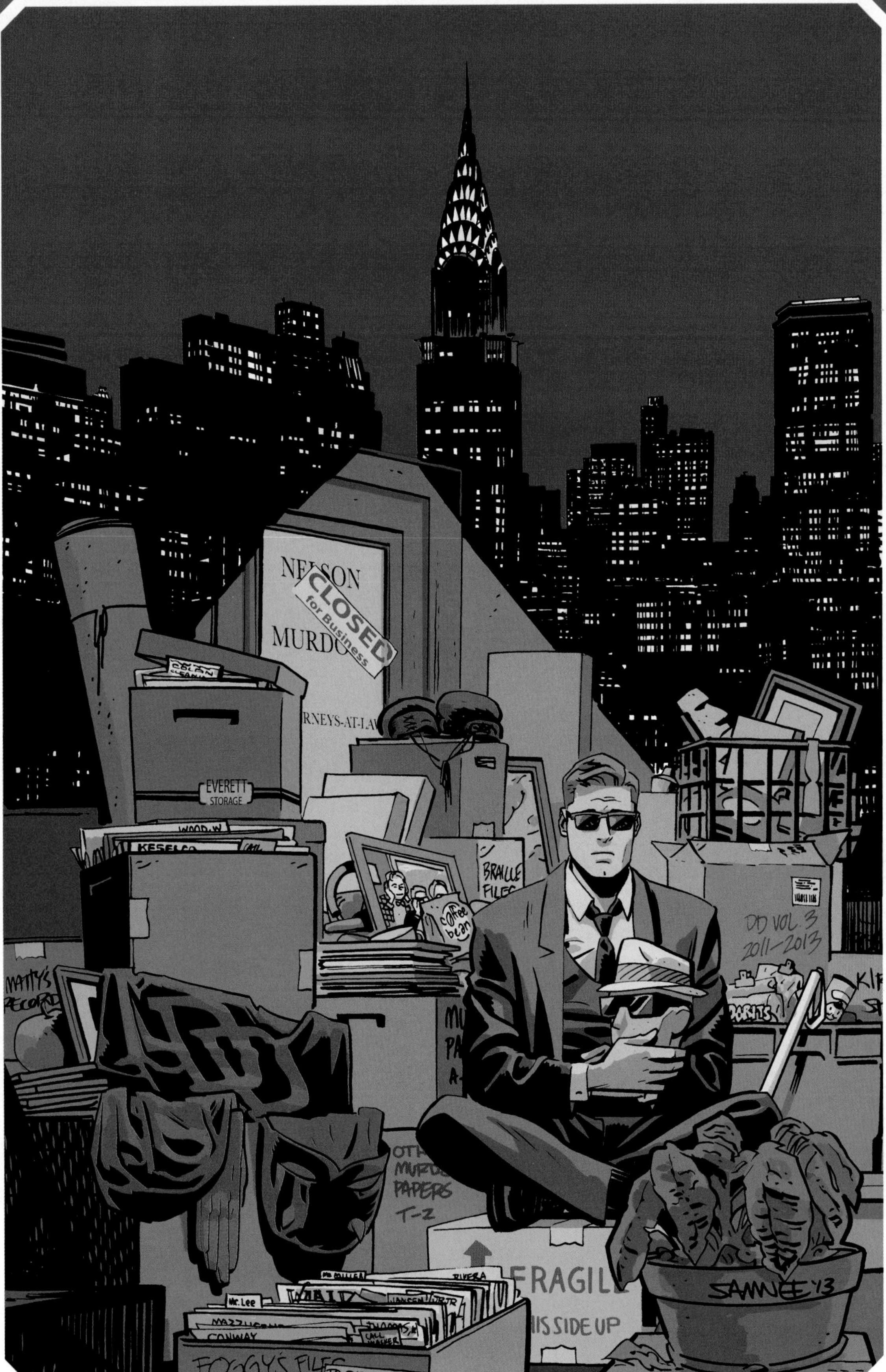
NELSON
CLOSED
for Business
MURDO
RNEYS-AT-LAW
EVERETT
STORAGE
WOOD, W
BRAILLE
FILES
DD VOL. 3
2011-2013
OTH
MURDO
PAPERS
T-Z
FRAGIL
IS SIDE UP
SAMNEE '13
Mr. Lee
CONWAY
RIVERA
FOGGY'S FILES
TO BE SORTED

DAREDEVIL #36

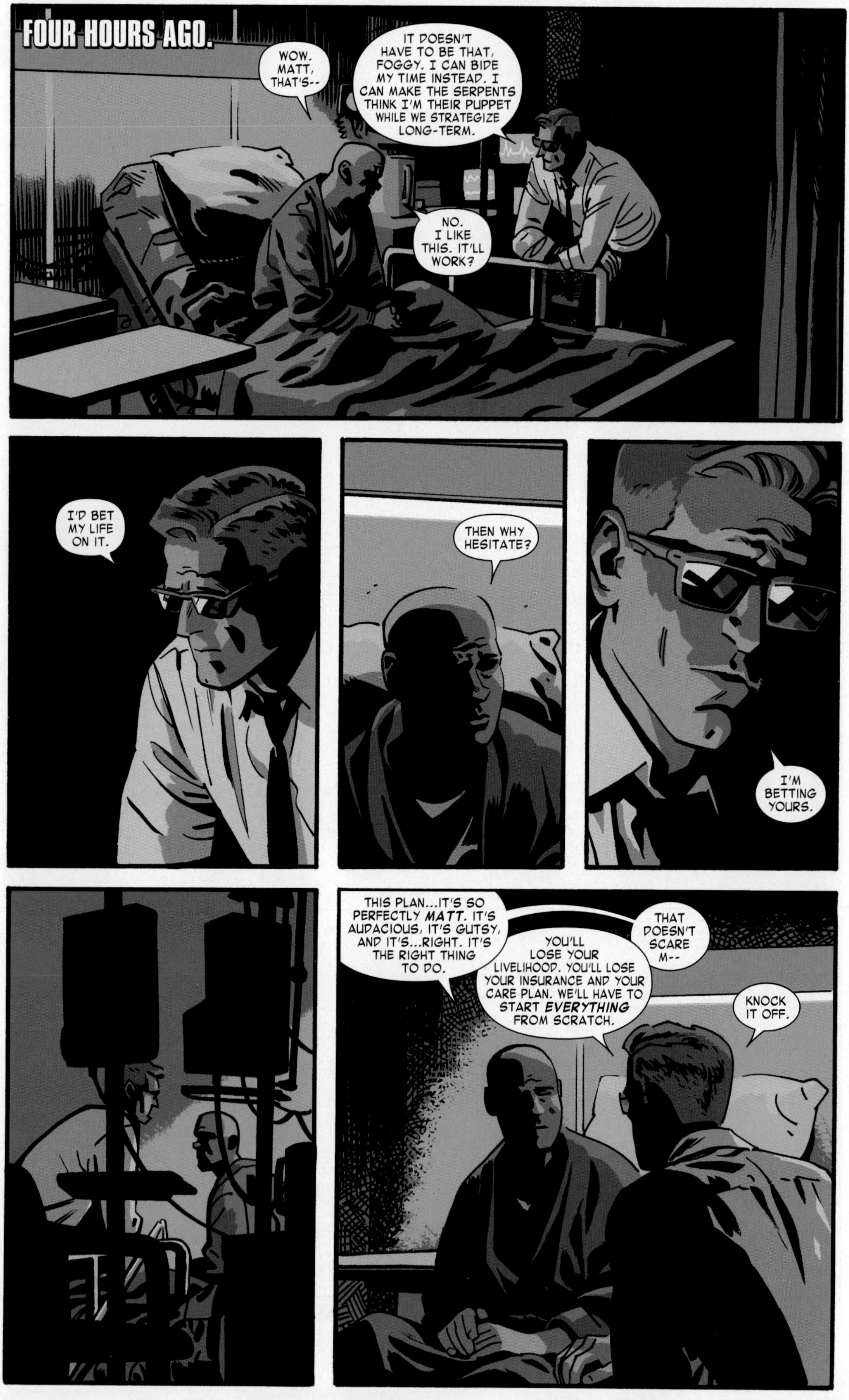
FOUR HOURS AGO.
WOW. MATT, THAT'S--
IT DOESN'T HAVE TO BE THAT, FOGGY. I CAN BIDE MY TIME INSTEAD. I CAN MAKE THE SERPENTS THINK I'M THEIR PUPPET WHILE WE STRATEGIZE LONG-TERM.
NO. I LIKE THIS. IT'LL WORK?
I'D BET MY LIFE ON IT.
THEN WHY HESITATE?
I'M BETTING YOURS.
THIS PLAN...IT'S SO PERFECTLY MATT. IT'S AUDACIOUS, IT'S GUTSY, AND IT'S...RIGHT. IT'S THE RIGHT THING TO DO.
YOU'LL LOSE YOUR LIVELIHOOD. YOU'LL LOSE YOUR INSURANCE AND YOUR CARE PLAN. WE'LL HAVE TO START EVERYTHING FROM SCRATCH.
THAT DOESN'T SCARE M--
KNOCK IT OFF.

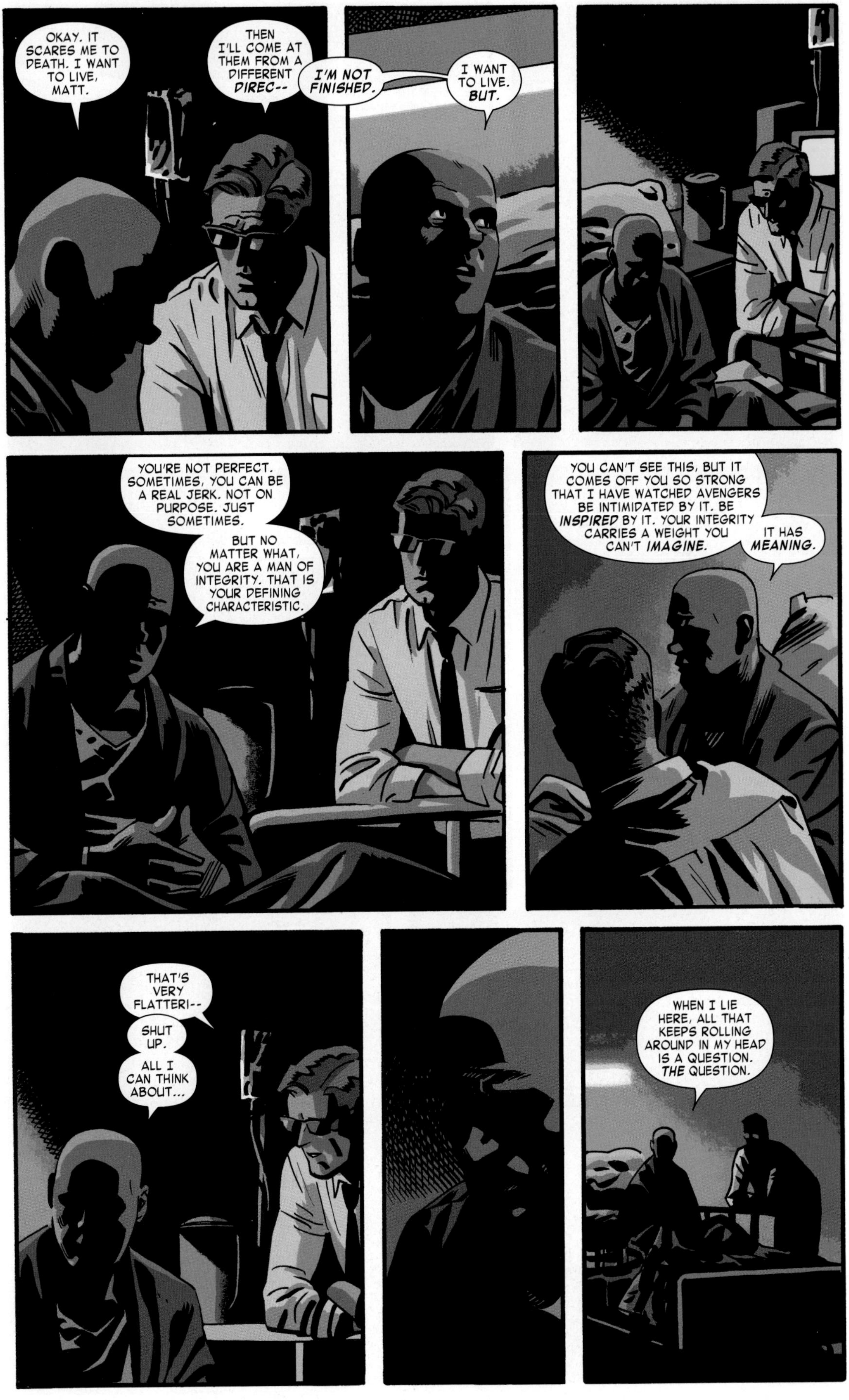
OKAY. IT SCARES ME TO DEATH. I WANT TO LIVE, MATT.
THEN I'LL COME AT THEM FROM A DIFFERENT DIREC--
I'M NOT FINISHED.
I WANT TO LIVE. BUT.
YOU'RE NOT PERFECT. SOMETIMES, YOU CAN BE A REAL JERK. NOT ON PURPOSE. JUST SOMETIMES.
BUT NO MATTER WHAT, YOU ARE A MAN OF INTEGRITY. THAT IS YOUR DEFINING CHARACTERISTIC.
YOU CAN'T SEE THIS, BUT IT COMES OFF YOU SO STRONG THAT I HAVE WATCHED AVENGERS BE INTIMIDATED BY IT. BE INSPIRED BY IT. YOUR INTEGRITY CARRIES A WEIGHT YOU CAN'T IMAGINE.
IT HAS MEANING.
THAT'S VERY FLATTERI--
SHUT UP.
ALL I CAN THINK ABOUT...
WHEN I LIE HERE, ALL THAT KEEPS ROLLING AROUND IN MY HEAD IS A QUESTION. THE QUESTION.

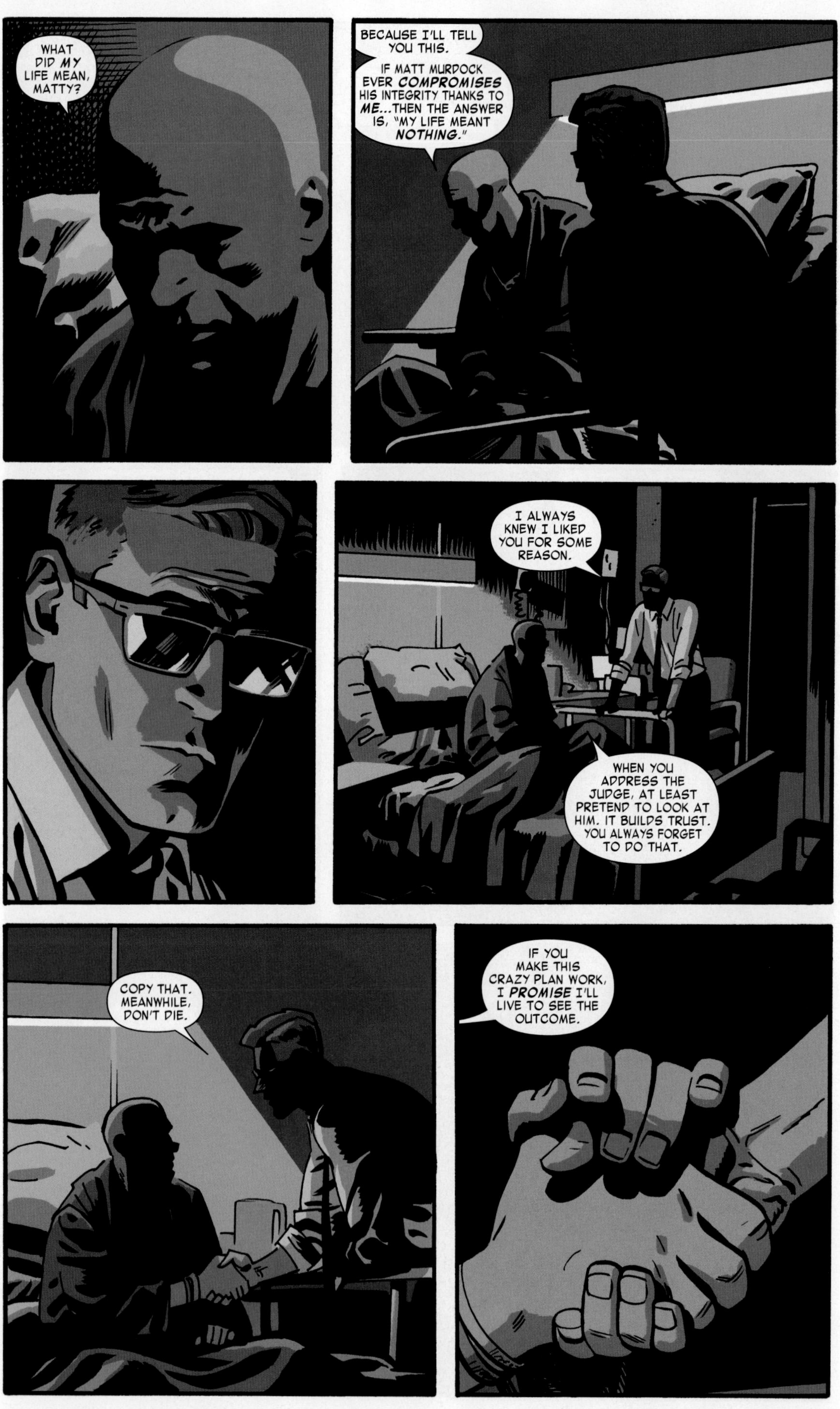
WHAT DID *MY* LIFE MEAN, MATTY?
BECAUSE I'LL TELL YOU THIS.
IF MATT MURDOCK EVER *COMPROMISES* HIS INTEGRITY THANKS TO *ME*...THEN THE ANSWER IS, "MY LIFE MEANT *NOTHING*."
I ALWAYS KNEW I LIKED YOU FOR SOME REASON.
WHEN YOU ADDRESS THE JUDGE, AT LEAST PRETEND TO LOOK AT HIM. IT BUILDS TRUST. YOU ALWAYS FORGET TO DO THAT.
COPY THAT. MEANWHILE, DON'T DIE.
IF YOU MAKE THIS CRAZY PLAN WORK, I *PROMISE* I'LL LIVE TO SEE THE OUTCOME.

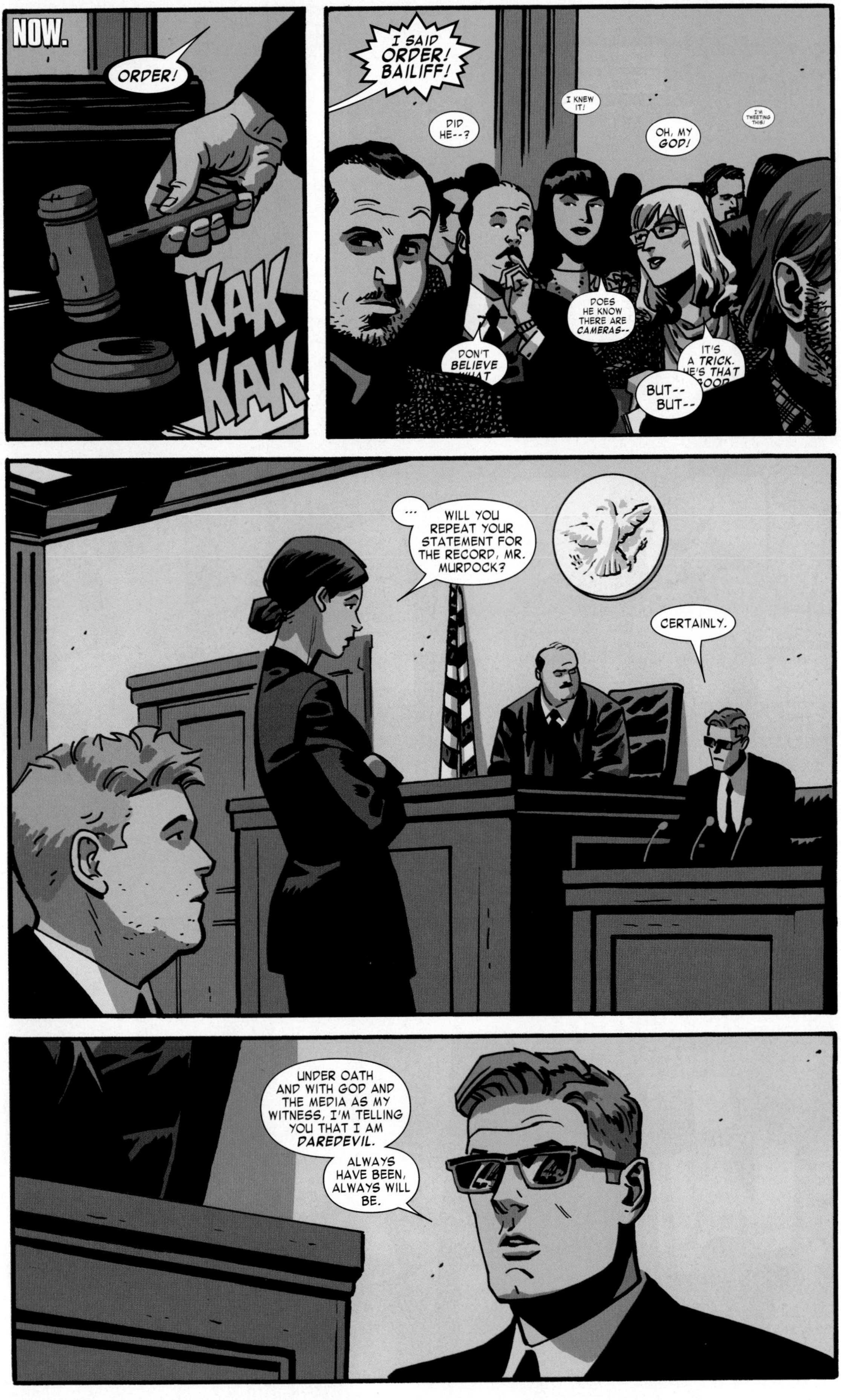
NOW.
ORDER!
KAK KAK
I SAID ORDER! BAILIFF!
DID HE--?
I KNEW IT!
OH, MY GOD!
I'M TWEETING THIS!
DOES HE KNOW THERE ARE CAMERAS--
DON'T BELIEVE
IT'S A TRICK. HE'S THAT
BUT-- BUT--
... WILL YOU REPEAT YOUR STATEMENT FOR THE RECORD, MR. MURDOCK?
CERTAINLY.
UNDER OATH AND WITH GOD AND THE MEDIA AS MY WITNESS, I'M TELLING YOU THAT I AM DAREDEVIL.
ALWAYS HAVE BEEN, ALWAYS WILL BE.

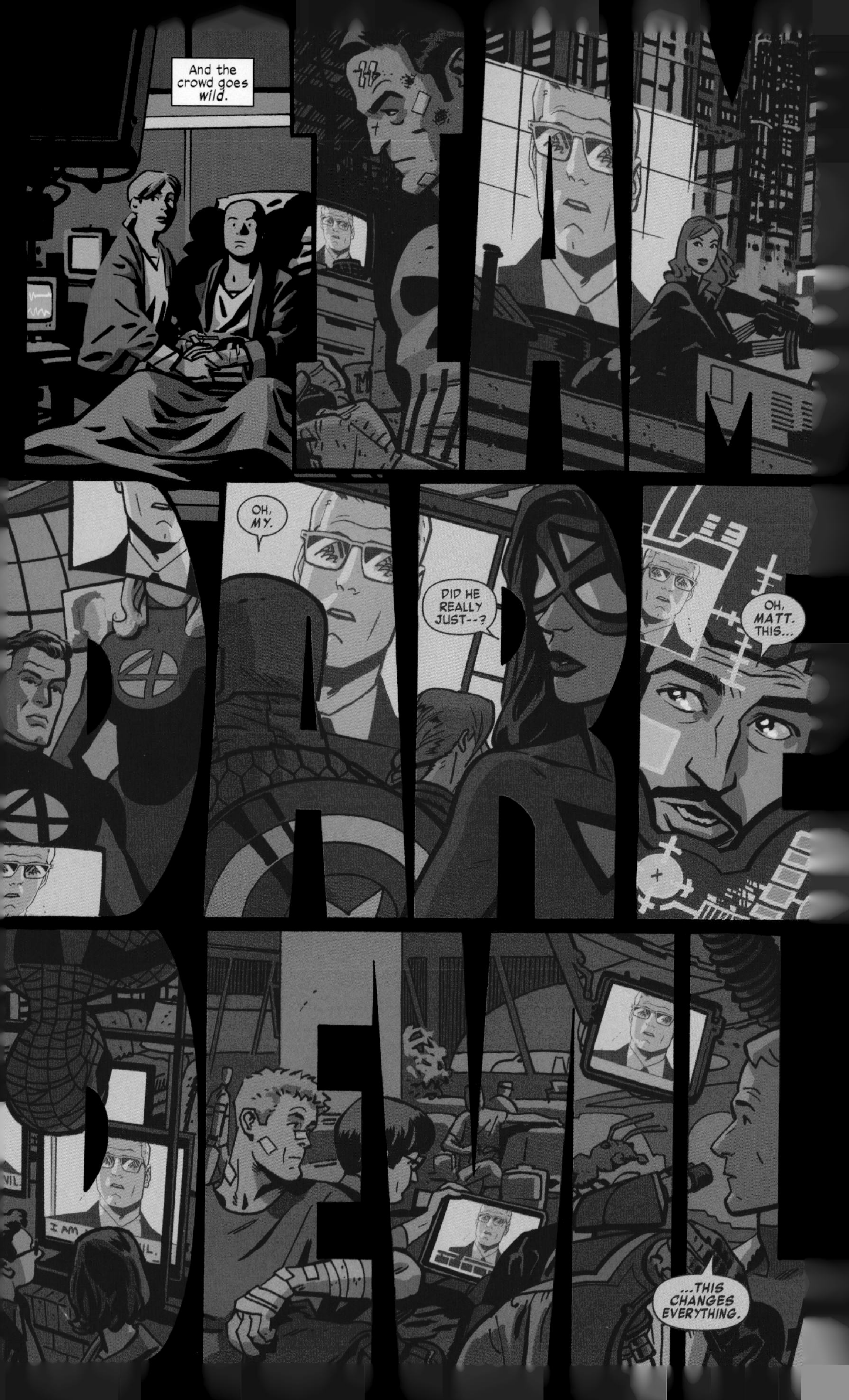
I AM
DAREDEVIL
And the crowd goes wild.
OH, MY.
DID HE REALLY JUST--?
OH, MATT. THIS...
...THIS CHANGES EVERYTHING.

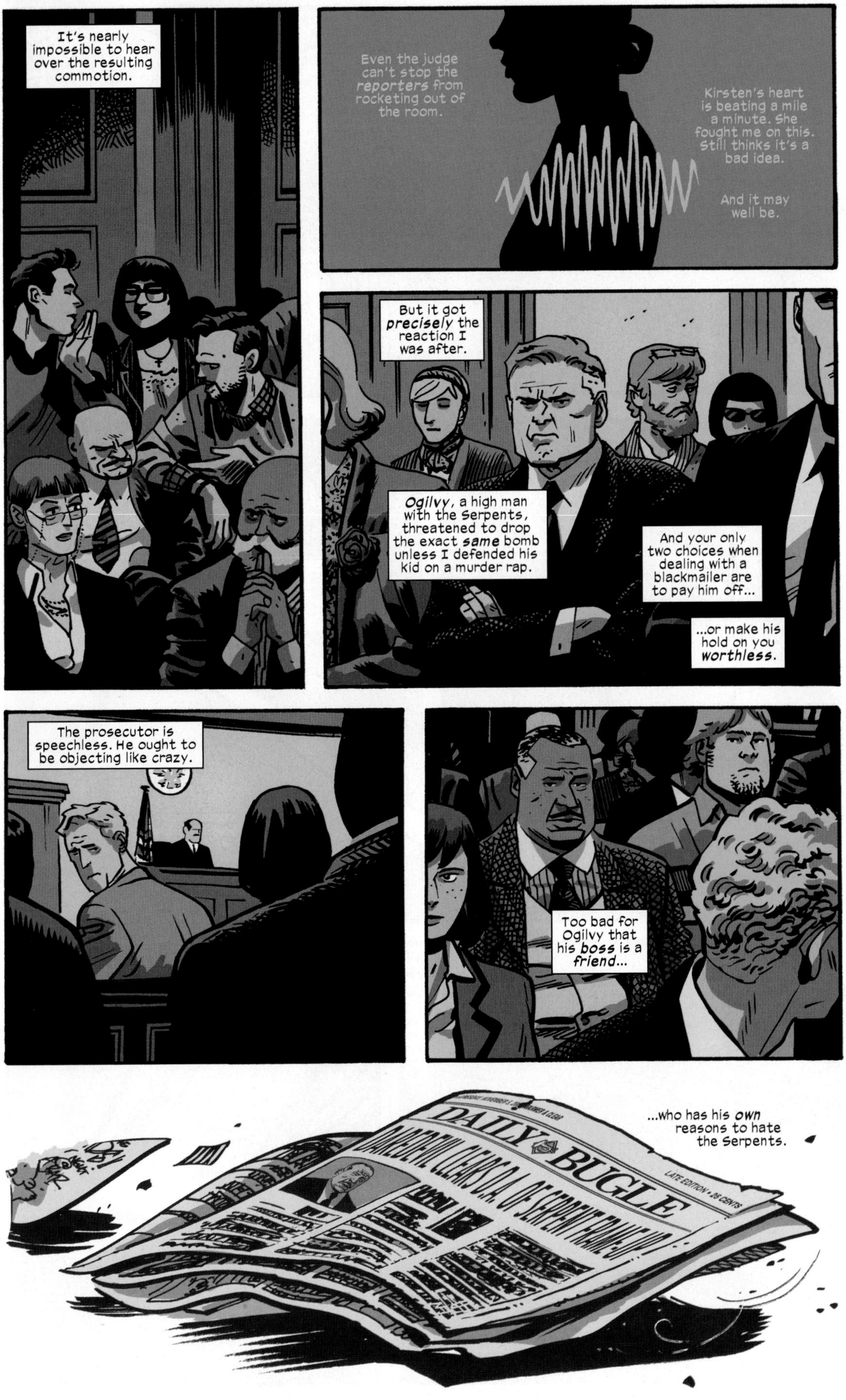

It's nearly impossible to hear over the resulting commotion.
Even the judge can't stop the *reporters* from rocketing out of the room.
Kirsten's heart is beating a mile a minute. She fought me on this. Still thinks it's a bad idea.
And it may well be.
But it got *precisely* the reaction I was after.
Ogilvy, a high man with the Serpents, threatened to drop the exact *same* bomb unless I defended his kid on a murder rap.
And your only two choices when dealing with a blackmailer are to pay him off...
...or make his hold on you ***worthless***.
The prosecutor is speechless. He ought to be objecting like crazy.
Too bad for Ogilvy that his ***boss*** is a ***friend***...
DAILY BUGLE
LATE EDITION • 25 CENTS
DAREDEVIL CLEARS D.A. OF SERPENT FRAME-UP!
...who has his *own* reasons to hate the Serpents.

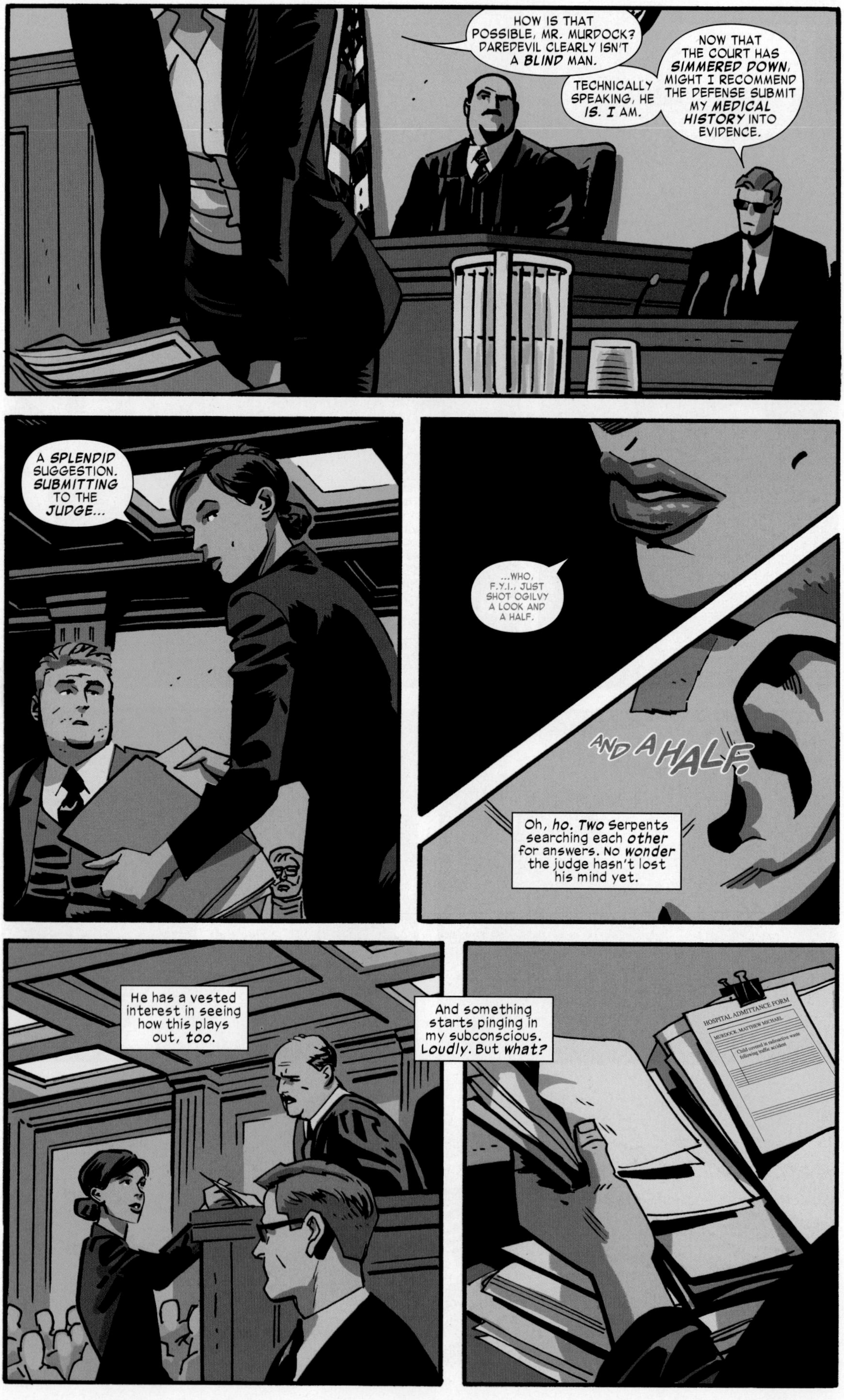
HOW IS THAT POSSIBLE, MR. MURDOCK? DAREDEVIL CLEARLY ISN'T A BLIND MAN.
TECHNICALLY SPEAKING, HE IS. I AM.
NOW THAT THE COURT HAS SIMMERED DOWN, MIGHT I RECOMMEND THE DEFENSE SUBMIT MY MEDICAL HISTORY INTO EVIDENCE.
A SPLENDID SUGGESTION. SUBMITTING TO THE JUDGE...
...WHO, F.Y.I., JUST SHOT OGILVY A LOOK AND A HALF.
AND A HALF.
Oh, ho. Two Serpents searching each other for answers. No wonder the judge hasn't lost his mind yet.
He has a vested interest in seeing how this plays out, too.
And something starts pinging in my subconscious. Loudly. But what?
HOSPITAL ADMITTANCE FORM
MURDOCK, MATTHEW MICHAEL
Child covered in radioactive waste following traffic accident

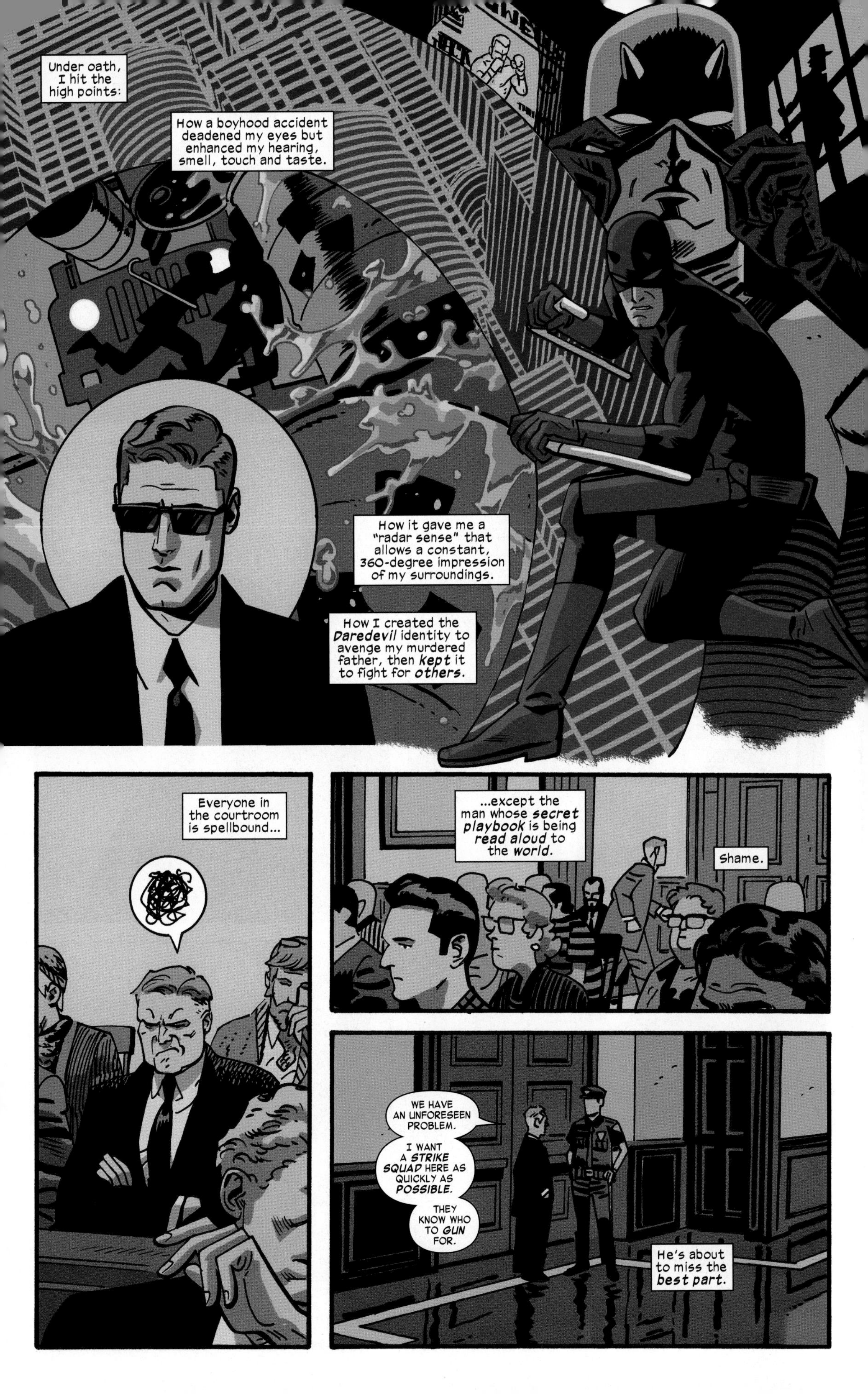

Under oath, I hit the high points:
How a boyhood accident deadened my eyes but enhanced my hearing, smell, touch and taste.
How it gave me a "radar sense" that allows a constant, 360-degree impression of my surroundings.
How I created the *Daredevil* identity to avenge my murdered father, then *kept* it to fight for *others*.
Everyone in the courtroom is spellbound...
...except the man whose *secret playbook* is being *read aloud* to the *world*.
Shame.
WE HAVE AN UNFORESEEN PROBLEM.
I WANT A *STRIKE SQUAD* HERE AS QUICKLY AS *POSSIBLE*.
THEY KNOW WHO TO *GUN* FOR.
He's about to miss the *best part*.

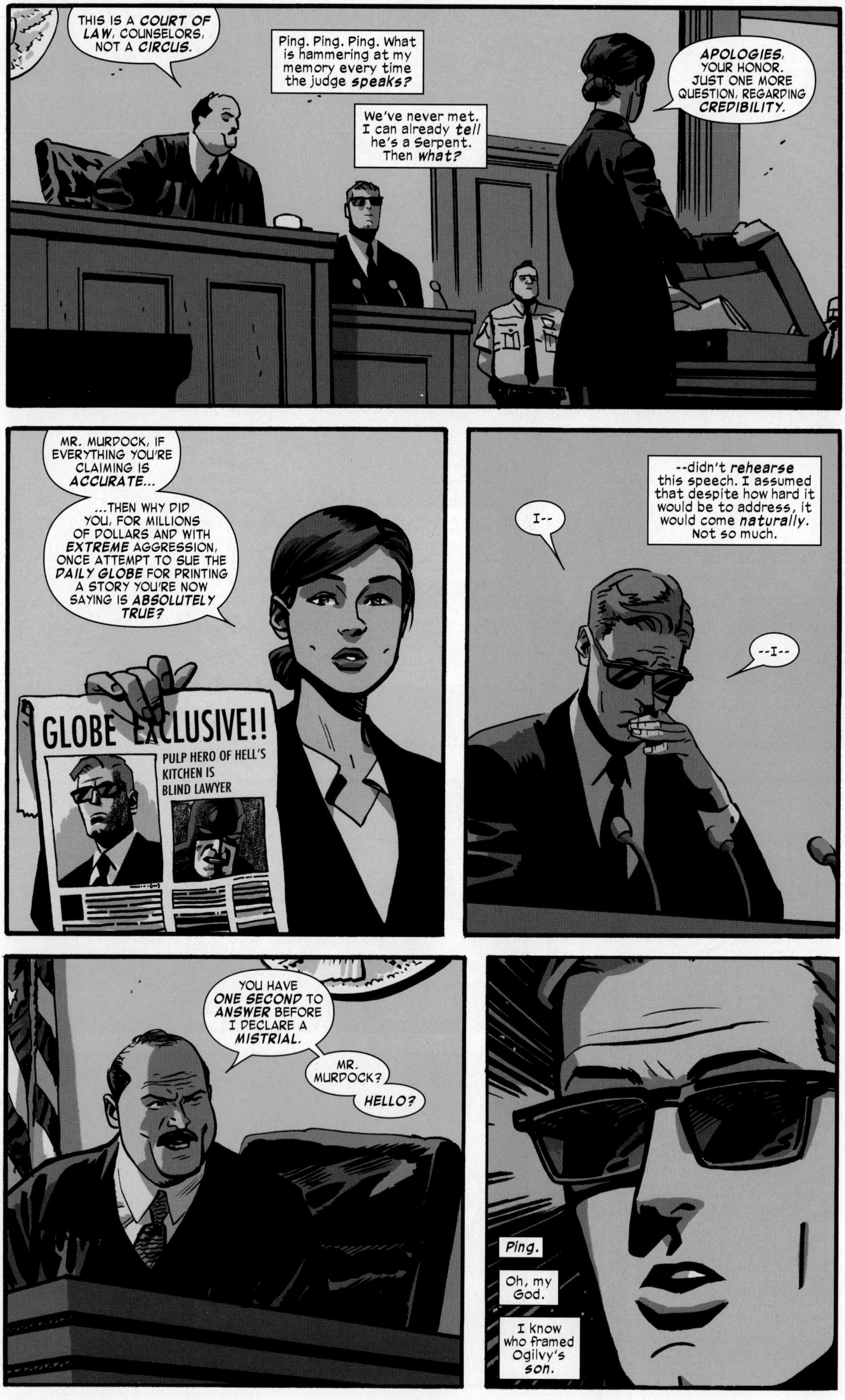
THIS IS A COURT OF LAW, COUNSELORS, NOT A CIRCUS.
Ping. Ping. Ping. What is hammering at my memory every time the judge speaks?
We've never met. I can already tell he's a Serpent. Then what?
APOLOGIES, YOUR HONOR. JUST ONE MORE QUESTION, REGARDING CREDIBILITY.
MR. MURDOCK, IF EVERYTHING YOU'RE CLAIMING IS ACCURATE...
...THEN WHY DID YOU, FOR MILLIONS OF DOLLARS AND WITH EXTREME AGGRESSION, ONCE ATTEMPT TO SUE THE DAILY GLOBE FOR PRINTING A STORY YOU'RE NOW SAYING IS ABSOLUTELY TRUE?
GLOBE EXCLUSIVE!!
PULP HERO OF HELL'S KITCHEN IS BLIND LAWYER
I--
--didn't rehearse this speech. I assumed that despite how hard it would be to address, it would come naturally. Not so much.
--I--
YOU HAVE ONE SECOND TO ANSWER BEFORE I DECLARE A MISTRIAL.
MR. MURDOCK?
HELLO?
Ping.
Oh, my God.
I know who framed Ogilvy's son.

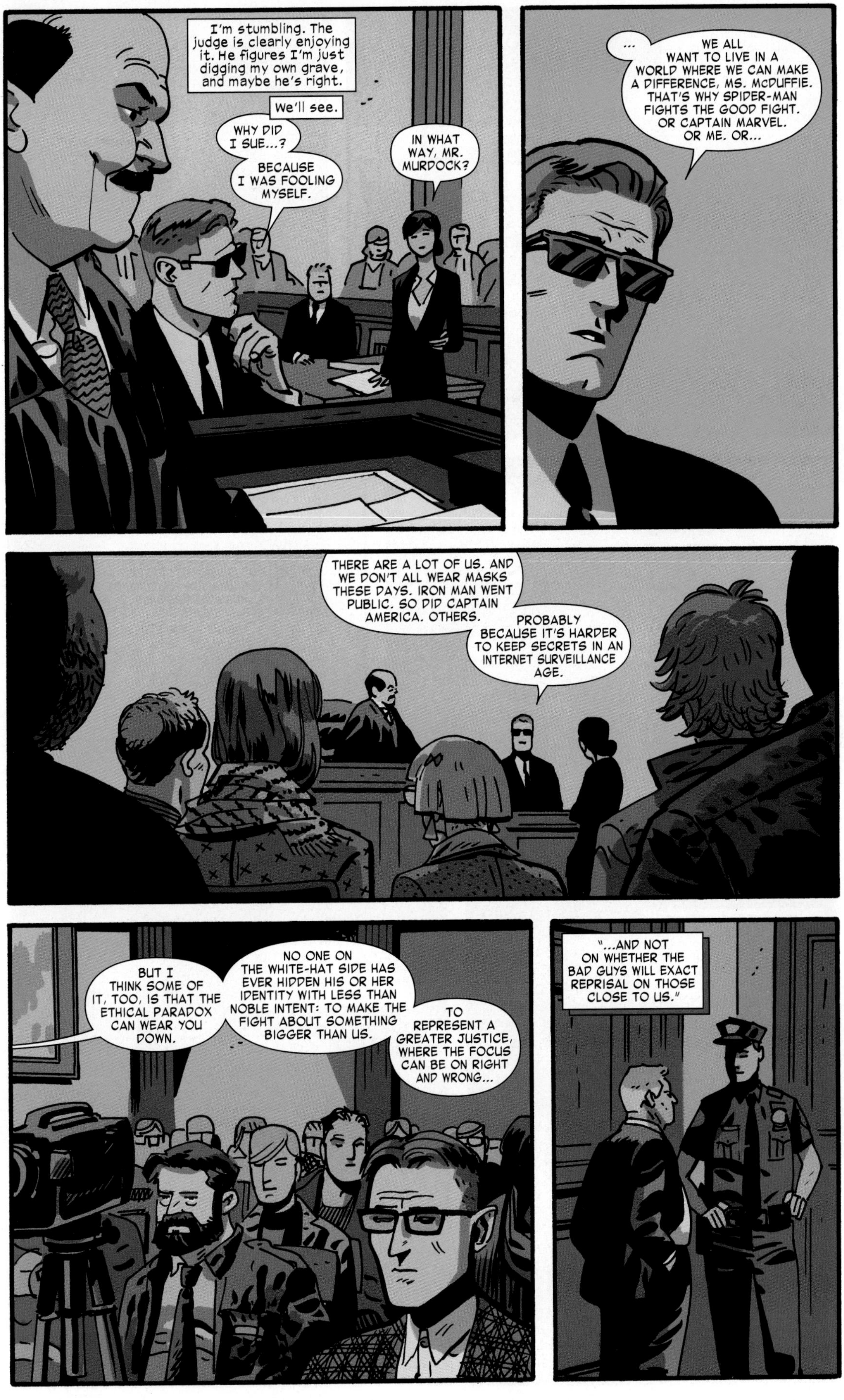
I'm stumbling. The judge is clearly enjoying it. He figures I'm just digging my own grave, and maybe he's right.
We'll see.
WHY DID I SUE...?
BECAUSE I WAS FOOLING MYSELF.
IN WHAT WAY, MR. MURDOCK?
... WE ALL WANT TO LIVE IN A WORLD WHERE WE CAN MAKE A DIFFERENCE, MS. McDUFFIE. THAT'S WHY SPIDER-MAN FIGHTS THE GOOD FIGHT. OR CAPTAIN MARVEL. OR ME. OR...
THERE ARE A LOT OF US. AND WE DON'T ALL WEAR MASKS THESE DAYS. IRON MAN WENT PUBLIC. SO DID CAPTAIN AMERICA. OTHERS.
PROBABLY BECAUSE IT'S HARDER TO KEEP SECRETS IN AN INTERNET SURVEILLANCE AGE.
BUT I THINK SOME OF IT, TOO, IS THAT THE ETHICAL PARADOX CAN WEAR YOU DOWN.
NO ONE ON THE WHITE-HAT SIDE HAS EVER HIDDEN HIS OR HER IDENTITY WITH LESS THAN NOBLE INTENT: TO MAKE THE FIGHT ABOUT SOMETHING BIGGER THAN US.
TO REPRESENT A GREATER JUSTICE, WHERE THE FOCUS CAN BE ON RIGHT AND WRONG...
"...AND NOT ON WHETHER THE BAD GUYS WILL EXACT REPRISAL ON THOSE CLOSE TO US."

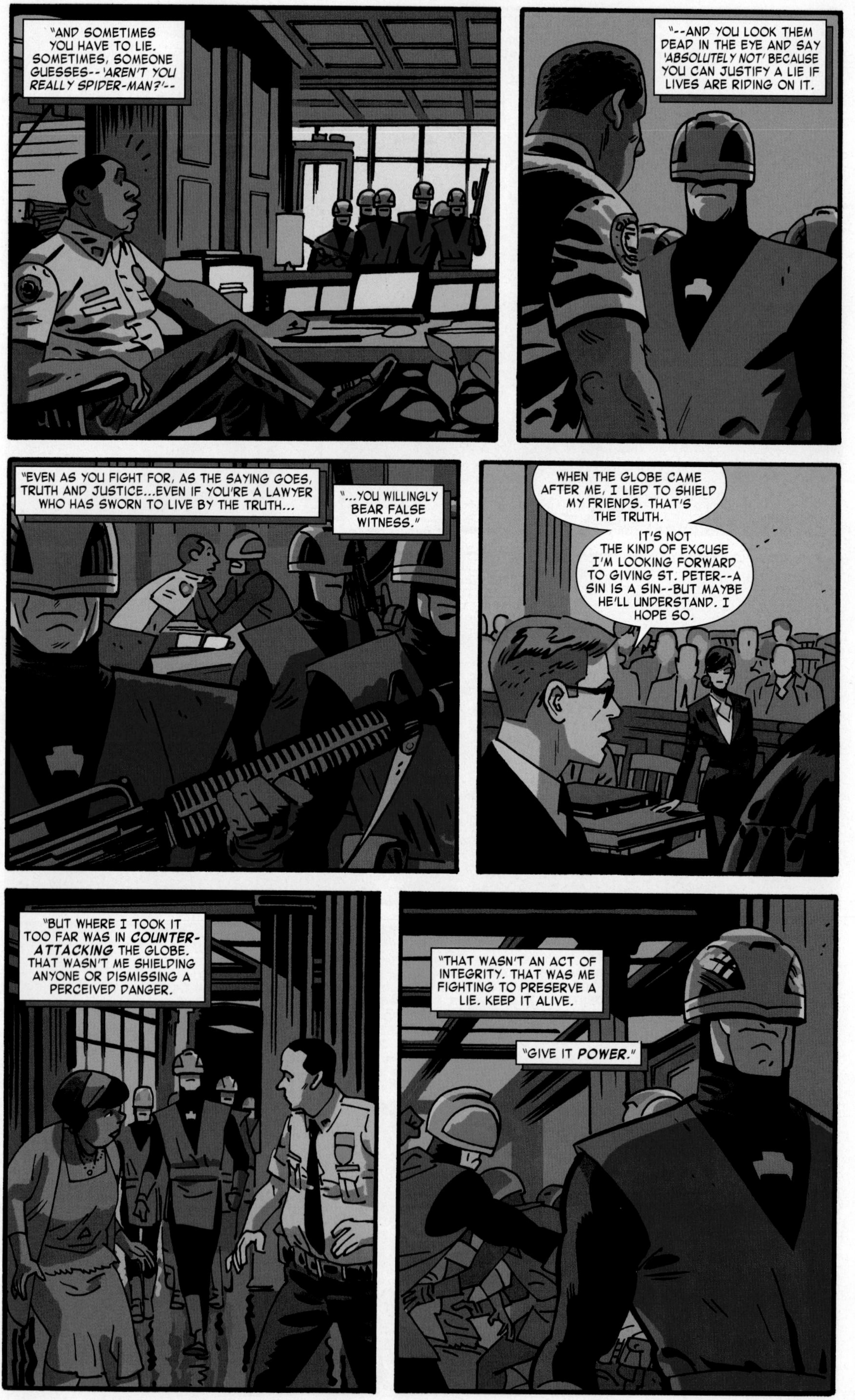
"AND SOMETIMES YOU HAVE TO LIE. SOMETIMES, SOMEONE GUESSES--'AREN'T YOU REALLY SPIDER-MAN?'--
"--AND YOU LOOK THEM DEAD IN THE EYE AND SAY 'ABSOLUTELY NOT' BECAUSE YOU CAN JUSTIFY A LIE IF LIVES ARE RIDING ON IT.
"EVEN AS YOU FIGHT FOR, AS THE SAYING GOES, TRUTH AND JUSTICE...EVEN IF YOU'RE A LAWYER WHO HAS SWORN TO LIVE BY THE TRUTH...
"...YOU WILLINGLY BEAR FALSE WITNESS."
WHEN THE GLOBE CAME AFTER ME, I LIED TO SHIELD MY FRIENDS. THAT'S THE TRUTH.
IT'S NOT THE KIND OF EXCUSE I'M LOOKING FORWARD TO GIVING ST. PETER--A SIN IS A SIN--BUT MAYBE HE'LL UNDERSTAND. I HOPE SO.
"BUT WHERE I TOOK IT TOO FAR WAS IN COUNTER-ATTACKING THE GLOBE. THAT WASN'T ME SHIELDING ANYONE OR DISMISSING A PERCEIVED DANGER.
"THAT WASN'T AN ACT OF INTEGRITY. THAT WAS ME FIGHTING TO PRESERVE A LIE. KEEP IT ALIVE.
"GIVE IT POWER."

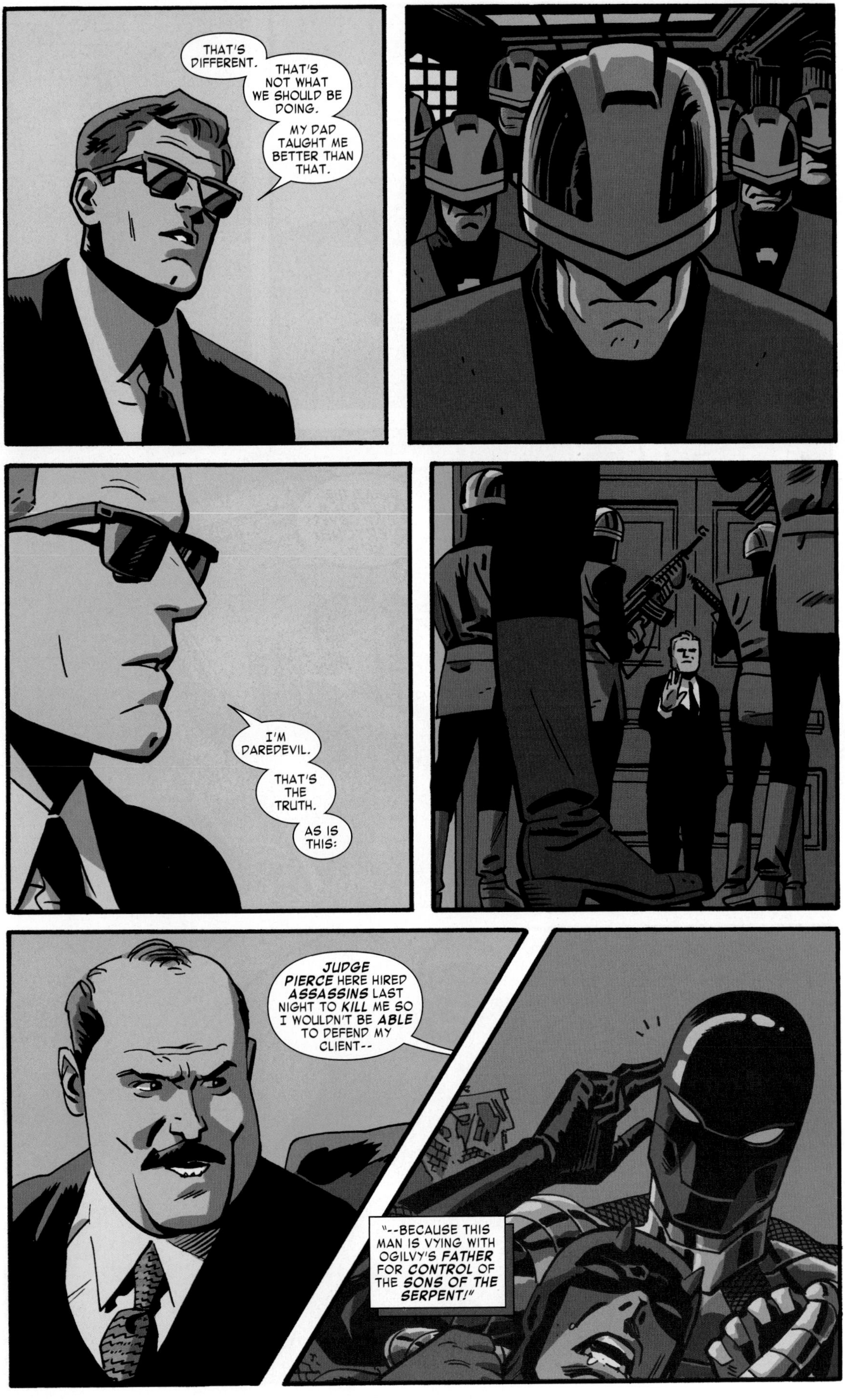
THAT'S DIFFERENT.
THAT'S NOT WHAT WE SHOULD BE DOING.
MY DAD TAUGHT ME BETTER THAN THAT.
I'M DAREDEVIL.
THAT'S THE TRUTH.
AS IS THIS:
JUDGE PIERCE HERE HIRED ASSASSINS LAST NIGHT TO KILL ME SO I WOULDN'T BE ABLE TO DEFEND MY CLIENT--
"--BECAUSE THIS MAN IS VYING WITH OGILVY'S FATHER FOR CONTROL OF THE SONS OF THE SERPENT!"

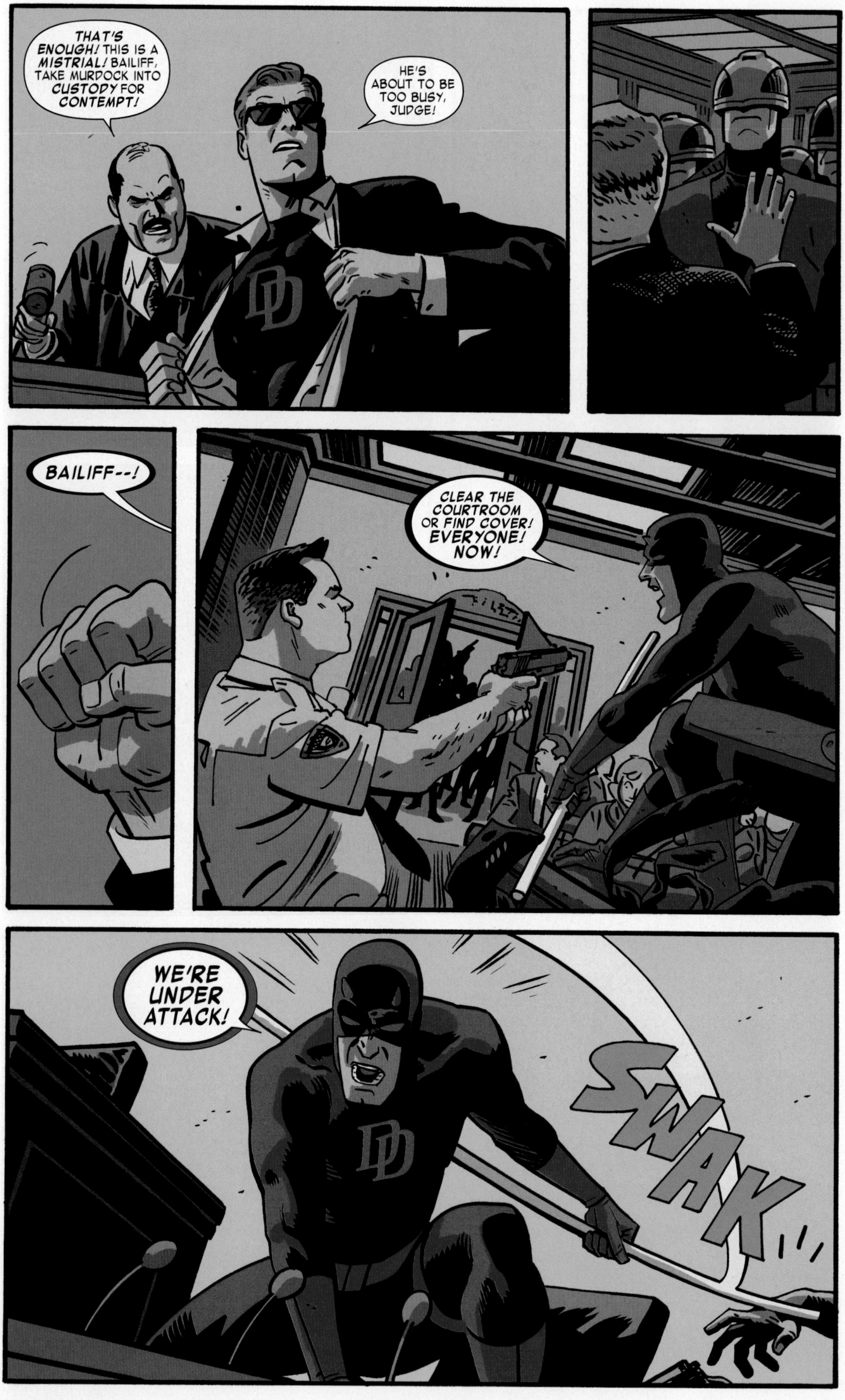
THAT'S ENOUGH! THIS IS A MISTRIAL! BAILIFF, TAKE MURDOCK INTO CUSTODY FOR CONTEMPT!
HE'S ABOUT TO BE TOO BUSY, JUDGE!
BAILIFF--!
CLEAR THE COURTROOM OR FIND COVER! EVERYONE! NOW!
WE'RE UNDER ATTACK!
SWAK

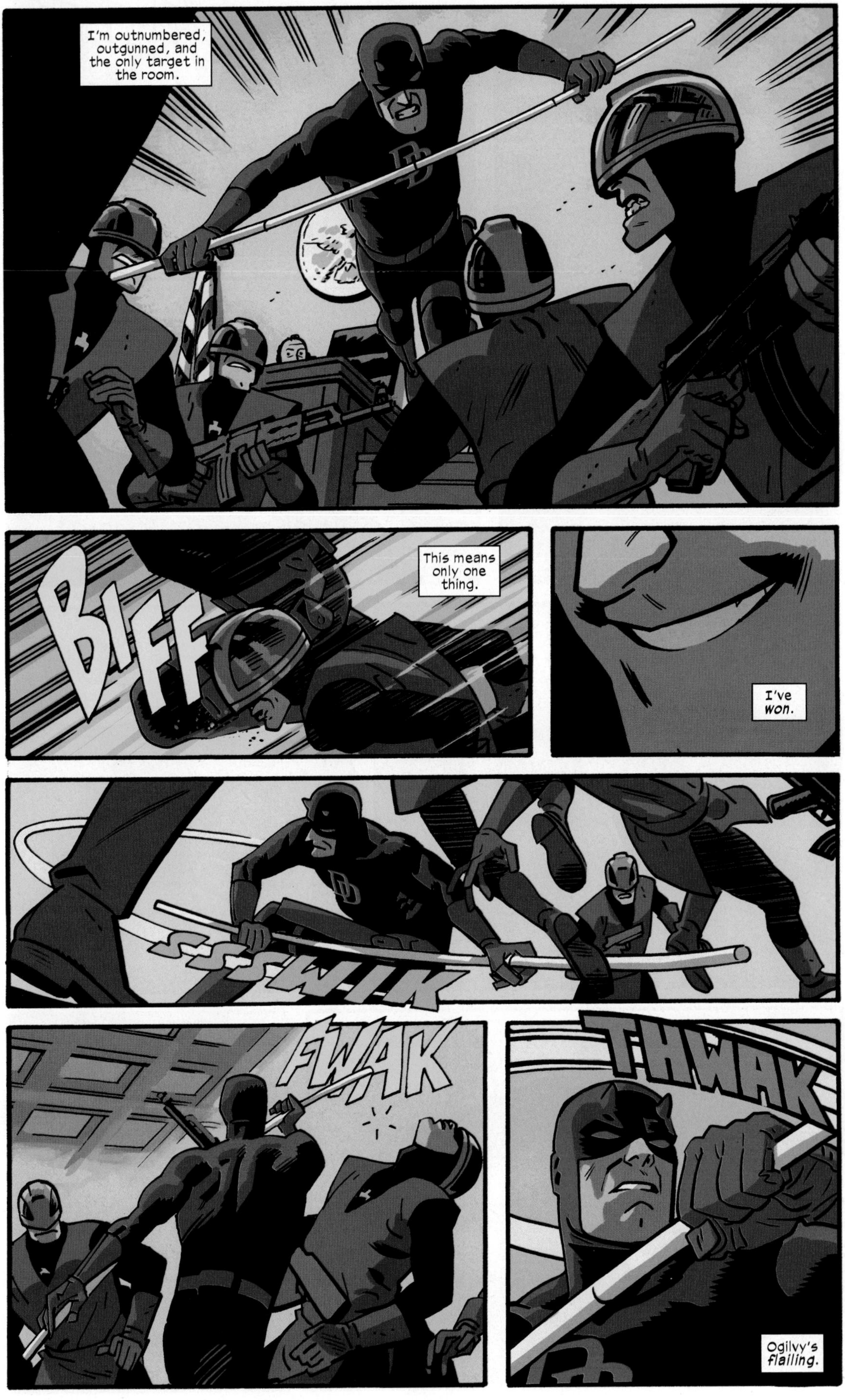

I'm outnumbered, outgunned, and the only target in the room.
BIFF
This means only one thing.
I've *won*.
SSSWIK
FWAK
THWAK
Ogilvy's *flailing*.

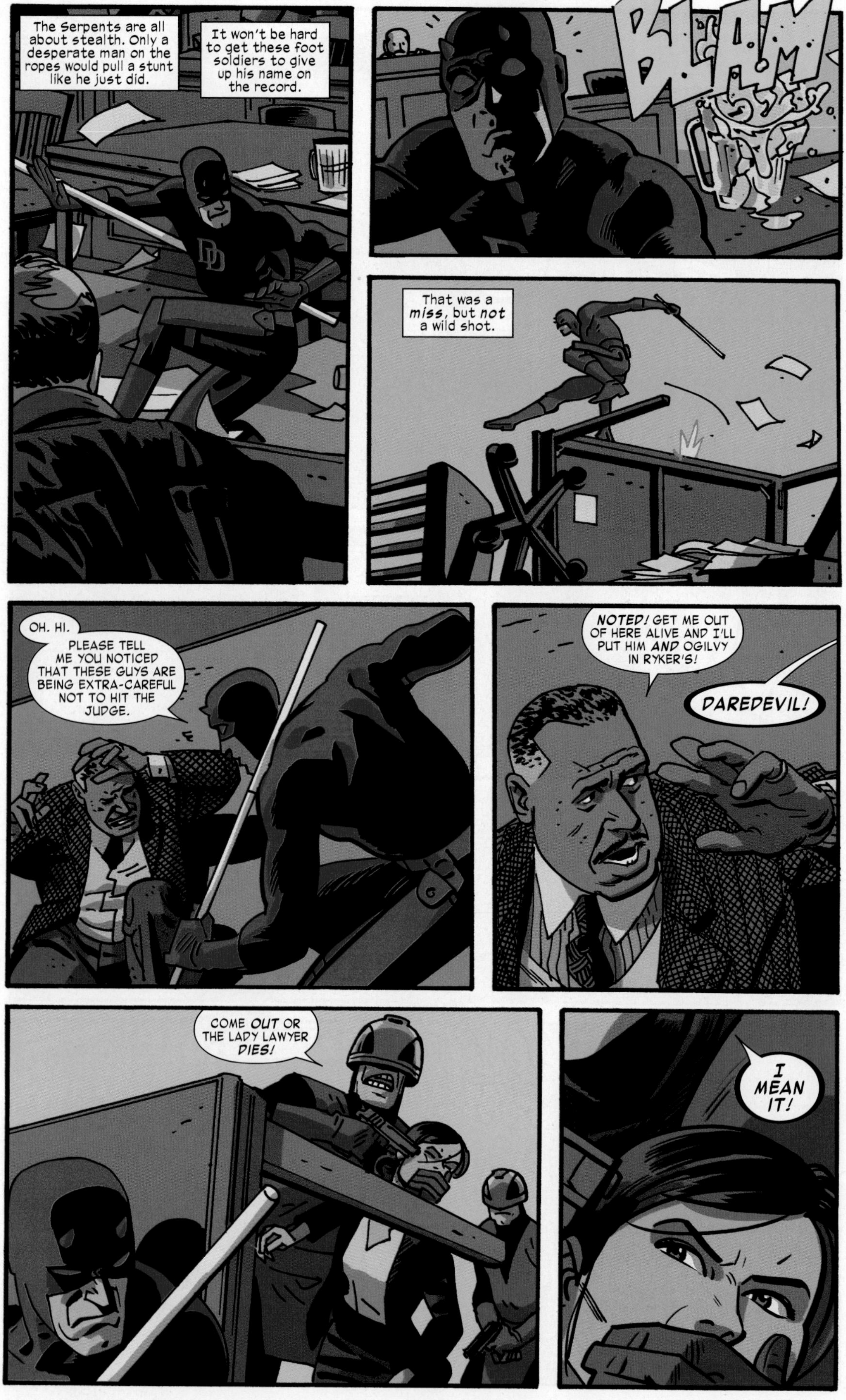

The Serpents are all about stealth. Only a desperate man on the ropes would pull a stunt like he just did.
It won't be hard to get these foot soldiers to give up his name on the record.
BLAM
That was a *miss*, but *not* a wild shot.
OH. HI.
PLEASE TELL ME YOU NOTICED THAT THESE GUYS ARE BEING EXTRA-CAREFUL NOT TO HIT THE JUDGE.
NOTED! GET ME OUT OF HERE ALIVE AND I'LL PUT HIM *AND* OGILVY IN RYKER'S!
DAREDEVIL!
COME *OUT* OR THE LADY LAWYER *DIES!*
I MEAN IT!

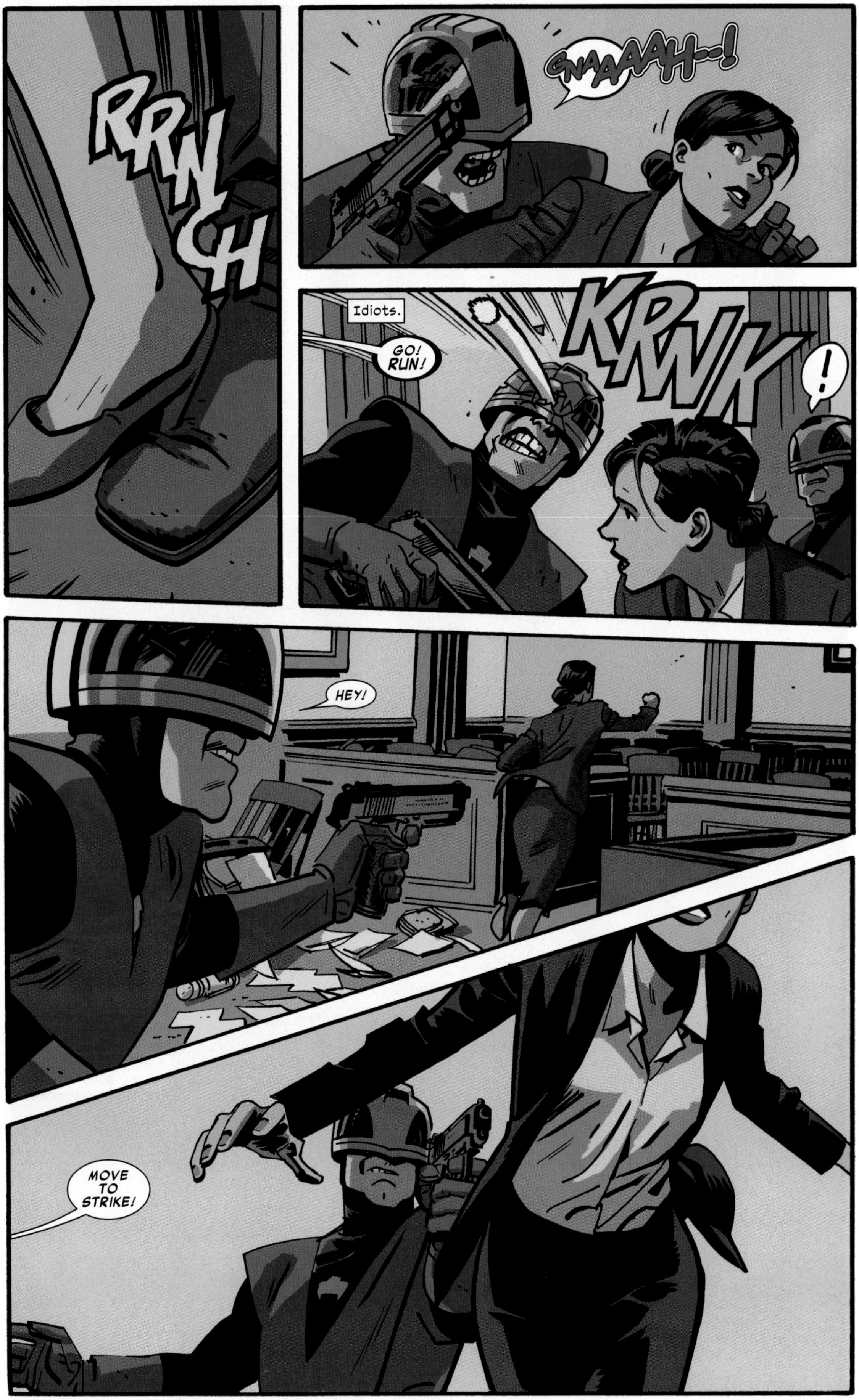
RRNCH
GNAAAAH--!
Idiots.
GO! RUN!
KRNK
!
HEY!
MOVE TO STRIKE!

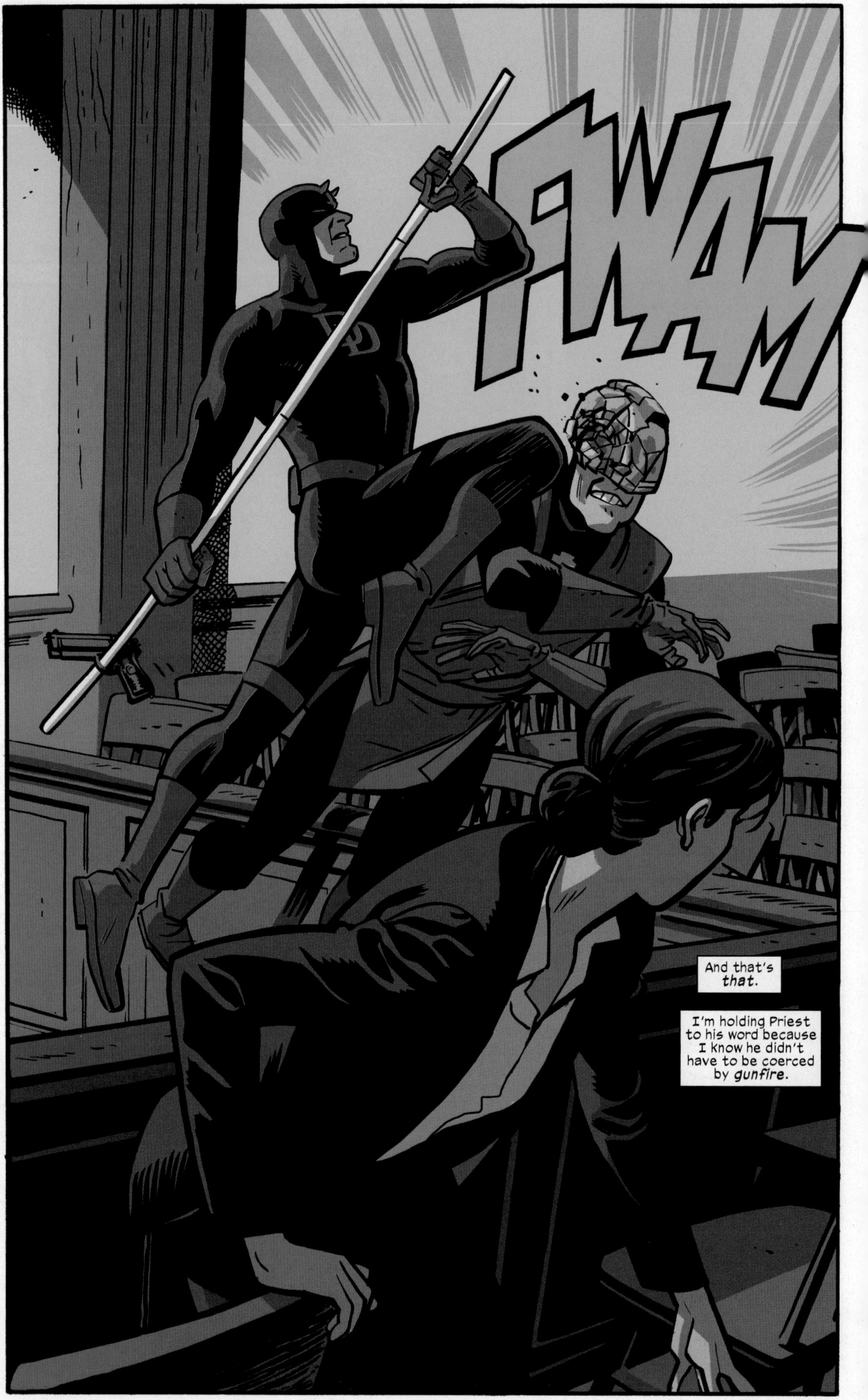
FWAM
And that's *that*.
I'm holding Priest to his word because I know he didn't have to be coerced by *gunfire*.

SNAKED!

D.A., Dept. of Justice Clean (Court)House

Secret Society Driven Out

by Abner Abernathy

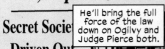

He'll bring the full force of the law down on Ogilvy and Judge Pierce both.

He'll also offer to pull some strings for *me*...

Daredevil Murdock Faces Ethics Charges

by Maggie Lorca

NETTY IMAGES

NEW YORK STATE SUPREME COURT APPELLATE DIVISION

...but I won't let him.

MR. MURDOCK, THEY'LL SEE YOU NOW.

MR. MURDOCK, YOU KNOW WHY YOU'RE HERE. HAVE YOU ANYTHING TO SAY BEFORE THIS COURT RENDERS JUDGMENT?

That I'm glad you're Serpent-free.

ONLY THAT I AM AWARE OF THE GRAVITY OF THIS SITUATION, YOUR HONOR...FOR WHAT THAT'S WORTH.

UNDERSTOOD. MR. MURDOCK, THIS COURT IS NOT UNMOVED BY YOUR YEARS OF SERVICE TO THE CAUSE OF JUSTICE BOTH PUBLICLY AND PRIVATELY.

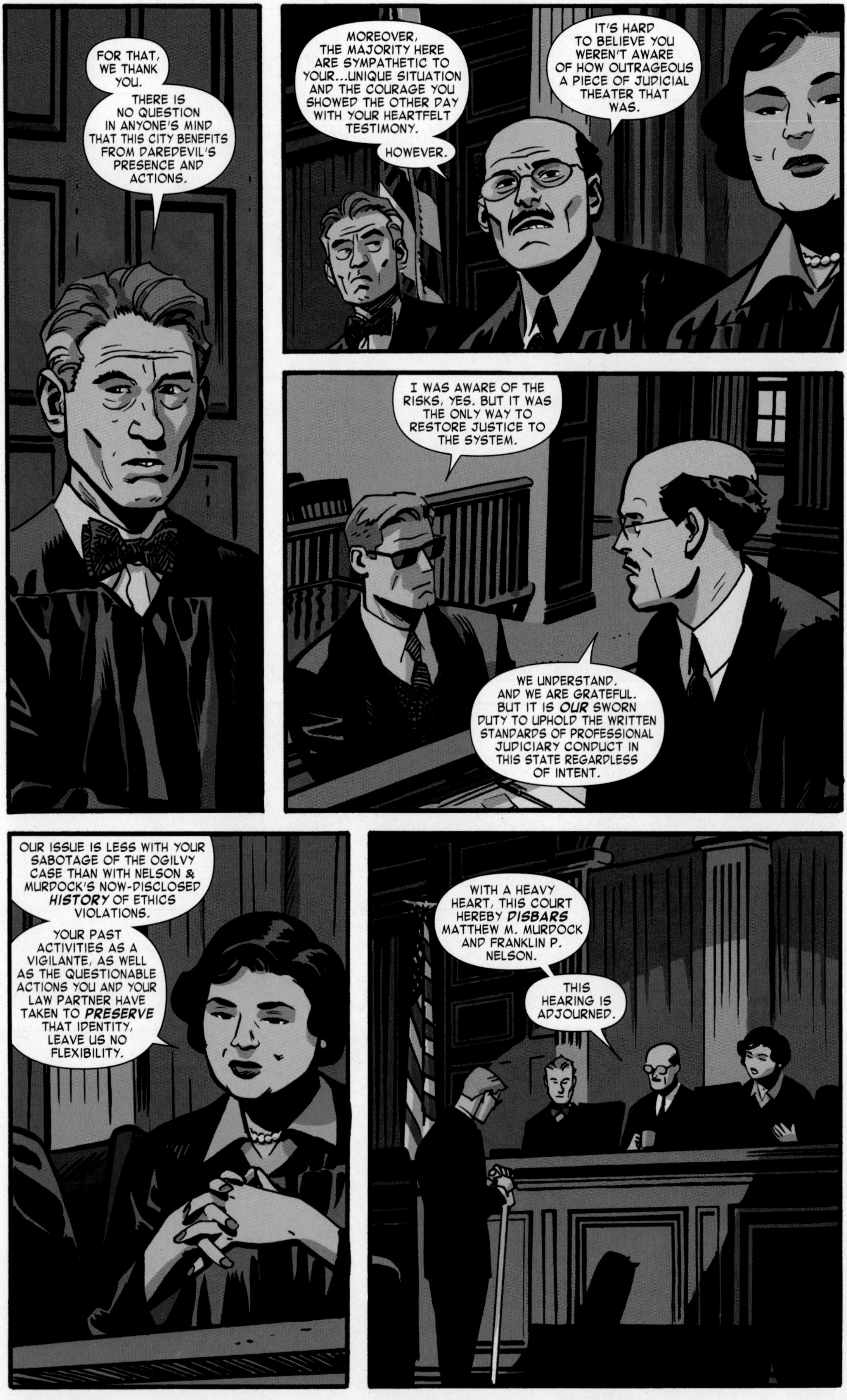
FOR THAT, WE THANK YOU.
THERE IS NO QUESTION IN ANYONE'S MIND THAT THIS CITY BENEFITS FROM DAREDEVIL'S PRESENCE AND ACTIONS.
MOREOVER, THE MAJORITY HERE ARE SYMPATHETIC TO YOUR...UNIQUE SITUATION AND THE COURAGE YOU SHOWED THE OTHER DAY WITH YOUR HEARTFELT TESTIMONY.
HOWEVER.
IT'S HARD TO BELIEVE YOU WEREN'T AWARE OF HOW OUTRAGEOUS A PIECE OF JUDICIAL THEATER THAT WAS.
I WAS AWARE OF THE RISKS, YES. BUT IT WAS THE ONLY WAY TO RESTORE JUSTICE TO THE SYSTEM.
WE UNDERSTAND. AND WE ARE GRATEFUL. BUT IT IS ***OUR*** SWORN DUTY TO UPHOLD THE WRITTEN STANDARDS OF PROFESSIONAL JUDICIARY CONDUCT IN THIS STATE REGARDLESS OF INTENT.
OUR ISSUE IS LESS WITH YOUR SABOTAGE OF THE OGILVY CASE THAN WITH NELSON & MURDOCK'S NOW-DISCLOSED ***HISTORY*** OF ETHICS VIOLATIONS.
YOUR PAST ACTIVITIES AS A VIGILANTE, AS WELL AS THE QUESTIONABLE ACTIONS YOU AND YOUR LAW PARTNER HAVE TAKEN TO ***PRESERVE*** THAT IDENTITY, LEAVE US NO FLEXIBILITY.
WITH A HEAVY HEART, THIS COURT HEREBY ***DISBARS*** MATTHEW M. MURDOCK AND FRANKLIN P. NELSON.
THIS HEARING IS ADJOURNED.

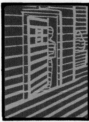

"YOU ARE NO LONGER *LICENSED* TO PRACTICE LAW IN NEW YORK STATE."

ELSON & MURDOCK

OFFICE FOR RENT

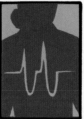

MAN, YOU REALLY DO LEAD WITH YOUR FACE, DON'T YOU?

THAT PART ISN'T NEWS.

SORRY YOU'RE OUT OF A JOB.

EH. IT WAS JUST A TEMP GIG. ALSO, LIKEWISE.

WHAT NOW?

KEEP FOGGY ON THE MEND? SELL EVERYTHING I OWN? I'M OPEN TO SUGGESTIONS.

TOUGH CALL. IT'S ALMOST IMPOSSIBLE FOR A DISBARRED LAWYER TO BE ADMITTED TO ANY *OTHER* STATE BAR...

...UNLESS, OF COURSE, IT'S A STATE WHERE THEY'VE PREVIOUSLY *PRACTICED*...

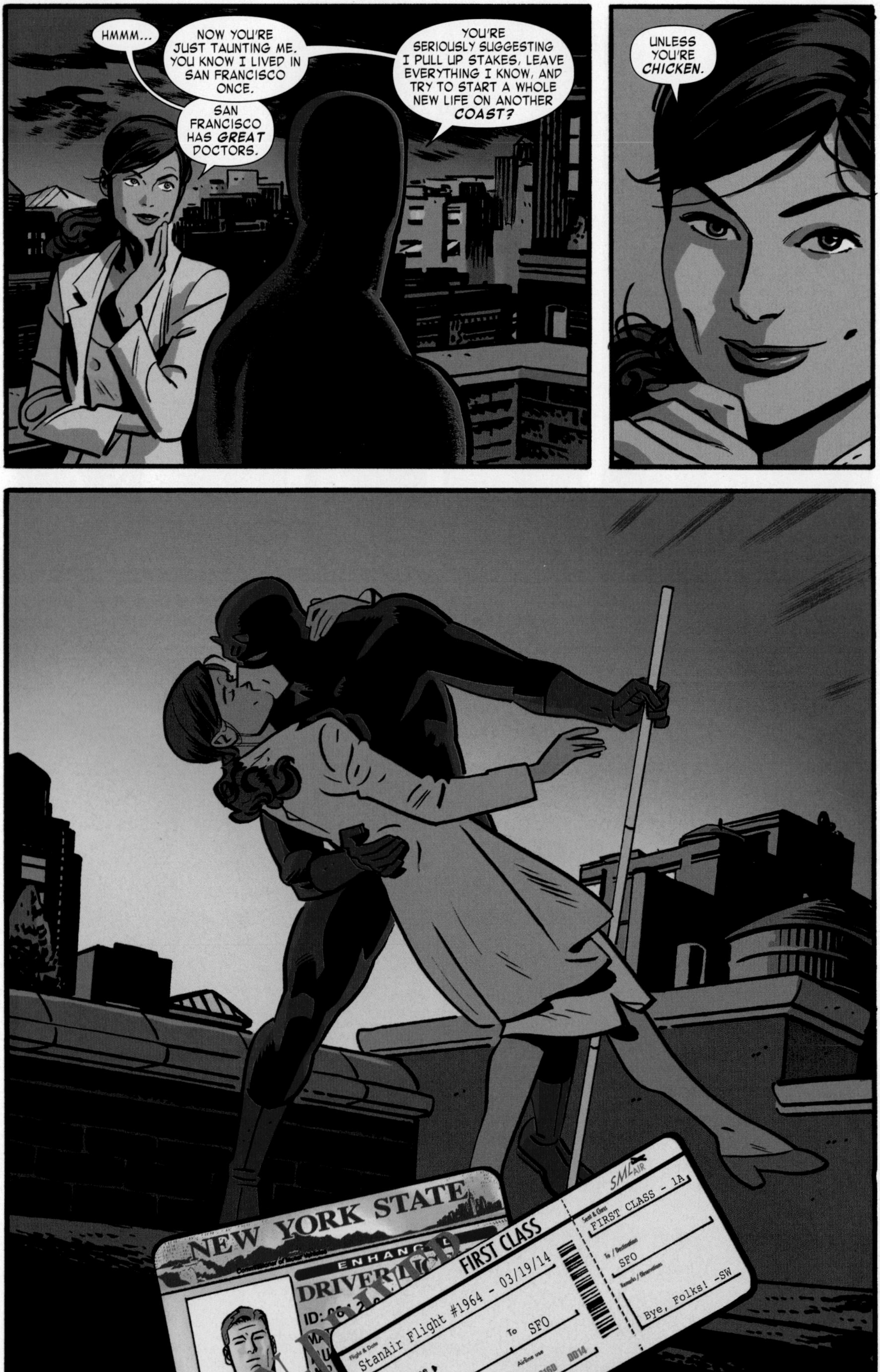
HMMM...
NOW YOU'RE JUST TAUNTING ME. YOU KNOW I LIVED IN SAN FRANCISCO ONCE.
SAN FRANCISCO HAS GREAT DOCTORS.
YOU'RE SERIOUSLY SUGGESTING I PULL UP STAKES, LEAVE EVERYTHING I KNOW, AND TRY TO START A WHOLE NEW LIFE ON ANOTHER COAST?
UNLESS YOU'RE CHICKEN.
NEW YORK STATE
FIRST CLASS
FIRST CLASS - 1A
SFO
Bye, Folks! -SW
StanAir Flight #1964 - 03/19/14
To SFO
Boarding time
From NYC
MATTHEW M. MURDOCK
Boarding Pass

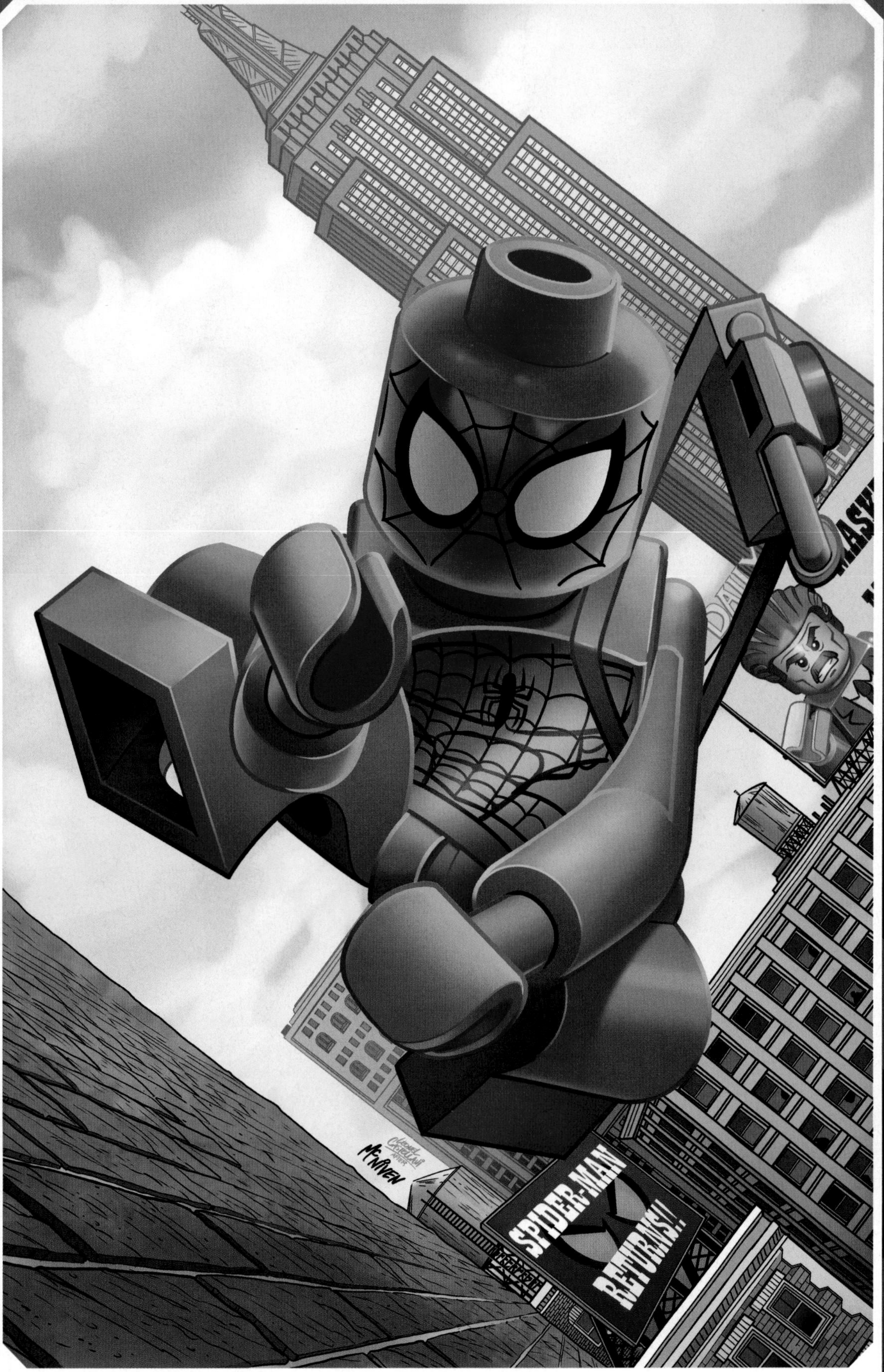
SPIDER-MAN
RETURNS!!

LEGO VARIANT
BY LEONEL CASTELLANI

DAREDEVIL #36

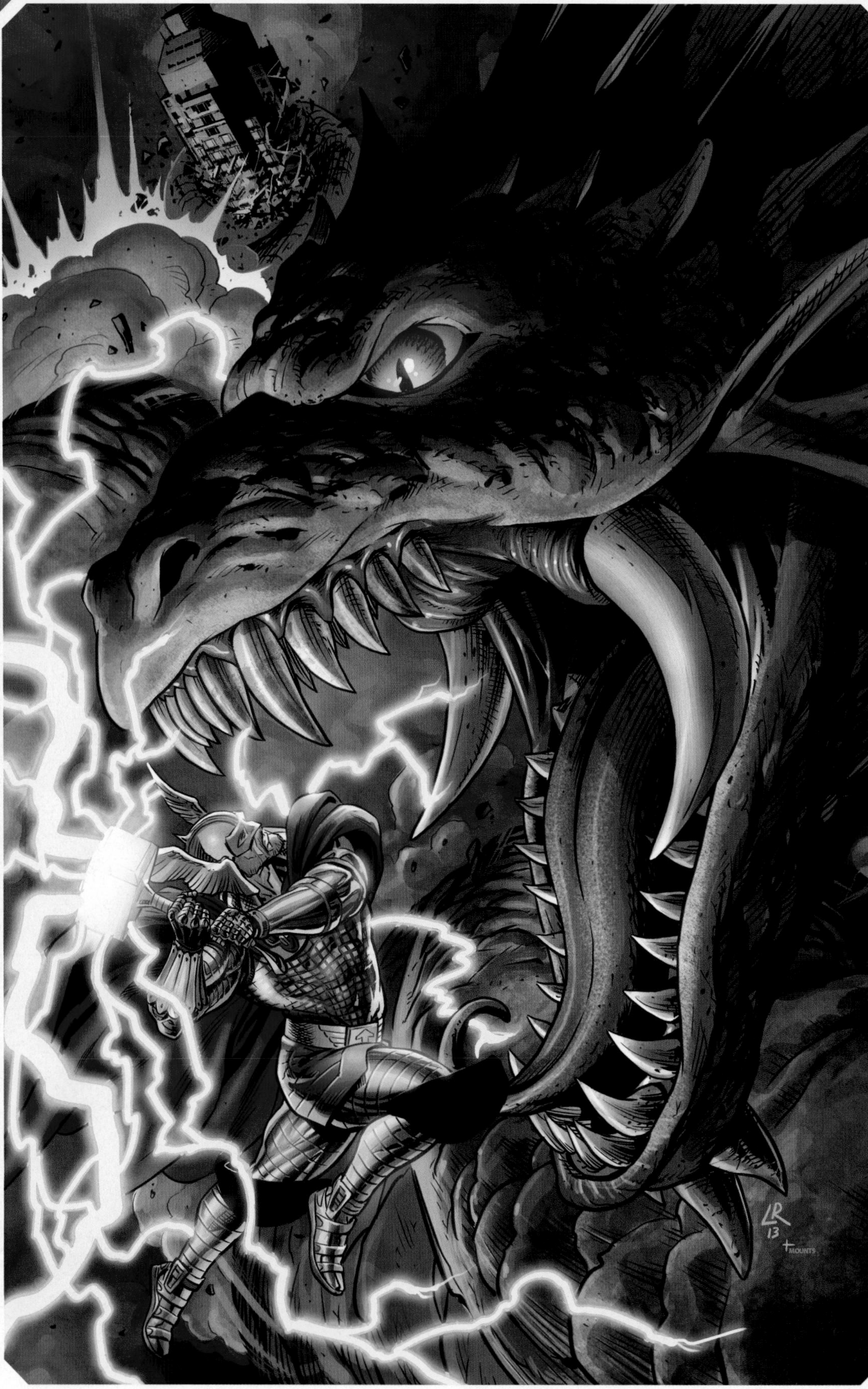

DAREDEVIL #32

VARIANT
BY LUKE ROSS & PAUL MOUNTS

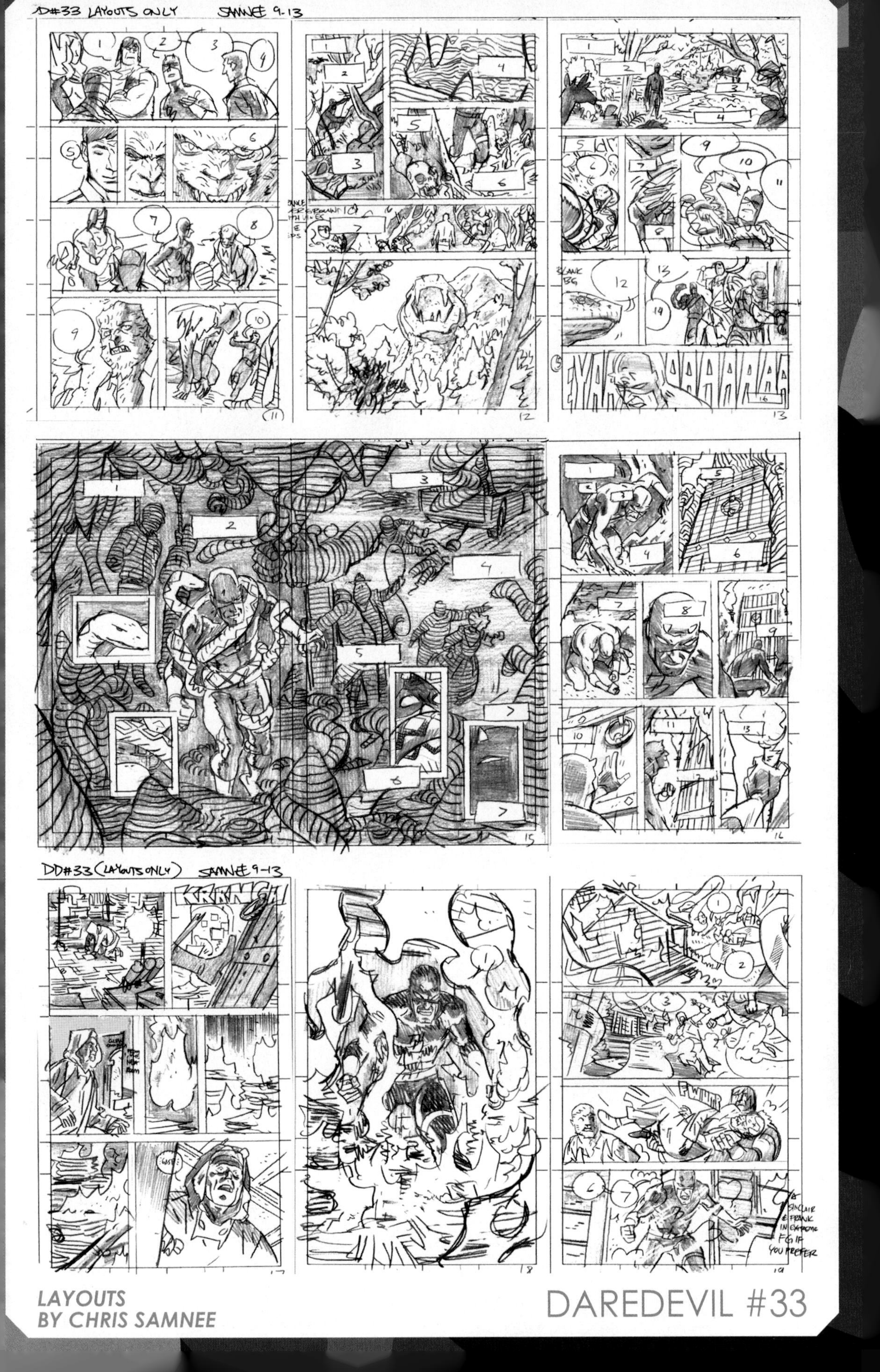
DD#33 LAYOUTS ONLY SAMNEE 9-13
BLANK BG
DD#33 (LAYOUTS ONLY) SAMNEE 9-13
SINCLAIR & FRANK IN EXTREME FG IF YOU PREFER

LAYOUTS
BY CHRIS SAMNEE

DAREDEVIL #33

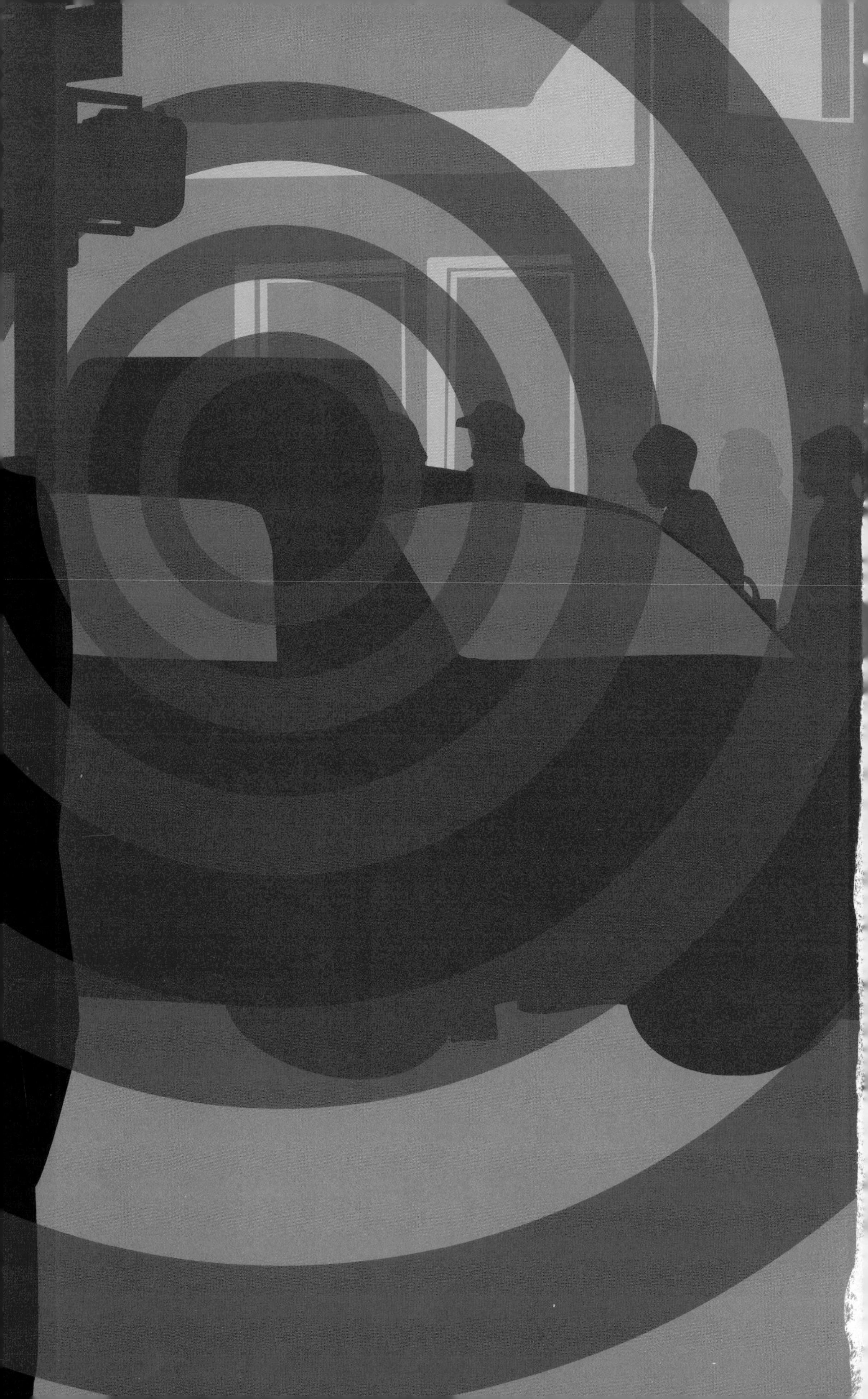